BURY ME
IN MY
JERSEY

BURY ME
IN MY
JERSEY

A Memoir of My Father,
Football, and
Philly

Tom McAllister

Villard Books
New York

While all of the incidents in *Bury Me in My Jersey* are real, certain dialogue has been reconstructed, and some of the names and personal characteristics of the individuals have been changed. Any resulting resemblance to persons living or dead is entirely coincidental and unintentional.

Published in the United States by Villard Books, an imprint of The Random House Publishing Group, a division of Random House, Inc., New York.

VILLARD and "V" CIRCLED Design are registered trademarks of Random House, Inc.

Library of Congress Cataloging-in-Publication Data

McAllister, Tom.
Bury me in my jersey : a memoir of my father, football, and Philly / Tom McAllister.
p. cm.
ISBN 978-0-345-51651-0
eBook ISBN 978-0-345-52200-9
1. Philadelphia Eagles (Football team). 2. McAllister, Tom. 3. Football fans.
4. Fathers and sons.
I. Title.
GV956.P44.M43 2010
796.332'640974811—dc22   2010007204

Printed in the United States of America on acid-free paper

www.villard.com

2 4 6 8 9 7 5 3 1

First Edition

Design by R. Bull

Photo on page ii courtesy of the author

For LauraBeth

Many people need desperately to receive this message: "I feel and think much as you do, care about many of the things you care about, although most people don't care about them. You are not alone."

—KURT VONNEGUT

CONTENTS

BURY ME
IN MY
JERSEY

CHAPTER ONE

SUPER BOWL XXXIX

THIS BOOK, like so many other stories in this city, begins and ends in the same place.

It's early February 2005 and eight of us are huddled in the basement, all dressed in green, desperately leaning toward the TV like plants toward the sun. Stacks of chicken bones and pizza crusts clutter the two end tables, and empty bottles and cans line the perimeter of the room. We're all engaged in varying degrees of prayer. The Eagles are on TV, and they're going to win the Super Bowl.

If you're from Philly, you know the story already. By the time you're old enough to throw a football, you can recite the history of futility, the failed trades, the untapped potential, the many pitiful losses. But let's not dwell on that right now. The fans in Boston and Chicago may have embraced their history of failure and sold it to the highest bidder, but Philly fans would give anything to forget it, to overcome it and never look back.

Swanson, my best friend since first grade, sits between his father and his uncle on the big couch. Next to them, in a recliner that hasn't actually reclined in years, is Swanson's brother-in-law. Three more close friends—Quinn, Big Kev, and Anthony—sit rigidly on the floor or on folding chairs.

There I am. In the corner, wearing my father's sweater (over a Brian Dawkins jersey, number 20, faded and tattered), drinking Molson Golden, tonight's celebration beer, because I'm convinced the team does something good every time I open a bottle.

I'm the only one drinking. In my defense, I may also be the only one helping the Eagles.

I open a new bottle, my seventh, and gulp a mouthful. I'm too full on wings and pizza to drink much more, but I don't have a choice. Donovan McNabb completes a thirty-six-yard pass to Terrell Owens, who wasn't even supposed to be able to jog on his broken leg, let alone play in the Super Bowl. I take another swig and pound my fist on my thigh. We've moved well beyond the high-fiving and group cheering that marked the first half; now we're into aggressive, personal celebrations, like punching the floor or clapping so hard it stings. I drink again.

The Eagles are mounting a comeback; they're behind by ten, but marching easily down the field. They'll score here, get the ball back, and score again. They'll hold on to the lead, maybe even add an insurance field goal. And we'll count down the seconds until the final gun before we charge into the street in an orgy of whooping, shouting, hugging, drinking, and champagne dousing that might never end, and I'll break free from the pack and sprint two blocks to my aunt's house, where my family is watching the game, and my brother and I will scream incoherent things that make perfect sense to us as we're mobbed by neighbors and strangers, and normally I'm not one to be comfortable with strangers, but tonight it's okay, because the Eagles won, the Eagles won, the Eagles won the Super Bowl and everything is okay. I might never stop, sprinting all the way back to my apartment in Iowa City just to let everyone know what they're missing, then turning back home and running through the cheesesteak shop where I worked for so many years, and maybe charging straight into heaven, where I'll finally relax with my Dad and his dad and always relive the moment, that second when the game was clinched and the city erupted in civic pride and true, legitimate brotherly love maybe for the first time ever.

EXCEPT NONE of this happens. There is no celebration. The next pass is poorly thrown, intercepted by Tedy Bruschi, a player I despise. The Patriots go on to win their third Super Bowl in four years, and we're left empty-handed. The celebration rages in Boston. Only rage remains in Philadelphia.

JANUARY 2004: The Eagles have just lost their third consecutive NFC Championship Game. They weren't even competitive this time. I'm slumped on the couch in the house I rent in Philly with Big Kev and Anthony, trying to figure out why I even bother with this team. I feel abandoned and forgotten; I want to give up on everything. I want to lock myself in my bedroom until I starve. I boycott the Super Bowl and vow never to watch football again.

JUNE 2003: I'm alone in the bathroom in a Toronto bar, punching the paper towel holder until it's dented and dangling from its mount; kicking the trash can across the room; and ripping the toilet paper dispenser off the wall, doing my best rock-star-at-the-Ritz. I'm Ted Nugent after a bitchin' show. I'm Jim Morrison after a gallon of whiskey and a bottle of pills. I'm nobody. My friends and I have just engaged in a heated argument with a group of Buffalo Bills fans about whose team is a bigger disappointment, and we've decided to go drink up the courage to find them later and start a real fight. I'm too drunk to remember that, though; all I'm thinking about is how I miss my Dad. I leave the bathroom with hands buried in my pockets so no one will see the blood on my knuckles. When LauraBeth, my girlfriend, asks what's wrong, I ignore her.

JANUARY 2003: The Eagles have just lost their second consecutive NFC Championship Game, this time to the Tampa Bay Buccaneers, a loss so shocking and heartbreaking that years later replays of the game's signature play—an interception returned for a touchdown by Tampa's Ronde Barber—will make me ill. I'm in the driveway by myself, cursing every Eagle and smashing empty beer bottles against the wall. Nobody stops me. When I'm out of bottles, I slink back into the house and wish we owned a broom.

DECEMBER 2002: Four days after Christmas, I'm huddled around a trash can fire with six other guys, waiting overnight for

Eagles playoff tickets. We've just caught someone cutting in line, and I'm throwing an empty beer bottle at him from twenty feet away. Just a few minutes ago, I spat at a family of four trying to sneak past us, and led the *Asshole* chants that rained down on them. It feels good to be a part of the crowd.

JANUARY 2002: The Eagles have just lost the NFC Championship Game to the St. Louis Rams. We're in my apartment in North Philly, and even though we're disappointed, we're also hopeful. This is a team on the rise, a team bound for a championship. We're already excited about next season, even if it is eight months away. Outside, a skinny white kid calls for help while an enormous black man squats on his chest, shouting something about money, presumably a bet on the game. He punctuates his demands with fierce open-hands to the face. Two of his friends kick the white kid in the ribs. We close the blinds and watch the post-game show, while one of the girls at our party insists that *it's not fair* that the Rams won't give the ball back and let the Eagles have one more chance to score.

EVERY YEAR, it's the same story, although in the seasons since Super Bowl XXXIX, the Eagles have been kind enough not to get my hopes up too much. They did sneak into the playoffs in the '08 season and played well enough to lose another conference championship game, but I never really believed they could win then, not after another mediocre regular season. Maybe I didn't allow myself to believe in them because I couldn't handle another letdown like the ones we had from '02 to '05. Or maybe this game is more complex than I ever realized when I was a kid. Now we're in the midst of another off-season, the buildup to another Super Bowl campaign, and I'm wishing I could stop caring. But I know that's never going to happen. The desperation in the city's air is contagious; it's a collective civic longing to be part of something great, even if we had nothing to do with it. I want that moment, that city-wide catharsis that will follow a Super Bowl. I need it.

CHAPTER

TWO

CONFESSIONS OF
AN OBSESSED FOOTBALL FAN

CONFESSION NUMBER ONE: I've been known to occasionally stalk pro athletes. When driving on the Schuylkill Expressway last summer, I saw Eagles cornerback Sheldon Brown cruising just ahead of me in his Escalade. I gassed my little Honda Civic and pushed as hard as I could to catch up with him. I didn't really have a plan from there, but I knew I wanted to watch him as he drove, to see where he positioned his hands on the wheel, to see if he sang along to the radio, if he talked on his cell phone, if anyone was with him. I caught up to him about two miles from the exit for Packer Avenue, the last exit before you cross the Walt Whitman Bridge into New Jersey, and also the exit that leads to the NovaCare Complex, where the Eagles practice. In two miles, he would be gone and I would probably never see him again, at least not in real, everyday life.

I stayed even with him and was glad to note that he was a careful driver—focused on the road, moderate speeds, no distractions. I was not careful, leering through my passenger window at my favorite football player, my car drifting off course like a shopping cart with a broken wheel.

I hoped he would look at me, but then I didn't know what I would do if we made eye contact. Would I wave dumbly? Would I ask him to pull over so I could explain that he's my favorite player, and I wear his jersey every Sunday? Should I call him Sheldon or Mr. Brown? And how would he react to all of this? Surely, he'd be as frightened as he was flattered.

I turned the radio down and opened the window to hear the music he was playing, but all I heard was the faint bass line of a rap song. There weren't many other cars on the road, and it felt like Sheldon and I had the stretch of highway to ourselves.

Two miles passed quickly. I fumbled with my cell phone to try to snap a picture of him, but soon we were at Packer Avenue. I veered across two lanes to follow him all the way to the NovaCare Complex. If he knew I was following him, he didn't show it. As we sat at a red light, I lightly tapped my horn, hoping he would look over, and I could point to the Eagles jersey I was wearing. But he looked straight ahead, leaning on his left hand and looking cooler than I've ever looked. At the next light, he was gone, turning into the NovaCare and leaving me behind. I turned around and headed back toward the bridge. When I got home, I would log on to the Eagles' Internet message board and tell everyone the story about my close encounter with greatness.

LauraBeth—then my fiancée, now my wife—was in the car with me, and she was extraordinarily tolerant, especially considering that I didn't talk to her the whole time Sheldon was there. She laughed at me, but she didn't complain when I pulled off the highway to follow him. She knows how much I care about the Eagles, how much I like Sheldon Brown, and she probably also knew I would follow him whether she approved or not.

One of these days, she's going to demand that I grant the same devotion to her as I do to the Eagles, and she'll be right to do so. I'm lucky to be married to her, but I suspect the Eagles will always be my mistress.

CONFESSION NUMBER TWO: The last real conversation I had with my Dad before he died was about the Eagles. We didn't talk about love, father-son bonds, or regrets—the regrets we saved for later, after I delivered the eulogy, after we put him in the ground and turned away and had to go back to living our lives as if nothing had happened, as if we weren't scarred and miserable.

He had cancer. A big, evil lump in his esophagus that spread all the way down to his stomach, rooted itself in his liver, and sucked the life out of him. Who knows how long he actually had cancer, but we knew about it for almost two years. When he was diagnosed, I turned it into a joke. When a friend asked if my apartment floor had a tumor—water damage had buckled the floor and caused an unusually large lump to form next to my couch—I said, "No, but my Dad does." Everyone laughed. It was funny at the time, but mostly they laughed because I had implicitly given them permission to laugh, and they needed it as much as I did. When we joked about it, it was less real. It was easier to face, to forget.

When people asked how Dad was doing, I didn't know, because I was too focused on life at college to call him and get real updates. I said he was doing fine, and, in fact, might be even healthier than before because he'd lost some weight and now he wasn't bothered by the diabetes or high blood pressure anymore. I'm not sure whether I was oblivious, stupid, or if I really did know he was dying and just tried to rationalize the whole thing away. Whatever I was thinking at the time, it forced me to distance myself from him. Even in his final five weeks, when he checked into the hospital and got progressively worse, his face becoming an unrecognizable putty mask, each organ shutting down one at a time, I only visited a handful of times. I acted like I wasn't concerned, but I was. I acted like I had more pressing things to do, but I didn't. I talked about what we would do after they discharged him from the hospital. And LauraBeth, knowing intuitively that he wasn't ever going to come home, urged me to visit. She made me go at least twice a week, which is five less weekly trips than I should have made, but still better than nothing.

He called me one day, left a message on my voice mail—a delirious, morphine-addled plea for me to come visit. His voice a near-whisper, he told me he missed me and was wondering where I was. He said he was scared and that he loved me.

I've never felt worse about myself.

And still, I didn't call back. What would I say? *Please don't die, Dad, and, by the way, sorry I'm too busy to see you before the cancer kills you.*

I did visit the next day. I was the only one there, and I told him

I'd gotten his message. "Oh, that was nothing," he said, "don't worry about it." Sitting next to him, I didn't know what to say, so I turned on the TV instead. The NFL draft was on, and I realized that he hadn't even heard the big news—the Eagles had replaced Hugh Douglas, one of the league's best pass rushers, with Jerome McDougle, a hotshot rookie from Miami. I told him the good news, and he smiled. He was broken down and nearly unrecognizable, but his smile was still the same, even if he was beardless and his teeth were stowed in a bedside container.

"Think he can play?" he asked.

"Definitely," I'd said. "All those guys from Miami are awesome. Like Jerome,* Warren Sapp, Ray Lewis, Dan Morgan—"

"I don't know how you kids keep up with all those names," he said, fighting to keep his eyes open. The drugs made it hard for him to stay awake for long stretches. "You're a smart kid."

"It's easy," I said, shrugging. "All you have to do is watch the highlights and check out the message boards online." I stood and stepped away from the bed. "Best thing is, a lineman can help out right away. If he's any good,† we'll be a lot better this year." He smiled again and closed his eyes. I left the room and would never see him lucid again.

CONFESSION NUMBER THREE: I've probably spent more time in my life thinking about the Eagles than all other subjects combined. Since registering on the Eagles message board in February 2003, I've posted over fifteen thousand messages, an average of seven per day. On the EMB, as board regulars call it, I'm known for my long, detailed messages, which average about 250 words each. While this may not seem like a lot, it's important to remember that reading 250 words on an Internet message board is like reading the Book of Genesis. I've written countless 1,000-word

---

* To Eagles fans, "Jerome" will always refer to Jerome Brown, an Eagles legend who died in a car crash in 1992, in the prime of his career.

† He wasn't good. He was terrible. The most noteworthy thing he did in five years as an Eagle was to get shot by a carjacker.

posts, even though I know everyone stops reading after the first paragraph, and even though writing them usually requires a half hour of research, plus an hour of typing and editing.* I feel guilty as I write them, because I know I should be spending that time on actual, useful writing, or on my family, or reading, or anything else besides analyzing the special teams coach's tone of voice in his mid-April press conference. But I can't. I'm driven there compulsively, every day.

My name on the message board is swamistubbs—which is Rerun's name when he becomes a used-car salesman on *What's Happening!!* I have no particular connection to Fred "Rerun" Berry, and no particular love for the show. I only picked the name because I thought it was funny, and at the time of registration, I'd had no intention of becoming an EMB regular. If I'd realized my identity would become tied to a sitcom character best known for his red beret and goofy dancing, maybe I would have spent more time considering my name, come up with something a bit more representative of who I am, but it's too late for that.

Since registering, I've established a reputation on the message board, and each of the hundred-thousand-plus members knows who I am and how I think. I say with a real mixture of pride and shame that I'm well respected on the EMB. I'm considered one of the voices of reason, one of the more intelligent posters who will really analyze a situation and then break it down clearly. Others have given me a five-star rating as a poster, and I've received several votes in the "Who's the best poster on the EMB?" poll.† Board administrators have asked me to be a moderator, an offer that was simultaneously flattering and depressing. When big Ea-

---

* I'm confident that I put more research and effort into my EMB posts than most professional analysts put into their own work. This probably reflects poorly on both me and the analysts.

† Of course, not everyone likes me, and I've actually received death threats from three different people. One particularly frightening threat came from a Vietnam vet whom I'd antagonized in a political debate—he had tracked my IP address and made it clear that he could find me. The other threats came from people who—misled by my name and the picture of Rerun that

gles news breaks, I feel obligated to go to the EMB and add my two cents. LauraBeth hates all of this, and I kind of hate it too.

The person they respect, though, isn't Tom McAllister, but swamistubbs. Tom McAllister is a neurotic guy who teaches college composition and admires the hell out of Kurt Vonnegut and loves donuts and can't ride a bike and has two obese Welsh corgis and a very tolerant wife. Swamistubbs is some dude who hides behind the face of Fred Berry and talks about football. On the EMB, I'm rational and well spoken and always calm. In real life, I throw things and break toes kicking tables. I give people the finger when I'm driving, and once, when my Dad was dying, I had to be restrained from attacking a priest in a hospital. I stammer and I talk too much and I'm socially awkward. I never went to the Internet with the intention of creating a new self, but it's what happened. It's what happens to all of us.

The deeper we dive into our online personalities and try to hide ourselves behind clever pseudonyms, the more we expose ourselves. We haven't created a new character; rather, we've indulged another aspect of our being. With each word I type, I realize just how obsessed I am, just how skewed my priorities are. When I wrote, after an ugly loss to the Jacksonville Jaguars, that "this team makes me feel like a battered wife—no matter how bad they treat me I always come back for more," it was supposed to be a joke. But this is exactly our relationship. I'm neglected and mistreated, yet I continue to follow them, always wishing I could be a part of what makes them so special, hoping that they would just look me in the eye once and tell me I mean something to them. I would never say these things, but swamistubbs says them every day.

Last year, I wrote that "I have a serious man-love for Sheldon Brown." Physically, I have more in common with him than most non-punters—we're the same height, he's got about fifteen pounds

---

accompanies my posts—thought I was black and didn't appreciate that I was getting so uppity. One sent a private message saying, "Listen up, black-ass, why don't you shut youre [sic] nigger mouth if you know what's good for you." I told the guy I was white, and he responded by saying, "my bad."

on me, and he's black, but it's not easy for a guy like me to find a good body double on a football team. He's soft-spoken, but when he does speak, people listen — the conviction and intelligence in his comments have won him the ear of both teammates and fans. Still, he's underappreciated, because he's not half as flashy as the other highlight-reel players on the Eagles. He just does his job every day with a quiet dignity and an impressive determination.

I wear an authentic Sheldon Brown jersey, a Christmas gift from LauraBeth, every week.* For three hours a week, I live inside the shell of Sheldon Brown; after a particularly good game, I'll wear the jersey until I go to bed. I never bring Sheldon into bed with me, but that may be because I don't want to share him with my wife.

I don't know exactly how much she paid for the jersey, but I do know authentics cost about $150 more than replicas, because we fans want our football costumes to be as realistic as possible. The only ones that cost more are actual game-worn jerseys, some of which go for over $1,000, just so someone can wear the sweat of another man.

The fantasy goes beyond just playing dress-up, though; it's a constant mind-set that drives us as fans, and that finds itself articulated on the message board. How many nights have I closed my eyes and dreamed about being on the field between Brian Dawkins and Sheldon Brown, laying down a monster hit on some fool halfback, and then celebrating with high fives and chest bumps? I've envisioned the Super Bowl in a thousand different ways — sometimes I'm in the locker room, and sometimes I'm in my best friend's basement, where we shower each other in beer. I spend hundreds of dollars every year on fantasy football, in a desperate attempt to edge my way onto the sidelines somehow, to win games alongside my heroes.

But why do we get so lost in the fantasy? What's so appealing about being with these athletes? Much of it seems to be rooted in

---

* Not completely true — sometimes I wear Brian Dawkins' number 20, depending on who needs the most support that day.

our obsession with the players' bodies, their impressive physical stature and what it represents: strength, invincibility, sexual prowess. Consider the EMB thread devoted to discussing the "sexual prowess [sic]" of 49ers tight end Vernon Davis.

Davis is an extraordinarily large, dreadlocked black man. He's stronger and faster than most NFL players, and could easily pass as a professional wrestler. The thread features about three dozen pictures of him, half of which are close-ups of his face, and the other half of which are wide-angle shots of him shirtless and/or flexing. To be fair, the thread started as a lighthearted attempt to make some cheap black guy/big dick jokes, but now, at 272 posts, it stands as a testament to something altogether different. One poster writes, "According to scouting reports, Vernon weighs 260 pounds and thirty percent of that weight is his genitals." Another says, "Rumor has it that Vernon wields his enormous member like a sword during games, using it to fight off opposing defenses." Sure, the guys are joking. But at the same time, it's a massive thread devoted to a bunch of guys discussing the size, shape, and effectiveness of a football player's penis.

Although overtly sexual threads like this are the exception on the EMB, there are still plenty of similarly revealing posts:

- Someone posted a picture of then-rookie Brodrick Bunkley in nothing but black boxer briefs. Dozens of posts followed with people using only an animated emoticon to indicate that they were drooling over his cartoonishly muscular upper body. Imagine a man calling a sports radio station and saying, *I get so excited at the thought of Bunkley topless that I'm drooling on my phone right now.* Imagine if it were said in a bar, or a locker room.

- In a thread titled "Who has the best Eagles wife?" one guy brags that "I get a bj at halftime of every game." Three others quickly follow suit* and it is generally agreed that after

---

* And, of course, they're all completely full of shit.

watching the Eagles for an hour, not only should we all have raging hard-ons, but women should be there to service us at halftime and then get the hell out of the way.

- Professional alcoholic Tara Reid appears at an Eagles game wearing a tight Eagles jersey, and is pretty obviously not wearing a bra. People drool over her like they did over Bunkley. They go on to proudly post pictures of their own wives and girlfriends in form-fitting Eagles jerseys. Eagles fans are more sexually attracted to women when they dress up like the players themselves. A wife is okay, but a wife in a Jeremiah Trotter costume is perfect. Fuck sexy nurses; we want sexy linebackers.

- When the Eagles sign free-agent linebacker Takeo Spikes, one poster writes, "I have to admit I am starting to get a little bit of a chubby thinking about [Spikes]." When the Eagles are rumored to be on the verge of trading for defensive tackle Kris Jenkins, he says: "I'm going to sleep but when I wake up we should have Jenkins or I just had a wet dream." Another poster responds: "I know man, if they get Jenkins I'm gonna totally cream my pants."

These are the kinds of things someone would only feel free to say online. In fact, most people wouldn't even allow themselves to *think* like this if they weren't on the EMB. Let's be clear: posts like these don't make their authors gay; in fact, if they *were* gay, their comments wouldn't be interesting at all. The fact that otherwise completely heterosexual men are saying these things reveals another layer of complexity to this whole ordeal, to our own responses to the game. They're sharing thoughts they would never share with other guys in real life. Freed by their anonymity, the posters' inhibitions fall by the wayside. And here, they may finally be finding out how they truly feel about the game, about the players.

CONFESSION NUMBER FOUR: A week ago, I walk into the Whole Foods supermarket with LauraBeth. It's not exactly my kind of place, but we go there because we have to, thanks to her celiac disease,* which necessitates the purchase of all kinds of specialty products you can't find at your standard grocery store. I see a massive black man in a blue sweat suit pull a cart out of the line. He wheels around and I get a quick glimpse of his face; he doesn't look at me, because he's so tall he probably doesn't even see me, and because he seems conditioned to ignoring crowds. Immediately, I recognize him as Eagles offensive tackle William "Tra" Thomas.

When I whisper to her that Tra is here, she laughs and then asks how I know. How would I *not* know, I ask. She asks if I want to follow him. I say no, but she knows I mean yes, so she asks again and I nod, a little ashamed that my idolatry is so transparent.

So we follow him as he picks up an orange. In his hands, it looks like a Ping-Pong ball. I pretend not to watch him squeezing it. At the time I think I'm smooth in my stalking, but probably I'm like a drunk teenager trying to do the sober walk past his parents on the way back into the house—a parody of self-awareness.

Tra loads his cart with fruits and vegetables, and I'm glad to see he's taking care of his body. I'm the only one stalking him, but others are watching. I resent their watching him; they're not fans like I'm a fan. They don't care like I care. They probably don't even know who he is—or that he's had back problems, and blood clots in his legs—and they're only staring because he's the first black guy they've ever seen in Marlton, New Jersey, or because he's a giant and we can't help staring at giants.

When it comes time to pay, I get in line behind Tra to see the money in his hands. I follow him through the parking lot to see him get in his car—an SUV, somewhat disappointing in its lack of ostentation except for the spinning rims. He drives off and I'm left in the parking lot with my fiancée and our bags of gluten-free

---

* Celiac disease is an intolerance to gluten, a protein found in wheat, rye, and barley. As we've learned over the past few years, gluten is in pretty much everything that tastes good, except for Cap'n Crunch and M&M's.

cereal. I don't remember anything else about the trip to the store, and I don't remember if I even talked to her while I was stalking. She's surprisingly comfortable with this, and I get into the car knowing full well that I ought to be ashamed of myself. As we drive, she sees how badly I want to call my friends and subject them to the *guess who I just saw* routine. Seconds later, I'm on the phone, like a fifteen-year-old girl with a crush, relaying every detail to friends who are equally interested in the quality of fruits Tra Thomas eats.

CONFESSION NUMBER FIVE: I'm a depressingly ordinary white guy in his mid-twenties. I'm so embarrassed by my own body that I actively avoid swimming pools and beaches, so I won't have to take my shirt off in front of other people. I was fat in high school, and my greatest athletic triumph was losing sixty pounds just to become a backup on the soccer team. I was seventeen when I peaked as an athlete, and now I'm just another doughy guy with limp arms and the upper-body strength of a corpse. My body is a constant source of disappointment and shame, and I naturally envy the appearance of men like Jevon Kearse, Brodrick Bunkley, and Terrell Owens, who are built like comic book characters. Their bodies are so perfectly sculpted, it's hard to believe they're even human. They look like they're indestructible, like bullets would bounce off of their chests and fall steaming to the ground. When you see people like Kearse, Owens, Dawkins, and Sheldon Brown, it's hard to imagine them ever being injured, sick, dying. How could a body like *that* ever harbor a tumor? How could they ever fall apart? What could possibly knock Goliath down? Sure, they get injured and sick, but it's always a shock, because you can't help being amazed by their appearance, the way they've perfected the human form. Hell yes, I envy their bodies, and I know I'm not the only one.

CONFESSION NUMBER SIX: I once told a friend, while drinking, that although I didn't cry when my Dad died, I would cry if the Eagles won the Super Bowl. I was partially lying when I said this: of course I cried when my Dad died. But the second part is true—not only would I cry if the Eagles won the Super Bowl, but I'm pretty sure I would cry more about the win than the death.

This half-truth seems particularly relevant for two reasons. First, it's fucking weird, and I know this. It's bizarre and inhuman and disrespectful. This all seems so straightforward that it barely warrants discussion.

But here's the second point: my macho chest-pounding in the bar (real men don't cry!) and my intense, thinly veiled vulnerability (this football team means more to me than my own family) are both eerily reminiscent of the tenor of the rhetoric on the EMB.

The EMB is marked by an aggressively masculine ethos, an exaggerated version of locker room bravado. Every post featuring the picture of a woman is guaranteed, within ten minutes, to elicit one specific response: "I'd hit it." Of course, the poster wouldn't just have sex with "it"; he would hit it, because even when he's being intimate, it's violent and painful, and he's totally in charge, like a real man would be. Like the Eagles would be.

Posters on the EMB spend so much time exposing their weaknesses—the emotional venting over losses, the desperation for a winner, the fetishizing of male physiques, etc.—that the remaining posts are a parody of hyper-masculinity. Literally every day, someone starts a new thread about the team's cheerleaders, so people can post the same old pictures, scrutinize their bodies, declare them hittable, and then say something like, "I see twenty hotter girls than that every day." And, as with the guys who claim to get blow jobs during every game, these people are liars, unless they live inside a rap video. Still, every man on the EMB will insist that not only is he surrounded by more beautiful women, but they've done the old in-out with those women and left them behind in tears, because that's what real men do.

It's a locker room atmosphere without the requisite checks and balances. In the locker room, we're limited by our appearance, and by our peers' personal knowledge of us. A guy like Tom McAllister could never get away with the claims swamistubbs can make. Swamistubbs could be a *GQ* model who works at NASA on weekends. No one has ever met DaveTheStud*—maybe he is a stud, and maybe he has bagged all of the Eagles cheerleaders in the past month. Even if one wants to call people on their BS, they can't make the accusation stick. So no one bothers, and then we're all up to our eyes in testosterone. Suddenly, every woman is an open receptacle waiting to be filled by Eagles fans. If any angry boyfriends or husbands get in the way, they'll take their beating and move meekly aside. Everyone on the EMB could kick everyone's ass. Everyone is a ninja.

It's a teenage boy's playground. Unlike with talk radio, you can always get the last word in and make yourself sound reasonably intelligent. You can hide behind false identities and you can pretend to be a legendary lothario, an ass-kicking machine who's built like Brodrick Bunkley. No one tries to stop others from lying, because they don't want to be stopped themselves. If you ruin one person's fantasy, then you ruin everyone's.

Here's what the Internet does: it promises to bring us together, but then it drives us apart from one another and ourselves. It promises anonymity, and yet it reveals parts of ourselves that we've hidden our whole lives.

These players embody so many of our fantasies, and they represent for us some unattainable ideal. Pro sports, ultimately, are about the worship of the human body, and the NFL is about the worship of the male body specifically. It's not about homosexual eroticism so much as it is about wish-fulfillment. We go online to pretend to be someone else, and yet we unwittingly betray the reality that none of us is close to the man we claim to be. This is a dichotomy that can only exist on the Internet, the only place in the world where you can be two people at once and yet still not even be one complete person.

CONFESSION NUMBER SEVEN: I've chosen to list seven confessions here not because of any biblical significance, and not because we rest on the seventh, but because former Eagles

---

* An actual name used on the EMB.

quarterback Ron Jaworski, The Polish Rifle, wore jersey number 7. I wish I were joking.

Jaworski was pretty good, not great, and he has had no direct influence on my life. But he was the predecessor to Randall Cunningham, who was the first really exciting athlete I ever watched, and he was the quarterback on the teams my Dad loved, which makes him part of the extended family. Before I ever watched football, I watched my Dad watching football. I learned how to think and talk about football. Although I hung on to every word he and my older brother, Kevin, shared during the games, I never heard the unspoken words that hovered in the conversational gaps. We watched the games because they did things we could never do, and because the Eagles showed us that it is possible to overcome the limitations of the human body.

One particular game stands out vividly. It's 1996, late September. The Eagles are 3-1 and hosting the hated Dallas Cowboys, who are 1-3 and on the verge of collapsing, so the excitement in the city is palpable. A win buries them for the season and finally puts an end to their loathsome dynasty—they've won three Super Bowls in the past four years—plus it catapults us toward our own championship.

When the Eagles jump out to an early ten-point lead, Kevin and I run around the living room like our shirts are on fire, high-fiving, jumping into walls, screaming. Dad is not a runner or a jumper but he yells along with us and high-fives us and he looks as giddy as I've ever seen him. When the Cowboys score consecutive touchdowns to take the lead, I sulk and complain that the Eagles always blow it, that they're screwed now. And Dad tells me, like he does every week, not to give up, to quit whining in the middle of a game when there's still a chance. Dallas hits a field goal, I sulk more, and Dad glares at me because I should know better.

The Eagles mount a drive, looking like they're about to tie the game before halftime. Quarterback Rodney Peete drops back to pass and he collapses, untouched. The ball trickles out of his grasp and sits less than two feet away from him, taunting him, taunting us. Instead of grabbing the ball, he grips his knee. Cowboys swarm to the ball, dive on it, dive on him, and we know now that the game is over. They will take the ball and score again before halftime. They will go on to turn their season around, finish tied with the Eagles, and win the division by virtue of a tiebreaker. They will host a playoff game and win it. The Eagles will lose a playoff game on the road.

The people on TV tell us Peete collapsed because his cleat got caught in a seam in the turf and his patellar tendon was torn. "Well, that explains the fumble," I say, amazed that something as simple as a rift in a carpet can so easily crumple a great athlete. My brother calls me an idiot and says that's no excuse, he blew it, the season's ruined. I look to Dad, expecting him to rebuke my brother, but he's nodding. "So what he hurt his knee?" Dad says. "That's no excuse for dropping the ball!" I say that when you're in severe pain, you're not thinking about the ball or the team. You're just grabbing your knee and hoping you'll walk again someday. We would all do the same thing, we would all focus on the pain instead of worrying about everyone else. My brother insists that he would have held the ball, and, again, Dad agrees. "They're going to fall on him anyway," he says. "Why not take the pain for another two seconds?" He's sitting on the edge of his seat now, fiddling with nail clippers like he does when he's nervous, and scowls at the screen. If his kids weren't with him, he would unleash a mighty stream of profanity, but he maintains his composure, mostly.

Peete gets carted off and Dad, usually the rational one, tells him to never come back. Then he flops back in his chair. When I begin a new defense of Peete, he glares at me silently and I know the subject's not up for debate.

CHAPTER

THREE

LIFE ON THE SIDELINES

I'VE NEVER played football myself. At least not for real, with pads and helmets and playbooks and swooning cheerleaders. I thought about playing once, but never went to a single practice because my parents had a rule that if you joined a team, you were obligated to stick with them for at least one full season. A full season of football meant months of daily practice, soreness, and exhaustion. I hated running and practicing and pain, and, besides, I had homework to do during the week. Instead of football, I played soccer on Saturdays and kept the rest of my week free. My friends and I did, however, make time to play football after school at least once a week.

Our playing field was near everyone's house but mine. Through some quirk in diocesan laws and plenty of bureaucratic hoop-jumping, the details of which are not at all interesting, I was enrolled at a Catholic school four miles from my house instead of the one at the top of my street. On football days, I'd hitch a ride on Swanson's bus with my duffel bag, do a quick change in his bathroom, and we'd be on our way to the field, each clad in sweatpants, cheap cleats, and a replica NFL jersey. Back then, I wore either number 92 for Reggie White—the evangelical superstar defensive end, one of the greatest Eagles of all time—or number 34 for Kevin Turner, a gritty fullback who even then was an obscure choice.

When we named captains and picked teams, I was usually among the first to go because I was manageably fat—too girthy to tackle easily, but just quick enough to keep up with the game. Like Kevin Turner, I caught short passes and tried to bull through people because I had the agility of a three-legged dog. My skills were invaluable, because first downs had nothing to do with yardage, but rather were earned by making three catches in four downs. On defense, I was either the designated blitzer or I covered the other team's fat guy. When we didn't have another fat guy, I covered Swanson because I think everyone saw us as being more or less interchangeable, an idea with which I generally agreed. I was a serviceable offensive player, but it was defense that I loved. I liked to think I was a punishing tackler, a real tough guy, the Chuck Bednarik of seventh-grade football.

Bednarik was the captain of the Eagles' last championship team, all the way back in 1960. The NFL's last Ironman, the last of the two-way players, he exemplified everything we loved about football. Even though I'd only recently become a serious Eagles fan, I knew everything I needed to know about Bednarik. I had never watched him play, and still have only seen a handful of grainy video clips, but that was more than enough to understand the legend. His nickname, Concrete Charlie, still stands as one of the coolest—both from a metaphorical standpoint, and from an ass-kicking standpoint—in Philly sports history.* And his entire career is encapsulated in the famous photo of him celebrating over Frank Gifford's crumpled body. Gifford had caught a swing pass and scrambled toward the sideline to stop the clock when he was blindsided by Bednarik, who was running full speed and took him down with a move that was more clothesline than tackle, more aggravated assault than fundamental football. Gifford collapsed and lay sprawled like a chalk outline while the ball bounced away.

An aside: a quick trip to the thesaurus reveals that there may not be an adequate adjective to impress upon the reader how dev-

---

* Narrowly edging out "Dr. J" Julius Erving, and beating the following by a wide margin: Shawn "The Stormin' Mormon" Bradley, Rod "He Hate Me" Smart, Rex "The Wonder Dog" Hudler, and Clinton "Pumpy" Tudors.

astating the hit on Gifford was. The pandemic of sports talk radio and the cultural saturation of shouted sports opinion have so cheapened the language and overused some words that they're rendered almost meaningless: "decimate, dominate, crush, kill, pummel, explode." We use these words because they're familiar and easy, even if they don't really mean what they used to mean, and even if we're constantly reminded that those words belong to a wholly different world, one in which *real* soldiers are in *real* battles and suffering *real* injuries, with *real* explosions and murder and death surrounding them. It doesn't take much for us to forget what words really mean, that not too long ago the Blitz was a horrifying assault by the Germans that rained hell down on the British, or that chucking bombs used to mean something completely different—and used to be much harder to justify—than hurling a football downfield willy-nilly. Somewhere along the line, the ideas got conflated and we lost sense of what everything means, to the point that most weeks at least one NFL game will feature a famous variation on the bomb play—the Hail Mary—in which the grisly imagery of war and the sanctifying imagery of the Virgin Mary become hopelessly intertwined and combine to mean something so much more hollow than ever before. War imagery and religion always have gone hand in hand, but applying either to a football game cheapens them both, and to allow them to be combined and used as simple sports metaphors seems almost hopelessly sad and misguided. The NFL, more than any other league, has co-opted our spiritual and nationalistic ideals, watered them down, repackaged them with a catchy soundtrack and tricky camera angles, and sold them back to us at triple the price. And we gladly pay them whatever they ask.

So this all leaves us with stale language that makes Bednarik's life-changing hit on Gifford sound like any old run-of-the-mill tackle, like the ones you see every week on the highlight shows. But this was a hit that caused Gifford to retire immediately. He returned to the NFL over a full season later, but, for a while, the hit had completely eradicated Gifford's will (and ability) to play football, transforming him from *Frank Gifford, star halfback* to

Frank Gifford, has-been. But still, that's not too spectacular; players get injured every day and they don't all become legendary. What makes this injury so legendary is that Gifford's teammates legitimately thought he was dead. Before Gifford was hit, a Giants fan had had a heart attack and was rushed by paramedics to the Giants' locker room, where he died. After the game, the Giants players walked into the locker room just in time to see medical personnel covering the heart attack victim with a sheet. Several Giants have since admitted that they thought the man under the sheet was Frank Gifford.

Back to the field—post-hit, Bednarik stood over Gifford in what has become a famous pose: Bednarik stares down at him, his weight on his left foot as he lands after a celebratory jump, fist cocked at about ear level as if he's about to drive a trident into Gifford's heart. He's predatory, exuberant in the violence of the moment, a barbarian just after the kill. Supposedly, he's in the midst of screaming, "This fucking game is over!"

This photo is one of the NFL's iconic images. Black-and-white, it harkens back to the days when men were men, a symbol for an entire era of football that's long dead, disappearing along with thirty-game winners in baseball and short shorts in the NBA. It exemplifies so much about what draws us to the game; it practically radiates with rage, justifiable violence, conquest, a euphoric manifestation of our animal instincts. Search online and you'll find thousands of these pictures available, most bearing Bednarik's autograph. I own one, although it's not autographed, and Swanson has a poster-sized version hanging on his bedroom wall.

So when we played football, I strived to emulate the legend of Concrete Charlie. I wanted to be the hardest-hitting, fiercest SOB any seventh grader had ever seen. I let people catch passes just so I could hit them. On offense, I preferred not to touch the ball because I wanted to block people downfield. I wanted to send my friends home bruised and limping, too sore to sit.

Once, I overheard someone complaining about being covered by me because he said I was a headhunter. I realized then that I wasn't playing hard so much as I was playing dirty and spearing peo-

ple with their backs turned. Instead of earning my friends' respect
with my aggression, I'd provoked their scorn. Still, it was the only
way I knew how to play, and I loved hearing the gasps on the field
when I laid down a particularly brutal hit. Nothing was more satis-
fying than a sudden violent eruption and the cheers that followed.

WE WERE in eighth grade when we staged one of our biggest
games ever: seven-on-seven instead of our usual four-on-four, and
the extra guys were some of the coolest kids in class, the kids with
swimming pools and Ping-Pong tables, the ones who'd seen real
breasts and tasted stolen cigarettes. Seven-on-seven meant offensive linemen and cluttered passing routes. It meant a greater
chance of fights breaking out. It meant greater glory to the winners.

I played well that day. Scored a couple touchdowns, had an interception and a couple sacks. If the larger rosters meant there
was more pressure, then this may have been the only time in my
life I handled pressure well. My diving interception of a batted
ball was the play of the day. I even got in a fight with Swanson. It
was nothing more than a cartoon dust rumble, and I have no idea
what caused it, but it would have made every network's highlight
reel. We rolled at least twenty yards, clubbing each other weakly
on the back and trying to rub the other's head in the dirt. The
other guys eventually pulled us apart. We retreated to our respec-
tive huddles, spat, and then played as if nothing had happened.

My team won, and it wasn't close. I looked forward to the next
morning in the schoolyard when we would recount our game and
reminisce about how great I had been. I would inch our little circle closer to the jump-roping girls so they could overhear us talking about my sacks, my diving catch, the fight. They would beg for
details and I would graciously, humbly shrug and defer to my
friends, who would regale them with the specifics of my prowess,
my manliness.

Normally, we would have played a second game, but nobody,
except maybe me, was interested that day. Everyone wanted to go

back to Keith's house, the real reason we had a bigger crowd than usual. Keith, a tiny kid who cried through most of our games, lived a minute's walk from the field, and his parents wouldn't be home until late. More important, his parents had an illegal cable box that gave them access to every channel, including Playboy and Spice. He promised we could all go back to his place and watch porn together. Since this was long before the Internet became a deep reservoir of free, easily accessible pornography, we had to capitalize on this opportunity.

Everyone except Swanson went to Keith's house. He didn't say why. I knew it was because he felt awkward watching porn with thirteen other guys and that he was afraid to get in trouble, but I stayed with the group instead of following him. Mick called him a fag as he walked away and everyone laughed. We went down into Keith's basement and left the lights off. The anticipation was palpable. I was breathing heavily, as if I'd just run for a long touchdown, and my stomach twisted into a painful knot. Thanks to careless older brothers and benevolent cousins, we'd all seen our share of centerfolds, but to see naked women in action was completely different. It was more *real*.

Thirteen of us went down to that basement and arranged ourselves in a half-moon on couches and beanbag chairs. At first, we chattered nervously, laughing at everything even if it wasn't funny.

"Damn, those tits look like basketballs!"

"Why are they still wearing high heels?"

"We gotta get some cheerleaders at our games."

We spoke into a void. There was no call-and-response; we spoke mainly because we wanted to act nonchalant about the whole thing, as if sex was routine. Each comment was nearly unrelated to the last, but we kept talking because we wanted everyone to know we were still watching. Nobody took their eyes off the TV or the bouncing breasts of a frisky cheerleader in the locker room shower with the star quarterback. Another cheerleader walked in on them, shrugged, and stripped. During the frenzied commentary of disembodied voices, someone noted that the new girl looked kind of like Molly, one of the popular girls in our class. Both Molly and Cheerleader had dark curly hair anyway, but only one of them had gargantuan breasts and a pierced clitoris.* But, still, close enough.

"I wish Molly was here right now," someone said. "I'd bone her in the closet."

Someone else chimed in: "I'd rather have Julia."

"What about both? I'd do them both."

"Julia's face is nasty," O'Connell said. "All big-nosed and shit." Still no one turned from the TV, but the initial shock had subsided and now we were able to focus on the conversation.

Tony jumped into the fray: "Yeah, but I'd put a flag over her face and fuck her for my country." We laughed, and a few guys imitated the funky porn music while Tony stood and humped the air.

"Why don't we call them up?" O'Connell said.

We looked around the room, waiting for someone to explain that you can't just invite girls over to your parents' basement to watch porn with a bunch of dudes. But no one said that. "Nah," Keith said. "By the time they get here, my parents will be home."

"Damn."

"But if they were here, it would be awesome."

"I bet Julia would wear those tight shorts, and she'd be all up on Bill like she always is."

"Molly would be over here on the couch with her titties hanging all out and shit." Tony jumped up and did the air-humping number again while everyone lost themselves in their fantasies. We fell back into the porn trance. The cheerleader bit had ended and now some nurse was, predictably, being naughty.

"I think Alexis is pretty hot," I said, but no one responded. "I'd fuck her." I looked away from the screen and saw Mick, crammed between two other guys on the couch, slipping his hand down his pants. Nobody spoke. The silence, punctuated by on-screen groans, threatened to choke us. Mick asked Keith for a blanket, which Keith tossed across the room. His lap covered, Mick slid his pants down to his ankles.

---

* Not that I knew what a clitoris was at the time.

Next, O'Connell asked for a blanket, then Tony, then Rich. I couldn't believe anyone could have so many blankets; it was like watching stolen porn in the basement of some Persian palace. The only two still wearing pants were me and Bill. I announced that we were going in the other room, but I doubt they heard me. Bill followed me upstairs, where we hooked up the Sega Genesis and popped in a football game. I closed the door and Bill turned up the volume so we couldn't hear the moans of the naughty nurse. The next day, nobody talked about what had happened. The girls never heard about my heroics, and I wasn't sure I wanted anyone to know.

CONVERSATION IN the schoolyard* almost always focused on one of two subjects: girls and sports. Gossip about girls followed typical patterns: who's hot, who's not; who's a slut, who's not; and where's the best place to sit if you want to see up their skirts? We were experts in the study of skirted women's legs, although we continually learned that the whole Catholic schoolgirl thing works differently in real life than it does in the movies.

If we had played football the day before, we would rehash the game's big plays: the dropped balls, the broken fingers, the time Pete ran the wrong way and scored on his own end zone. But we also envisioned the girls as cheerleaders swooning over our athletic prowess. We concocted elaborate fantasies—about Alexis, Molly, Julia, whomever—showing up just in time to see us all sweaty and muddy and glorious in our victory, swigging Gatorade as blood trickled down our knees and stained our socks. Alexis, of course, would be so impressed that she would tackle me and pin me right on the field, her hands roaming over my developing mus-

---

* Full disclosure—schoolyard, in this case, does not refer to some idyllic hopscotched and swingsetted field that overflowed with the hopes and dreams of youth. It refers to a slanted, gum-dotted parking lot edged by dumpsters and a line of trees that reputedly housed at least two crazy drifters.

cles, and mine frantically groping every part of her that I could touch, parts I'd strained so hard to see from every angle in the classroom. Sweat and saliva would mingle on her tongue, the dirt and blood pressed between us, but we wouldn't care. I would hold on to her and never let go. I would own her.

We took turns going around the circle, offering different names, different scenarios, all with the same end result—football glory, lustful girls, heroic conquest on the field and off. The fantasies gradually became more graphic as we raided porn stashes in brothers' closets and parents' sock drawers; watched shoplifted porn videos in groups of twenty, tight-lipped and saucer-eyed; and huddled around pay phones to hear the moaning of a phone sex operator who didn't just want us, but needed us inside her.

It probably goes without saying that our fantasies never came true. Twice, while I was in high school, I invited girls to watch me play football. In both cases, my friends and I had banded together to play groups from other neighborhoods in eleven-on-eleven real football with playbooks, offensive lines, and high-stakes gambling for either money or beer. The first time, we won in a blowout, but the girl I'd brought spent half the game talking to our quarterback on the sideline before leaving with him. The second time, we got trampled by a team that was bigger and faster than us, and on the last play of the game I missed a tackle, collided with a teammate, and cracked my head just above the eye, spilling more blood than I care to remember. Caked in mud and failure, I sat in the ER for three hours with a rag pressed against my head, waiting to get twenty-one stitches above my left eye. The two girls I'd invited did not stay with me, and, before leaving, one told me not to look at her because I was disgusting. They left with a couple of guys from the other team, and I called Mom to tell her I was in the hospital with a broken head.

STILL IN eighth grade, a few of us got together to play football on a Friday night at our usual field—Apartment Hill, a sloping, uneven hill adjacent to a row of apartments, terribly suited for football, but very close to most of my friends' houses. Early in the game, a group of the cool kids in our class showed up uninvited and demanded that we give them our ball. Quinn stood defiantly on the field while five of us shuffled off to the sideline. There were three of them—Joe, Coady, and Bobby—and I think they were drunk. They shoved Quinn and slapped at the ball, but he held on to it. I pretended not to see; I wanted to be friends with the popular guys, and I knew they would make fun of me later for being out with this crowd. When I wasn't with Swanson, Quinn, and Anthony, I was with Joe, usually doing things I knew were wrong. We shoplifted as much candy as we could fit in our Eagles Starter Jackets. We stole beers from our parents and sipped them in the woods, cringing like we'd just stepped on a nail. We ran a shopping cart through the show window at Pep Boys and then tried to set their wood fence on fire. When that didn't work, we kicked down the entire fence, one section at a time. We ran from the cops a lot. These guys hung out with easy girls and drank beer, smoked cigarettes and raised hell. Swanson and I played football and video games, drank orange soda, and watched bad horror movies like *Killer Klowns from Outer Space* in his basement.

Quinn was as stubborn as he was outnumbered, so they offered a deal: we'll leave you alone if you can score a touchdown on us.

Quinn agreed. They punted it and all three sprinted toward him. He avoided one tackle and then had a clear lane to the end zone. Easy touchdown. Six points, game over, get the hell off our field. I moved closer to my friends. But wait, Coady said, I wasn't ready, that one didn't count. Fine, Quinn said, let's do it again.

Another punt, same result. Quinn spiked the ball and glared at them from the end zone. Joe charged and tackled him. The other two piled on. Quinn wriggled out from beneath them, and then Coady kicked him in the head.* They picked the ball up and

---

* Quinn now claims he was never kicked in the head, but I'm pretty sure that's because his memory is fuzzy from having been kicked in the head.

spiked it on his chest. As they walked away, I stared into the dirt as if looking for a dropped contact lens. Later, when Quinn asked why I didn't do anything, I lied and told him I thought Bobby had a knife. The other guys helped Quinn to his feet. I stayed behind, unable to look him in the eye.

FOOTBALL WASN'T the only sport I cared about back then; there was also soccer. Because I was too slow to play in the field, and because I was closest to the net when our original goalkeeper had quit mid-game, I was a goalie for the Roxborough Indians. We'd won two championships—one indoor and one outdoor—and I was actually pretty good. I even collected a couple all-star T-shirts, won a few big games, and still remember the time when we were playing West Philly in the playoffs and I stopped five consecutive shots at point-blank range, the final four while contorting and writhing on my back because I didn't have time to get back on my feet. There were only twenty people on our sideline, but I remember the cheers as an eruption, as if we were in a packed arena. I remember walking away from that game with Dad as he told me—as he always did—how many saves I'd made: forty, on forty-one shots, a pair of numbers I scrawled in the margins of my notebooks and in my desk for the next week, calculating and recalculating my save percentage.

Mom and Dad attended every game I ever played, even years later when Dad was sick and I was playing in a men's league in North Philly. Afterward, Dad liked rehashing the game with me. He seemed to have a photographic memory, recalling plays and details that even I couldn't. These post-game dialogues represented the first and easiest bond we had; although I was a weak conversationalist and we had differing interests, we could always talk about sports.

After that game against West Philly, Dad took me to Dunkin' Donuts, a reward usually reserved for shutouts. He ordered a coffee and a chocolate frosted, I got a chocolate milk with a vanilla sprinkled. Conversation had always come easier for us when there was good food on the table,* and now we discussed the game, my starring role in the win. Behind us, a weathered old man in a black hat mumbled into his coffee, just as he did every morning and night. Dad knew him and had bought him the coffee. His name was Cal-Cal, and they had been business partners lifetimes ago. They didn't speak otherwise. Everything that ever needed to be said between them had been said long before I was born, back when Dad risked his life to save Cal-Cal's.

We went home that night and I felt good about myself. I probably should have felt good about Dad too, but I had no idea how he knew Cal-Cal; I assumed they'd met when Dad was working for the Post Office. The next day, my heroics were the hot topic in the schoolyard, and I basked in my momentary glory.

Unfortunately, in the schoolyard, soccer talk rarely lasted very long, and usually by lunchtime other items were on the agenda. Namely, bicycles and baseball.

I hated both.

I never learned how to ride a bike. It scared the hell out of me when I was younger and, even after I took the traditional training wheel ride where Dad guided me by hand and secretly let go, thus tricking me into riding on my own power, I was reluctant to take that bike out on the streets where other people could see me. When I finally did join the other kids in riding around the block, I realized, in a sudden awful moment, that I'd never asked how to stop a bike. This ride ended with me screaming "Where's the brakes?" as I sped downhill toward a neighbor's garage. Everyone saw, or at least heard, me plow into the garage door. And everyone thought it was hilarious. I limped home, dragging my bike behind me and hearing the echoes of their laughter.

I have since learned where the brakes are, but I never rode a

---

* Although neither of us was a good chef, we both loved good food. In the years since Dad's death, LauraBeth has taught me how to cook—beyond boiling water and adding noodles—and I've become reasonably good at it. During big family meals, I sometimes regret that I can't share my newfound skills with Dad.

bike again. As an adult, it's not much of a hindrance to be bikeless. But when you're twelve, the whole world seems to be about bikes. Except for Swanson, everyone rode them almost every day. They all had fun and met girls and caused mischief, and I never had access to any of it. Still, I could have tolerated being shut out of the world of bikes if it weren't for baseball.

Kevin had played baseball for two years and never gotten a hit. Dad thought baseball was boring, and Mom thought it was worse. We only watched games when my grandmother was around, and I didn't own my first real glove until I was ten. I was so ignorant of even the most basic baseball strategies that when we played Wiffle ball in the neighborhood, I once bunted with the bases loaded and two outs, just because someone had told me to. When we picked teams, I was always the last one chosen.

Unfortunately, we may have been the only family in the whole neighborhood that didn't love baseball. Roxborough* is flooded with guys who made it to the low minor leagues and had their careers derailed by bad luck, injury, arrest, or surprise pregnancy. It's also flooded with kids who dream of making it to double-A ball and flaming out at age twenty-six with a torn rotator cuff and a drinking problem. So when baseball started, everything else ended.

Everyone played except for me and Swanson. Even most of the girls played softball. Most weeknights, I knew Al Pearlman Field was flooded with my classmates, either playing a game or watching other teams' games. Guys spent more time with their teammates than with their families, and they lingered at the field long

---

* Philly is one of those cities that is divided into many distinct neighborhoods. If someone asks you where you're from, you don't say Philly; instead, you say Fishtown, or Kensington, or the Main Line, and so on. I'm from Roxborough, or Manayunk, depending where you draw the border, and both towns are generally considered very blue-collar and very white, although both are currently being gentrified and diversified, the discussion of which would necessitate the writing of another full book. The name Manayunk, I should note, comes from the Lenape word "manaiung," which means "where we go to drink."

after their games to stare at the girls' breasts as they bounced down the baseline. They ate pizza and soda, and their parents left them alone. On any given night, I could sit alone in my bedroom and know that Jones was throwing a shutout, Brian was flirting with Alexis and she kinda liked it, and everyone in the neighborhood had seen O'Connor (or Schrank, or DiBenedetto, it didn't matter who) hit a game-winning double. I was never there. At first, because I thought baseball was too boring, and later because I was too stubborn to admit I wanted to be a part of it. By the middle of high school, it felt like it was too late to join the party, like they'd closed ranks without me and left me at home with my books and my video games. I had family, even if I wasn't very interested in that. I had a friend, maybe two. And I hated baseball. During baseball season, I was alone. I needed something else in my life, but didn't know where to find it.

CHAPTER
FOUR

BEST OF PHILLY

HOT GREASE splashed into my eye for the third time that night, and I spiked my spatulas onto the griddle. "Uh-oh, Duff, he's breaking down," Fitz said. He and Duffy laughed. They were the veterans on the crew, the best workers we had. I was the new guy, about a month into my tenure at D'Alessandro's, the best cheesesteak shop in Philly.* Duffy and Fitz were called "pullers." They made the sandwiches. They got the glory, such as it was, and they cranked out orders so quickly that even the managers and customers couldn't keep up.

I was what they called a "feeder." I did everything else that wasn't making sandwiches—stocking the fridge, emptying the slop bucket, refilling the sauce pots, whatever they needed. Mostly, though, I stood in the corner, threw fifteen pounds of frozen meat on the griddle, and chopped the hell out of it while it sizzled. On my first day, they told me the meat should be chopped so fine you could snort it. The older guys made it look easy—Fitz could cook two full trays of meat and have them ground into dust within ten minutes. I was cooking a half tray and took at least twenty minutes to chop it well, by which time it was already dry and rubbery. A good feed pile was still moist, a corona of grease radiating from it.

---

* In my opinion, of course. Although it hasn't won the coveted Best of Philly award in a decade, it is routinely in the running. We never won Best of Philly while I was there, a failure for which the older guys blamed us, saying we didn't have the same work ethic or skills as their generation did.

Sweat dripped from the tip of my nose onto the griddle. We were almost out of cooked meat and the line stretched out the door. Fitz and Duffy refused to help. They joined the customers in staring at me as I hammered the spatulas against frozen beef, while everyone else in the tiny shop did nothing, nothing at all.

Everything about this job hurt. My wrist screamed with each swing, and my fingers locked themselves into a claw. My arms were dotted with burns from airborne beef, my thigh blistered from accidentally leaning against the grill. Grease had already shot up my nose, and now it had splashed my eye.

The inside of my eyelid burned, and I wondered if grease could blind someone. I heard them laughing. And I chopped some more. Fitz and Duffy didn't even offer me a drink when they filled their own sodas from the fountain.

Four hours later, the rush had subsided. I finished up another feed and slumped against the wall. Fitz told me to take a break, eat a sandwich. I thanked him and started eating. Then he notified the manager that I was slacking off, eating without permission. She rushed over and made me trash the sandwich. After being reprimanded, I slogged back to the griddle. Fitz and Duffy cackled again. I had liked them both prior to this shift—Duffy was the one who had gotten me the job, and Fitz had this enviable charisma that made all the customers love him. And, damn, they were good at their jobs.* But near the end of this Friday night shift, I hated both of them. I wanted Duffy to cut himself slicing a sandwich. I wanted Fitz to spill bubbling hot sauce on his wrists.

Fitz gave me a list of things he needed me to bring up from the basement. Two items on the list didn't even exist—a squeegee scraper and a left-handed spatula—but I still spent the next forty-

---

* A quality I've always admired, thanks largely to Mom and Dad, who were good at their jobs, and also emphasized the importance of taking pride in your performance. The people Dad respected were hard workers who did their jobs the right way, regardless of what the job was. If we got good service anywhere—restaurants, gas stations, convenience stores—he always sought out the manager and praised the employees. He was a born manager, and all he wanted was for people to take their work seriously.

five minutes carrying up tray after tray of meat, cases of ketchup, boxes of burgers—everything that could be carried upstairs was carried upstairs. Finally, they let me take a real break, and Fitz handed me a soda. I took a big gulp, and it burned all the way down. They'd spiked it with Tabasco.

Everyone in the shop, including the handful of late-night customers, laughed at me, but still, I tried to play it cool. "I don't appreciate your ruse," I said, referencing a line from the movie *Clerks.*

"What the fuck is a ruse?" Fitz said.

"Whoa, smart guy. We aren't all rich enough to go to *La Salle,*" Duffy said.

I told them it was a line from a movie, but Fitz shook his head. "You just made that shit up." He lifted a roll and said, "Hey, Duffy, you wanna help me ruse this sandwich?"

"You're not using it right," I said.

"Sorry," he said, grinning. "I didn't mean to ruse you."

"It's a real word. And that's not how you use it."

"It is in *my* book."

I said, "Is that the same book that got you stuck working here for the rest of your life?" For the first time all night, Fitz and Duffy were speechless. Fitz trudged into the back room, and Amanda, our hoagie girl, told me I was mean. Duffy shook his head, said they were just having fun, breaking me in, and I'd crossed the line by getting personal. I slumped against the wall and counted the seconds until I could go away.

I WORKED at D'Alessandro's for five years and left no friends behind when I finally quit. Two of the four hoagie girls spent most of their time talking about dropping out of high school, while I lectured them on the virtues of a good education. Not surprisingly, we didn't talk much. The other guys on the grill were okay—we got along well enough, but the differences between our high schools produced obstacles we couldn't overcome, even after I'd graduated. I went to a private Catholic boys' high school out in the suburbs. Almost everyone in Roxborough went to Roxborough High or Roman Catholic. Roxborough was the kind of school that spends half its time assuring people that there isn't a discipline problem, even while they're installing metal detectors and barring the windows. Roman is the school everyone's father, and most people's grandfathers, had attended. Dad went there, and I had visited the school with him. It looked dingy and old, rundown, like an orphanage. Not at all the kind of place where I wanted to spend the next four years. Still, it was where you were supposed to go.

So, when I, along with Anthony and Quinn,* ended up at La Salle High, people in the neighborhood disapproved. I did not enroll there to make any kind of statement; I wouldn't have admitted it then, but I went there because Kevin had also done so six years earlier. He was always better liked than I was—by classmates, neighborhood kids, cousins and uncles—and so I spent much of my life emulating him. So when it came to high schools, I never truly considered any other option, because it had always seemed to me that if La Salle was good enough for Kevin, then it was good enough for me. If he'd gone to Roman or Roxborough High, I would have gone there. I don't know exactly why he picked La Salle, but it was clearly the best high school Mom and Dad could afford, a place whose main mission was to prepare students for college. Although Mom and Dad hadn't gone to college—Dad couldn't afford it, and Mom went directly from high school to nursing school—their expectations for us were very clear: we would go to college and we would excel. There was no other option. They checked our homework every day, quizzed us on what we'd learned in classes, encouraged us to develop an intellectual curiosity. The teaching never stopped in our house. By the time I was ten years old, I knew never to ask Dad the meaning of a word, because he would just send me to fetch the dictionary anyway; many of our conversations consisted of him dropping ob-

---

* Swanson went to a suburban Catholic school that was not Roman or La Salle.

scure (but contextually appropriate) words in mid-conversation and me turning quietly away to grab the dictionary and figure out what he was saying.*

Point is, I liked learning, I was a really good student, and we all knew this was the best school for me. But that didn't matter to some people, like the kids from Roxborough High who chased me from my bus stop back to my house, shouting threats the whole way. They'd seen me in my uniform sweater and khakis and charged, calling me a fag and warning me to stay off their street.

Most of the people we knew were doing the same exact thing their parents had done, and we were doing something different, something outside the neighborhood, and this doesn't sit well in Philly, whose unofficial motto could be "What, you think you're better than me?" After a while, I did think I was better than them. The more they taunted me or threw cigarettes at me, the more I fired back at them, mocking their stupid tattoos,† telling them I went to my school because I wanted to go to college instead of being a roofer like everybody else.

One problem: I wasn't rich at all. Despite the partial scholarship I'd earned, my parents went deep into debt just to send me to high school. Dad worked seventy-hour weeks, Mom worked overtime. They rarely spent money on themselves, and they took out a second mortgage. We got the negatives of being rich and influential without the actual riches or influence. My co-workers looked down on my high school for being preppy and faggy, and I looked down on theirs for being inferior and trashy. Most of the people who worked there had either not gone to college or wouldn't graduate, so they prided themselves on their high school identities. The first thing new hires were asked was what high school they'd attended. They all said Roman, then spent the next

---

* Naturally, I made it my mission to stump him, spending whole days compiling lists of X and Q words, practicing their usage, and then casually testing him later in the day. I never got him.

† Always on the biceps, always one or more of the following: shamrocks, Italian flags, names (or nicknames) in Old English script.

half hour filling the other Roman alums in on all the school gossip. Meanwhile, I leaned over the griddle and chopped away at my meat pile, silently wishing I could take as much pride in my school as they did in theirs.

As impressive as La Salle High was academically and aesthetically—situated on fifty-seven suburban acres, it was more picturesque, and more demanding, than many colleges I've visited—it was never the place for me socially. I met kids with surnames like Von Medicus, Vandiver, and Halfpenny. Kids whose parents didn't work construction, but owned construction companies. Kids who got brand-new Mustang convertibles on their sixteenth birthdays, while I didn't even have a license because I couldn't afford insurance. I resented everything about them. I thought they were all spoiled, coddled, unfairly entitled. I didn't like or understand La Salle kids, and I didn't want to.

The end result of which was me and three other guys creating *The Scourge,* an underground newspaper we clandestinely distributed throughout the school. If underground papers are supposed to give voice to outsiders, offer alternative viewpoints, or challenge the administration, we were not an underground paper in the truest sense of the word. More accurately, we were four unhappy guys who bitched about school in a somewhat creative and very public way. Whereas most underground press is focused on the collective good, ours existed only to serve our personal needs. I wrote the front-page article, entitled "A Beginner's Guide to Life at La Salle." The article seethed with rage and listed every complaint I'd ever had against the school. It stereotyped every broad group of students—hockey players, stoners, trust fund kids, etc.—and insulted them as pointedly as possible. Near the end, I wrote:

> After you find your way around the school and all your grades are earned, remember La Salle's one golden rule and you'll be fine: Conformity Is Key. Being an individual does nothing but make the teachers' jobs harder and force we [sic], the students, to learn to tolerate different types of people. Our parents pay for every-

thing for us, just so that we can close ourselves off from the more inferior people in our world, and avoid the struggle that is always associated with learning and stretching the mind.

I showed this article to Dad, who would read almost anything.* Beginning with the play I'd written in second grade—titled *Dinosaurs,* it was about dinosaurs, mostly walking around in circles, complaining about the heat, and then fighting, which meant that about half of the dialogue was "Auuugh, that hurts!" or "Ow! I'm bleeding!"—he had always encouraged my writing, poring over everything, no matter how terrible, showing it to coworkers, and offering feedback. He took this all very seriously, treating me like a legitimate author rather than some bored kid who had written fourth-rate imitations of stuff he'd read in school. No matter what I wrote, Dad read it, putting down his latest Heinlein book and taking his editing pen to the page while I sat quietly on the couch awaiting his approval. It was these moments, more than any others, that made me want to become a writer. I pretended to watch TV, but I was really watching him, anticipating his laughter or his impressed nods. When he finished, he detailed the story's virtues. He gave a couple suggestions for improvement, or maybe said the story reminded him of some book he'd read by Heinlein, or Asimov, or Bradbury. Then he handed the story back to me, and I took it upstairs, where I worked on it some more. Or I dug through his mountain of books and started reading the one he'd referenced.

Later, in college, I wouldn't show him everything I'd written, but he would still ask to see my essays and stories, and we would go through the same process. Every time, I felt like a ten-year-old eagerly awaiting his praise and recognition. And when he was dying in the hospital, and I couldn't find the words to say good-

---

* One of my most enduring memories of Dad is how, every weekend, he fell asleep in his recliner, a half-finished book open on his chest. It was always a sci-fi paperback pulled from the waist-high stacks in his bedroom. After he died, we gathered his old books to donate them, and found seven copies of *Stranger in a Strange Land* stashed throughout the house.

bye, I wrote him a letter. I handed it to him, hoping he would read it while I watched, but he was too weak to hold it up. I had to read it aloud while he struggled to stay awake and hear me. I'm not sure how much he heard, because the last two paragraphs were read through a haze of tears and choked out between sobs. While I struggled, he grabbed my hand and held it weakly until I finished. This, as I would say during his eulogy, was the most difficult thing I've ever had to do. We would have one more conversation after that—the one about Jerome McDougle—but this was our official good-bye.

About three days before he died, he was barely conscious, in a drug-induced haze and mumbling something incoherent about a car. Mom patted him on the head and told him I had gotten an A in my Creative Writing class, his eyes opened, and he looked directly at me. He whispered, very clearly, "He's gonna write a best-seller someday." Now, I'm no believer in prophecy or magic or mysticism, and I doubt I'll ever write a best-seller, but this is what he said and it's not the sort of thing you forget. It's the sort of thing that gives you a direction, no matter how uncomfortable or frightening.

But let's get back to *The Scourge*. Despite the pretentious prose, Dad liked my article well enough, but suggested that it may not be a good idea to actually distribute the paper. Why not just write it, keep it to yourself, and ride it out until graduation? What were we going to gain by insulting everyone?

The tone of the rest of the paper was pretty similar to my article: three pages of watered-down Vonnegut and Joseph Heller, dashed with plenty of generic teenage angst. We distributed it, of course, because by the time Dad suggested that I rethink it, we were past the point of no return. People all over the school were talking about *The Scourge* by lunchtime. A member of the hockey team stomped down the hallway bellowing that he was going to kick the shit out of whoever wrote this fucking *Scourge*. We saw teachers reading it and heard administrators were investigating. We were sure we would get away with it. We were smug like that.

We got caught the next day. We'd told about thirty people that it was us, and one of my teachers recognized my writing style. Under normal circumstances we definitely would have been suspended, maybe even expelled. But we didn't even get detention.

The Scourge happened only a few months after Columbine. Everyone in the country was still convinced that the schools were filled with gun-toting little Harrises and Klebolds itching to go on a killing spree. Now La Salle had their own Trenchcoat Mafia, a term administrators actually used when talking with us. They never said so, but we were sure they didn't discipline us because they were afraid we would come back with automatic weapons and dirty bombs.

Instead of suspension, they created a student diversity council, which consisted of The Scourge conspirators, three of the school's seven black kids, the school's one Jewish kid, a gay guy, and a couple athletes. We sat in a circle and talked about diversity for a half hour, offering a few half-assed suggestions on how to better foster harmony on campus. Everyone shook hands and left. We never met again. This meeting accomplished nothing for the school, obviously, but it did force me to reflect on my own motivations.

I hadn't realized it then, but my simultaneous condescension toward both La Salle and Roxborough signaled the fact that I'd adopted the worst of my two cultures. At La Salle I tried to play the part of the violent thug, and in Roxborough, I was an elitist snob. I had always portrayed myself as an outsider. I wore my Jim Morrison T-shirts (twelve of them, total) almost every day, thinking my obsession with The Doors somehow set me apart from the kids of my generation who listened to crappy pop music. Later, I realized that *every* teenage boy goes through a Jim Morrison phase, but eventually they all understand that he was a self-indulgent, self-important man-boy who just happened to be a great performer. I sulked in the corners at parties, thinking my brooding darkness made me deep, but it just made me unpleasant. During classes, I compiled lists (138 names long) of people I hated at La Salle, but never included myself.

At lunchtime, I sat at the freaks table with the angry kids who played guitar, draped themselves in black, and smoked a lot of pot. We scowled through lunch and listened to the angriest music we could find—Metallica, Fear Factory, Deicide, Slipknot,* etc. I didn't have much in common with them: all suburban kids, they complained about their parents, talked about drugs, and drummed songs on the table with their fingers; I was from the city and liked my parents, didn't do any drugs, and had no musical ability at all. But they were the only La Salle kids with whom I got along, as we bonded over our shared anger. During one lunch period, they pushed me to confront Tony, a hockey player who had been sending me threatening online instant messages because I'd stolen his best friend's girlfriend.† I stomped over to him, threatened to break his jaw—regretting that I couldn't come up with a cool one-liner like Dad might have—and nothing happened. One of his friends warned, "Be careful, he's from Roxborough!" and Tony slunk away without saying a word. The guys at D'Alessandro's would have loved that line about me being from Roxborough; anyone who considered me tough or intimidating must be *really* weak. The contrast between the two places couldn't have

---

* Sample Slipknot lyrics: "Insane—Am I the only motherfucker with a brain? I'm hearing voices but all they do is complain."

† I'd done so in a particularly sleazy fashion, sending her a love letter while she was on a four-day religious retreat with her school. I'd gone on the same retreat myself months earlier, and found it to be somewhat pleasant but not at all life-changing as some classmates had claimed. We did a lot of praying, sharing, and venting. People smoked a lot of cigarettes, stayed up all night playing acoustic guitar, and ate terrible food. It was kind of an alcohol-free preview of dorm life. We were supposed to have been filled with the holy spirit, but I felt no closer to god than I had at any other time in my life. Also, there's something mildly sinister about a retreat that forces seventeen-year-olds to live a semi-monastic lifestyle, then bombards them with religious messages while they're vulnerable and exhausted and lonely. Maybe my ambivalence about the whole thing made it easier for me to justify abusing the system and sending the letter to her in the first place. Or maybe I had no qualms about it because she was the hottest girl I'd ever met, and I wasn't used to hot girls liking me. Ultimately, all of this drama turned out to be wasted energy, because I cheated on her over the summer and I haven't spoken to her in almost ten years.

been starker: in one, I was a fruity rich kid who didn't know his place; in the other, I was a hard-nosed city kid who didn't fit in.

Condescending to both groups the way I did was as much about judging them as it was a denial of who I was, what I did have in common with them. There was some truth in the things people said when they mocked me. I was an egotistical elitist. I was socially uncouth. I was out of place. Their taunts tapped into what was probably my biggest fear: I was afraid to turn out to be unremarkable, to be a nobody. At the very least, I hoped to be a spectacular failure—the Ed Wood of Roxborough. At both school and home, I was nobody, even if I refused to admit it, and I blamed them for it instead of blaming myself.

IN DECEMBER 2000, during our first Winter Break from college, Swanson and I camped out for Eagles playoff tickets, scoring four tickets each for a Wild Card playoff game against the Tampa Bay Bucs. My then-girlfriend seemed horrified by the fact that not only would I willingly spend a December night outside, but that I cared so much about football. "Oh, so you're like a pretty serious fan, huh?" she'd said, looking past me. "It's the playoffs," I'd told her, walking out the door. Not that we'd had a strong relationship, but I'm pretty sure this was the breaking point.*

Mom and Dad didn't want me to go, worried that I might get hurt, but they relented when I assured Mom (approximately three hundred times) that I would be careful, and I promised Dad that he could have one of the tickets. But once I had the tickets, things changed. Suddenly, everyone was my friend, and Swanson and I wielded a social power we'd never had before. Within a few hours, I had promised tickets to a dozen people, none of whom were Dad.

The next day Dad overheard me giving Kevin the rundown on

---

* By contrast, when I camped out for tickets before the '01 season, Laura-Beth packed me snacks, wished me luck, and called me at two A.M. to see how I was surviving the night.

my situation. Kevin and his girlfriend, Michelle, were going, and I needed to figure out who got the last ticket. I knew I'd promised one to Dad, but I wanted to take more friends with me. I was so focused on myself that I'd been willing to break my promise, a particularly egregious offense in our home, because Dad prided himself on keeping his word and expected us to do the same. One thing we'd always known about Dad was that if he said he would do something, it was going to happen, even if it didn't make sense, or if it meant sitting silently across the table from his eight-year-old son for four hours until he agreed to eat a single pea.

When he got mad, Dad had this way of radiating anger; you could feel it rolling off of him in waves, filling the whole room, weighing the air down and tainting it with his rage. As I spoke, I felt the angry waves crashing into me, and Dad didn't even need to say anything. I'd screwed him out of a ticket, and we both knew it. He was the one who had introduced me to football, made this whole thing possible. He was the one who had taken me to my first game and taught me how to be a fan. When I had begged him to get us tickets, he'd always come through. The only right thing to do was to give him a ticket, enjoy the game, and thank him for coming with me.

I spent the next several hours weaseling out of commitments to other people to free up the last ticket for Dad, and a week later the four of us were at the game together, next to Swanson, his dad, his brother-in-law, and Anthony. Dad never said a word about the ticket fiasco, but I could tell he was glad to go, and possibly relieved to learn that I wasn't quite as selfish as I had seemed.

This would be the first playoff game any of us had ever attended; on the drive to the stadium, we all chattered nervously, hoping the game could live up to a lifetime of expectations. We arrived just before the singing of the national anthem, which finished with the obligatory military flyover. Seconds later, a fan in a Bucs jersey climbed the stairs toward the upper level, and our entire section—except for our group, because Dad didn't believe in casual profanity and had no respect for people who lacked self-control—rose to chant, "*Asssss-hole*," stabbing the air between us with their index fingers. Someone hit him with a cup of beer, and he dropped his nacho tray. He complained to a nearby security guard, and the guard shrugged. The chant continued.

We were sitting in the 700 level, the upper deck of Veterans Stadium,* renowned for housing the fiercest, trashiest fans in the country. The infamy had grown exponentially after a 1997 *Monday Night Football* game, in which the Eagles had lost a nationally televised embarrassment to the 49ers. The fans had embarrassed themselves even more. Over sixty fights were broken up, hordes of fans were arrested, and someone fired a flare gun in the stands. Following that game, the Eagles established a court and holding cells in the bowels of the stadium. Now if you were caught fighting, you would be dragged down to the court and sentenced by an actual judge during the game.

Not that this deterred many people. Being in the 700 level was kind of a self-fulfilling prophecy. It was the ghetto of The Vet; once you were up there, you were expected to act a certain way, and if you didn't, you risked being not only marginalized, but also victimized. Besides, Eagles fans took pride in their reputation; people were afraid to come to Philly. The *Philadelphia Daily News* ran a semi-regular feature called "The 700 Clubbing," in which they tracked the criminal behavior in The Vet each week. After home games, it was a guarantee that the visiting team's newspaper would publish at least one story about the rowdy Eagles fans, sometimes complete with a picture of a black-eyed and fat-lipped fan. In '02, Thom Loverro of the *Washington Times* began such an article like this:

> They call it the Nest of Death. It is Section 700 at Veterans Stadium in Philadelphia, a haven for rabid Eagles fans. It is a place with a Dawg Pound–caliber reputation for toughness that can match any other in the NFL.
> One could argue that the Vet is one huge nest of death, a place

---

* Commonly known as The Vet.

where civilization has died and been replaced by green-and-silver-shaded anarchy.

"We like to put the fear of God in most teams and the fans that come into the stadium," said Bill Deery, a season ticket holder who sits in Section 700.

Maybe it wasn't the best way for Philly to gain notoriety, but at least people were paying attention to us.

Back to the game: the Bucs led 3–0 early in the second quarter. I ran to the bathroom, knowing I would miss at least fifteen minutes of action. The Vet must have been designed by someone with an enormous bladder, because there's no way a person who made regular restroom trips could have conceived of such a place. There were only a couple bathrooms on the entire upper level, with four toilets each, and a few pairs of port-a-potties scattered throughout. The port-a-potty line ran fifteen deep, and the guys in front shook the boxes to hurry people along. I rushed to the bathroom and waited in a line longer than I've ever seen outside of any women's room. In front of me, a guy in his thirties urinated in a trash can while three others used the sinks. Out on the concourse, one guy peed over the edge of the stadium, while another whipped it out and let it flow like a waterfall down the escalator.

A boy, maybe eight years old, and his father stepped in line behind me. The father checked his watch and bounced on his toes. In the stadium, there were cheers, the first in a long time. The father looked past me and grumbled something about how people better not be taking shits. On the wall next to me, a metal panel covered some sort of crawl space. The father pried the panel off the wall and pushed his son inside. The boy cried and said he didn't want to go in there, but his father stood firm. "This is your only chance to go," he said. He closed the boy inside the crawl space, checked back a minute later, and carried his crying son away.

A Bucs fan stood in line, brave enough to wear his jersey in the stadium and then to wander by himself. He got to the urinal, and before he even unzipped, the crowd unleashed their rage on him.

The *Asshole* chant started. A younger guy—probably high school age—with a shaved head charged the Bucs fan and shouted the chant directly in his ear. Another guy joined him on the opposite side. Hatred in stereo. A circle closed around him, chanting louder, jabbing him in the head with index fingers, shoving his face into the wall. The Bucs fan kept his head down and pushed his way out of the bathroom while slaps and punches rained on his back.

Before I left the bathroom, the Eagles took the lead on a touchdown run by McNabb. I heard the cheering, but wouldn't see the play until I got home. The concourse buzzed with activity as people tried to get a jump on the halftime concession rush. I joined as many Eagles chants as possible while I hurried back toward my seat. Another fan tried to start a *Fuck Howard Eskin* chant, but it didn't catch on. He took to hoarse ranting about how Eskin, a local sports radio host, had predicted an Eagles loss, and he couldn't wait to shove it in Eskin's face when the Eagles won. Someone else shouted, "Eskin's a fucking dope!" Then another voice joined in: "Eskin's a Jew!" And another: "The Jews killed Jesus!"

An older Eagles fan near the crowd interrupted. "Actually, the Romans killed Jesus," he said. The anti-Semite punched him in the face, and the crowd started another *Asshole* chant as the older guy crawled along the urine-veined concrete, groping for his glasses.

The Eagles won that game, but it ultimately meant nothing to the team, as they lost to the Giants a week later. But it meant everything to me—being there live for the first playoff win in five years was a defining moment in my fandom. Swanson and I agreed that we needed to attend as many games as possible in the future; we needed to be in the stadium whenever we could, just to feel that collective surge of pride that follows every big play. Counting playoffs, we went to nine more games over the next three years, earning our seats at every one of them. When we got first-round playoff tickets again next season, I invited Dad without hesitation.

WHEN I moved to college—La Salle University, in North Philly, five miles from home—I reduced my hours at D'Alessandro's, but still worked until closing every Friday night and opened the place every Saturday morning. By then, I was an important part of the team—a couple years' experience under my belt, I knew everything about the place, I could bang out feeds just as fast as Fitz, and they could trust me to run the show on Fridays. I rarely took off, calling out only three times in the five years I was there—once because I'd seriously sprained an ankle and could barely stand, once because I wanted to go out with LauraBeth and couldn't get anyone to cover my shift, and once because I was scheduled for a Monday night during an Eagles game that I had no intention of missing.* Point is, I was reliable and I was good. Much as I hated hard work, Dad had taught me that two of the most important things a man can do are to take pride in his job and to fulfill his responsibilities, so I was there every shift, doing the best I could.

ON FRIDAYS, I finished class around two o'clock, then immediately walked to the bus stop. I wore my work uniform to class— faded old D'Alessandro's shirt with basic cheesesteaky logo on the front, old soccer shorts, and my battered black Nikes that were coated in gristle and smelled so bad that I couldn't keep them in my apartment anymore. The sole of the left shoe bubbled oddly and made a clownish sucking sound every time I took a step. The toe cap of the right shoe dangled off like a hangnail, so I had duct-taped it down, periodically adding another layer of tape to keep things in place. The rolls of tape were layered so thickly that I was thrown off balance as I tottered, squeaking, to the bus stop with my book bag over my shoulder. Generally, I packed my

---

* After that Monday night game, I learned my lesson. From that point on, I made sure to check the NFL schedule in April and surreptitiously request days off months in advance, coinciding with any non-Sunday game for which the Eagles were scheduled. Thankfully, the place was closed on Sundays, so work rarely conflicted with football.

bag too full, thinking I would somehow get all my homework done during night shift, and making sure everyone knew that not only did I have to go to work instead of partying, but also that I was overwhelmed with schoolwork.

I waited for the bus on the busiest corner of campus, so everyone could see me—oversized bag strapped to my back, grotesque shoes on my feet—and I could tell them, "Sorry, can't do anything tonight—got to go to work. Yeah, it sucks. But you gotta pay the bills, right?" Then they would shake their heads and pity me, and I could feel like a martyr for the working class.

The bus was always crowded, and I was always the only white person on there. As it pulled away, I held my bag across my chest and clung to the pole, staring straight at the floor and desperately afraid to bump anyone. People on the bus seemed so lonely and surly. I was sure they were just waiting for an excuse to assault me.

When the bus stopped, I charged off, hands in pockets so no one could rob me, and I sat against the wall of a church, waiting a half hour for my next bus. I was never so conscious of my own whiteness, or my own latent racism, as when I rode the bus from North Philly through Germantown, and sat huddled in the middle of this run-down mess of endless dollar stores, wig shops, and beer distributors. The only other white people around were homeless. And there was me, in my ridiculous sneakers, hugging my giant book bag, suddenly very aware of how it feels to not belong. As much as I didn't want to acknowledge it, I saw every black man as a menace, a threat to my safety. When they walked too close to me, I balled my fists and uncapped my pen, planning to stab potential muggers. No one ever bothered me, and most people probably didn't even notice, or care, that I was there. But still, I eyed them all the way an antelope watches a stalking lion. When the ordeal was over, I was relieved to be safe, but mostly I was ashamed by my own obvious prejudices. The worst thing about taking the buses back to work every weekend was that it forced me to confront some of the uglier aspects of my own character.

On campus, it was easy for me to embrace the image of a Real

Working Man. Having been surrounded by actual blue-collar people my whole life, I could emulate their mannerisms and copy
their speech patterns. I could distinguish myself from the rest of
the Honors program, many of whom were privileged suburban
kids, just like my high school classmates. I could show them that
even though we might be in the same classes now, we had come
from totally different social classes. In my creative writing
courses I always wrote this friend-of-the-working-man bullshit,
stories about roofers overcoming obstacles, retired carpenters
coming to grips with the harsh realities of the world, and men ex-
periencing epiphanies while digging ditches. It was all okay, at
least for an undergrad class, but it was really patronizing junk because I didn't understand a thing about these people or what it
meant to be a working man trying to make it in the rough sections
of Philly. I didn't know what it was like to need four Vicodin just
to get through the day, or to really *need* that dime that I found at
the bus stop, or to have to work two soul-crushing jobs just to pay
for dinner and to keep the lights on. I tried to understand, but I
pitied them rather than empathizing. My stories romanticized
the life of manual labor in a way that would have made even my
own characters laugh at me. I pretended I would rather be laying
bricks or tarring roofs, but did so from the safety of my
$30,000/year liberal arts university. In the campus cafeteria, I
pretended to be a man of the people, but I ignored the workers
who served my food and washed my dishes.

I sat at the bus stop now watching real impoverished people
whose resentful glances told me all I needed to know about how
conspicuous I was here. Anyone who saw me could tell I was from
the college down the way, and they could probably tell that I was
judging them while they strolled silently past. I avoided eye contact with everyone and checked my watch every couple minutes.
On the rare occasions when a police officer rolled by, I breathed a
sigh of relief, glad to know I was in one of the poor neighborhoods
the city still cared about, and not lost in the Badlands of North
Philly, or in the neglected slums of Southwest.

When I got to work, I talked about the bus ride as if I hadn't

been afraid, as if I hadn't been hyper-aware of my incongruity in
my own city, an alien among the people I claimed to know so well.
I told endless stories about college life, the classes, the crazy pro-
fessors, the parties. I described tests I had taken, and I kept a
book on the cart behind me, between the ketchup and the hot
peppers. I never read more than a page or two during the night,
but I made sure to keep it on display, made sure to reference it and
the long paper I had to write about it. When my co-workers
shook their heads and said they wouldn't be able to do all that
writing, I shrugged and told them it was easy. And it was. School
was nothing. Working was hard. Trying to find a place where I belonged, that was hard.

EVEN AFTER moving on to college, I couldn't shake the stigma of
having attended La Salle High. Obviously, it didn't help that I was
still, technically, a La Salle boy, since I enrolled at La Salle University. The University's reputation differs drastically from the high
school's, but the name was all that mattered, and the taunts from
the Roman boys at D'Alessandro's persisted. After a couple years
of college, I'd stopped taking their prodding personally and generally it was all in good fun—co-workers bantering to pass the
time. But one new kid seemed to consider us real rivals, even
when I didn't reciprocate his trash talk. His friends called him
Stump; he had been a backup center on Roman's football team
when Roman beat La Salle for the Philadelphia Catholic League
championship. He wore his championship ring to work and
talked incessantly about how he'd beaten my school. I hated him.
Not because of anything relating to La Salle or Roman, but because he was utterly incapable of talking and working at the same
time, which was one of many reasons he was the worst co-worker
I've ever had. I rarely responded to him, because he was clearly
very stupid and he was also a gigantic goony endomorph, like a
massive baby, or like an unpleasant version of Lennie Small. Besides, most days he came to work drunk and on painkillers. So
who knew what might set him off? I kept working and let him

bombard me with insults about a football team that didn't mean a thing to me. I suppose it was strange that I didn't care at all about La Salle's team when I cared so much about the Eagles, especially considering that I actually knew the guys on this team. But maybe my knowing them is the reason I didn't support them. It's much harder to mythologize someone when you've met them, when you see all their flaws, and when you could easily talk to them whenever you'd like. The Eagles, even living in the same city as me, always seemed so distant, and it occurs to me that maybe it's a good idea to avoid them if I want to continue being a fan. Suppose I had met with Sheldon Brown and talked to him on the road that day I followed him, and he turned out to be ignorant, or obnoxious, or belligerent, or all three? Suppose he was boring, or even just petty and uncool, and not at all the classy, decent superathlete I've envisioned? No, some things are better left unexamined, viewed only from a distance.

One day when I was working with Stump, he disappeared into the basement for about thirty minutes. I actually hadn't noticed his absence for a while, as he wasn't interrupting my work, but we were running low on meat, and he was supposed to be the feeder. The line, as always, stretched out the door and curled around the corner, and everyone thought their order was the most important one in the stack. I rushed downstairs, fully expecting to find Stump accidentally locked inside the walk-in freezer. But he was sitting next to the meat slicer, tears streaming down his face, and talking to Mrs. Pinto.

Mrs. Pinto was a kindly old woman with an incomprehensible, high-pitched Italian accent. Most of my conversations with her involved her chirping a stream of possibly related syllables and me trying to read her body language so that I could know whether to nod and say "Yep, that's right!" or to shake my head and say ruefully, "I know, it's crazy . . ." Four nights a week, she chopped onions in the basement. I once asked her how many she chopped per night, but I didn't understand her answer. All I know is that she chopped for hours, filling bucket after five-gallon bucket, never shedding a single tear. She listened to an AM radio preacher the whole time, the voice of fire and brimstone rushing up the stairs to us during the quiet times. He was not at all a forgiveness-and-friendliness Christian; he was a hate-and-fear Catholic, who shouted condemnation at us almost every night we worked, damning us to hell while we thought we were already there. There was no place for god in my life, except in the basement of D'Alessandro's, where he forced his way in, and he seemed like an unpleasant character, not someone with whom I would like to spend my Sunday afternoons.

Stump was crying and talking to Mrs. Pinto about the preacher. His eyes were like marbles and I could tell he was high on something. He probably didn't even realize he was crying, and I'm sure he didn't understand a word Mrs. Pinto said. But she kept talking, possibly even lecturing him on all the ways he was angering god with his drug abuse. The woman was ready for the Rapture, but while she waited for Salvation, she kept busy by cutting onions and making people cry.

I called Stump a fat slob and told him to get the fuck upstairs, language that shocked Mrs. Pinto, who shouted incoherently at me as I ran up the steps. The customers were angry. All the workers had disappeared, no steaks were moving, and the managers had no answers. Stump stumbled to the corner, moving like a zombie, and I shoved him out of the way, throwing a feed on myself. This was my time to save the day, like Fitz and Duffy could have done during my first nights on the job. I chopped feverishly and Stump flopped on a chair in the back room, struggling to stay awake.*

Everyone in the shop waited on me. Nothing could happen

---

* Later that night, Dad told me he was in the crowd during this mess. He hadn't ordered anything. He had stopped by on the way home from work to see me in action, and was impressed by how well I'd handled the situation. He apparently did this not to spy on me, but to see how I operated in the real world, outside of his house. Perhaps this detail sounds creepy or unsettling, but it didn't bother me. I pictured him in the crowd telling people, "That's my son up there, making your dinner. That's my son working hard." And I knew he was proud. I knew he loved me.

until the meat was cooked. So our hoagie girl seized the moment, rushing out to the counter to make an impromptu sales pitch. She'd brought two boxes of T-shirts to work, raising money for some charity. The front of the shirt was simple: a police badge with a brief message remembering slain police officer Daniel Faulkner. But it was the back of the shirt that got everyone's attention:

Officer Danny
FAULKNER
was
MURDERED
by
MUMIA ABU-JAMAL
who shouldn't be in an
8 X 10 FOOT CELL
He should be
6 FEET CLOSER TO

HELL!

All of my co-workers had bought shirts, but I wanted nothing to do with it. When I'd told them I didn't have any money, they offered to pay me in advance, but I refused, explaining that I think it sends a very specific message about yourself when you're willing to pay twenty dollars for a T-shirt with (mild) profanity on it, and that wasn't a commitment I was willing to make. Also, I didn't know enough about the case, and I wasn't ready to make that kind of statement about something I didn't really understand. Our manager had rolled her eyes at me and asked me if I wanted more cops to get killed. This was the same manager who refused to take the orders of black customers because "they talk like they've got marbles in their mouth." She also had a habit of waiting until black customers had turned around, then brushing fistfuls of pepper and bread crumbs onto their backs. She always looked very proud of herself after she did this. The last thing I wanted was to be aligned with someone like her on any kind of controversial issue.

Naturally, she had no problem with the hoagie girl's sales pitch to the customers, even though she was trying to run a legitimate business, even though half the customers were black, and even though the Mumia thing is one of the most combustible, controversial issues in a city full of them. We're not just talking about any guy who was on trial for murder, we're talking about a radical black man convicted of shooting a white Irish cop in Philadelphia. We're talking about a murder that happened before I was born, and yet is still being hotly contested by people younger than me. It's one of those fights that's been going on for so long that many of the antagonists don't even know why they're fighting anymore.

If you drive through Philly, past the empty lots and abandoned warehouses, past the hollow shells of dead neighborhoods, there's one surefire way to tell whether you're in a white area or a black area. In the black sections of the city, the graffiti-tagged walls implore you to *Free Mumia*. In the white sections, the walls demand that you *Fry Mumia*. The Mumia case is a race riot waiting to happen. It would be much more convenient for all of the legislators involved if he just died without forcing them to make a decision. If he's released, white Philadelphians will explode; they might even try to kill him. If he's executed, the city might burn. The Mumia case isn't even about him or Daniel Faulkner anymore; it's about a simmering hatred between two disenfranchised groups that need a scapegoat for their city's troubles.

Huge swaths of the city have been totally neglected, left to decay, while billions of dollars pour into developing a few commercially viable areas. Even though at least twenty-five percent of Philadelphia high school students will not graduate, the city spends $200 million in taxpayer money to build a fancier football stadium and $170 million on a baseball park that features the largest Jumbotron in the league. Meanwhile, in the shadows of the stadiums, people are starving, people can't read, and people are killing one another. The continued gentrification of select neighborhoods is great, but it is usually synonymous with white-washing, and it leads to increased ghettoizing of other areas. Instead of solving problems, this is a city that likes to push them aside and ignore them, hoping they'll eventually disappear on their own. But that's the inconvenient thing about people—when you want them gone, they'll never leave, and when you want them around, they're never there.

In what is decidedly not a black-and-white issue, Mumia–Faulkner has become nothing but a black/white issue. You either want him dead, or you support cop-killers. This is the city where former mayor Frank Rizzo is a hero in the South, but in the North he's a villain, a proud figurehead of a racist, corrupt police department. This is the city where Wilson Goode, a black mayor, bombed an entire neighborhood in order to eradicate MOVE, the black separatist group with which Mumia was affiliated. This is the city where famous cheesesteak shops sell merchandise demanding that you learn English or get the hell out of America.

Our hoagie girl barely had to say anything before the first shirt was sold and the buyer proudly pulled it over his head. Some people walked out. Others looked like they wanted to leave, but not without their food. More bought shirts. People came in for cheesesteaks and left wearing T-shirts advertising their rage. I chopped steak while Stump slept. The faster I worked, the sooner we could end the T-shirt sale, and the happier I would be. The show went on, whether we liked it or not.

When Stump woke up, I made him fill the fridge and restock everything. When he was done, I told him to go home, and I would finish everything else for the night. He walked out, unaware that this was supposed to be a punishment, and I struggled through the end of the shift. While I frantically scrubbed the grill after closing time, the residual heat still rising up to meet my face, the manager asked me why I sent Stump home. I explained that he was lazy and incompetent, and he should have been fired hours ago. She told me that was stupid. Now she was late to get to the bar next door, and would be late to get home herself. Go home, then, I said, I've been doing everything all night anyway. She rolled her eyes and lit a cigarette. I cleaned the grill, while she and the hoagie girl watched from the back. I didn't say another word for the rest of the night. We had nothing to talk about.

I'm not sure exactly when I started actively hating that job, but I do know that was the first night I thought about quitting. Like many people, I had my daydreams about going out in a blaze of glory, telling everyone off, lecturing them on all their personal and hygienic flaws. But I held my tongue. Much as I didn't want to admit it, I couldn't afford to lose the job. The pay, after all, was pretty good, especially compared to what my friends were making. The hours weren't terrible, and we were closed every Sunday, a perk most jobs couldn't offer. The work was dull and draining, but it still had a certain prestige—as long as I worked there I had the ultimate trump card in establishing my Philly credibility, because I pulled the strings at one of the best steak shops in the city. Besides, work was supposed to be dismal and exhausting, wasn't it? You got a job partly so you could complain about how you hated your job—that's what adults did—and so people could know you were as unhappy as they were in their own crummy jobs.

Still, I routinely reminded my co-workers that I didn't need or want the job. When they called me at home and asked me to work extra hours, I told them I'm not a doctor and I'm not on call, especially not to make fucking cheesesteaks. Why the hell would I put myself through extra hours at a job I hate just to make your life easier?* Guys like Fitz and Duffy, they always showed up when they were called. They supported the place, respected it, treated it like a job they needed. I treated them like they needed *me*. By their own admission, all the managers and waitresses were lifers, and they didn't like my steady reminders that the place was only a temporary stop for me. I always got my job done—by the end, I was as good as anyone they had—but I didn't *care* about it like many of them did.

---

* This point highlights a crucial difference between me and Dad; regardless of the circumstances, Dad would *always* go to work if they asked him to. He wouldn't question it, because all he would care about was the job getting done correctly.

CHEESESTEAKS HAVE always been in my blood, both literally and metaphorically. In the most literal sense, I've eaten a lot of them, occasionally consuming two in a day during long shifts at D'Alessandro's. I've visited as many different steak shops as possible, including the insultingly overpriced tourist traps in South Philly, just to sample the product around the city. I order them at out-of-state restaurants even when I know they're going to be terrible.* It should come as no surprise, then, that my time at D'Alessandro's coincided with a massive weight gain.

But let's focus on the metaphorical angle here. Dad always loved cheesesteaks, much more so than anyone I've ever known. At restaurants, he invariably ordered either a cheesesteak or a chicken parm sandwich. At home, the only meal he cooked was cheesesteaks. And long before I knew him, before he moved on to computer programming and became a minority owner of a furniture warehouse, he managed steak shops. So it was particularly appropriate when Dad dropped me off for my first day of work at D'Alessandro's and I became a steak jockey myself. At the time, I wasn't even aware of how deeply ingrained the business was in the family, and I didn't really care. I had only applied for the job because Mom and Dad had made me do it. By the time I turned seventeen, all of my friends had gotten jobs and some had even bought cars, but I'd never had any interest in working. Mom and Dad pestered me into applying for jobs until I finally backed into a position at the steak shop. Duffy, a friend's older brother, recruited, interviewed, hired, and trained me in the same day. I failed to realize then how much this job had pleased Dad—besides the fact that I'd finally joined the workforce and taken the next step toward becoming a self-reliant man, the nature of the work was such that Dad and I could relate on a totally different level than we previously had. It felt almost like I'd taken my right-

---

* In San Francisco, I once ate an "authentic Philly cheesesteak" that was served on a croissant, which is wrong in every conceivable way.

ful place in the family business. We were peers now, two guys who could bullshit about the rigors and frustrations of making cheesesteaks in front of impatient, angry crowds. Now, when he picked me up after work, particularly after night shifts, we swapped stories and talked to each other like adults. During one of these rides, Dad revealed that many years ago, he'd nearly been killed over cheesesteaks.

Before Kevin and I were born, he'd partnered with Cal-Cal, the old coffee drinker from Dunkin' Donuts, and a guy named Fat Stuff. They were going to move to Florida and start a cheesesteak business called Fat Stuff's, making true authentic steaks with fresh Philly-baked rolls delivered every week. The three of them rode a truck down 95, hauling all of their meat slicers, refrigerators, and other necessary equipment to the new location. Not long after leaving, Dad learned two important business lessons: 1) don't trust guys named Fat Stuff, and 2) make sure your other partner doesn't have a major cognitive disorder.

During the trip, they ran into a number of problems, beginning with Dad being forced to drive the whole way. He liked driving and had a class C license, but he could have used a break from the sweaty tedium of trekking down the highway in a semi. On their only overnight stop, Fat Stuff stayed in a motel while Cal-Cal and Dad slept in the truck. The next day, somewhere in the Carolinas, they were pulled over and Dad had to restrain Fat Stuff from fighting with the police officer. That same day Fat Stuff picked a fight with a black trucker at a rest stop and pulled a gun on him while spouting racial slurs. Again, Dad was the peacemaker.

Meanwhile, Cal-Cal was upset by all the violence and yelling he'd endured on the drive. He missed his mom and wanted to go home. He was there to do the grunt work, but he wasn't capable of much more than that. Dad had known him as a loyal friend and a hard worker, but also understood that he functioned mentally at the level of a thirteen-year-old boy. So, they'd agreed to a deal: Cal-Cal would do whatever they needed from him, but if he wanted to go home and be with his mom, Fat Stuff had to give him

meal money and put him on a flight back to Philly. But now Fat
Stuff told him he couldn't leave until they had unloaded everything. After the truck had been unpacked, he deferred Cal-Cal
again, saying they couldn't afford a plane ticket right now. Dad
threatened to quit unless Fat Stuff stuck to the deal. The next day,
Cal-Cal was on a Greyhound with a can of soda and a cheese sandwich.

When Dad found out that Fat Stuff had cheaped out on them
again, he was livid. He agreed to finish setting up the store and to
return the truck to the depot, but after that, he was gone. Part-
nership over.

At night, Dad slept alone on the floor of the future steak shop
while Fat Stuff stayed in a motel again. Dad awoke to an odd rum-
bling. The soda refrigerator was moving. Dad rolled away just as
the fridge crashed to the floor where he'd been sleeping. Fat Stuff
was standing over it, swearing it had been an accident. Dad
picked up the cash register from the counter and hurled it into Fat
Stuff's chest before walking out the door. They never spoke again.

Years later, Fat Stuff was shot and killed, which is fine by me.
It's not so hard to hate people you don't know, and the fucker
could've killed my Dad before I ever had a chance to meet him,
before I even had a chance to exist. And as much as I hate the cancer for what it took from me, at least it waited until I had a chance
to know my Dad.*

When Dad finished telling his story, we went our separate
ways, he to the computer downstairs and I to the computer in my
room, where I waited for hours hoping to swap instant messages
with girls I knew.

We never talked about that story again, not for any particular
reason besides that there was nothing left to say, but since then

---

*This event was Dad's second near-death experience, as far as I know. In the
first, he was hit by a bus while trying to get to school. He flew twenty feet in
the air but he got up promptly, gathered his books, and boarded the bus.
Didn't even go to the hospital. He was sore and a little dazed, but wasn't
hurt badly at all, which seemed borderline miraculous. But maybe it took
some years off the end of his life without his knowing it.

I've often wondered what my life would have been like if I'd been born in Florida. What kind of person would I be? Would I still be a sports fan, does that mean I would have grown up loving the Tampa Bay Buccaneers? Or would Dad still have passed his Eagle fandom on to me? Maybe it would have been a major conflict between us, a house divided. On Sundays, we would watch football in rooms on opposite ends of the house — he in Eagles gear, and I in the pewter and red of the Bucs — and we would listen for the other's cheers. When the Bucs beat the Eagles in the NFC Championship Game, I would gloat and taunt him, rather than share in his heartbreak. I would be a front-runner with no history and no substance. Game days would be lonely. Football would be empty.

Maybe I would work at Disney World, be all smiles at the happiest place on Earth instead of sweating over a griddle in a city that falls on the complete opposite end of the happiness continuum. Maybe I would have died of awful, painful sunburn, or maybe shark attack. Would I have ever been a writer, or moved to Iowa, or met LauraBeth, or any of it? I never came up with any solid answers, although I ran plenty of alternate scenarios in my head. But location can't be the only thing that matters. There's still plenty of me that was genetically predetermined and filtered through my parents; if that weren't the case, why would so many relatives insist that I'm so similar to my paternal grandfather?*

Maybe the real question I've been juggling since hearing that story is this: how much of my character do I owe to my family, and how much do I owe to my city? What's the balance, and what does it even mean if I can determine who is responsible for what?

---

* Who died before I was born. All I know about him is listed here: he was short, about which he was defensive; he liked Michelob; he used to edit encyclopedias; he was an intensely devoted baseball fan, reading minor league baseball reports via Teletype and shouting at the TV screen during games; and I supposedly look just like him.

CHAPTER

DEATH AND REBIRTH

DAD, KEVIN, and I are in our usual seats in the living room, decked out in our game-day uniforms. It's January 2, 1993, and the Eagles are in the playoffs. This is the first playoff game I've ever watched, after the first season to which I've really paid attention. The weekly ritual is still relatively new to me, but Kevin has known it for years and Dad has known it longer. Since before we were born, Dad has spent his Sundays waiting anxiously by the TV for kickoff, his whole week having built up to the game, every nuisance and petty issue at work having been worth it because at least on the weekend he got to watch football. As long as we could remember, Sunday had belonged to the Eagles in our house. Dad never forced football on us, but the Eagles played such an important role in his life that we couldn't help emulating him. Besides, he worked such long hours that we rarely saw him during the week; if we wanted to really spend time with him, it had to be on the weekend. Kevin had fully committed his Sundays to football by the time he was ten, and now he was a starting defensive end at La Salle High. Nearly seventeen, already driving, he was now much more interested in going out with friends than staying home and playing video games with me. So, if I wanted to spend time with Dad and Kevin, I had to embrace football Sundays.

Last season was doomed from the start when superhuman quarterback Randall Cunningham had his leg more or less snapped in half during the first game. It was a sad introduction to the life of an Eagles fan: a season begins with unbridled hope, and then the quarterback gets broken on day one. Cunningham ran like a deer, absorbed hits like Gumby, slipped out of tackles like he was covered in Vaseline. He was one of the most exciting players we'd ever seen; at ten years old, I was sure Cunningham was not only uncatchable, but also invincible. So, then. First game versus Packers, second quarter. Bryce Paup hits him low and Randall's cleat catches in the turf. His leg bends into the shape of a boomerang and does not bounce back. He's crumpled on the field, carted off, season over just like that.

I should have walked away then, moved on to something else, but I couldn't. Eagles fandom was in my blood. Even if it made perfect sense to abandon them, I found myself unable, and unwilling, to do so. Neither Kevin nor I ever truly considered the possibility of *not* being Eagles fans. Fandom for us wasn't something you chose; it was something you had, something you did, and you didn't question it. Dad was born in October 1948, the same year the Eagles won their first NFL championship. They won another the next year, and Philadelphia officially became a football city. Everyone embraced football, a game whose violence and concentrated bursts of rage made it a perfect match for the city's temperament. Dad was born into the first generation of life-long Eagles fans; his father passed the obsession on to him, then he passed it down the line to my brother and to me. It's hereditary, a dominant gene in the family, just like acne, weak ankles, a slow metabolism, and a propensity for dying young.

So, even though they'd only won one more championship since then, and even though my first Eagles season was a failure from nearly the first play, I was still there in front of the TV when the 1992 season started. And that year got off to an even more inauspicious start than the previous one had. Things started going wrong even before the season had begun. Beloved blowhard head coach Buddy Ryan got fired and his loyal players were mutinous. Then, in June, star defensive tackle Jerome Brown flipped his Corvette on a Florida road and died, along with his nephew. This—aside from losing Grunt, our guinea pig, to natural causes—was my first real experience with death, and the only emotion I can remember is anger.

I don't even know where I was when I heard the news, but I know I was with Dad and Kevin, and I was pissed. The Eagles were built around defense. In '91, they'd become the first team in NFL history to win the so-called Triple Crown—fewest rushing yards, passing yards, and points allowed. Jerome, the fulcrum of a historically good defensive line, played a huge role in that accomplishment—few had ever seen such a combination of power and quickness at defensive tackle, and he had just the right mix of cockiness, swagger, and good humor to appeal to everyone in the city without alienating them. Sure, he was full of himself, but he'd earned the right to be full of himself. He hadn't quite lived up to his potential in the beginning of his career, but he was entering his prime and everyone *knew* he was on the verge of doing something special. Then, suddenly, death.

I was even more angry when I remembered that a couple of Phillies—Darren Daulton and Lenny Dykstra—had been involved in a drunk-driving accident the previous year and escaped with only a few broken bones. The Phillies had been terrible my whole life and I still hated baseball. I also knew that drunk driving was bad, so they were morally more wrong than Jerome was for driving a little fast, because, hey, who doesn't speed? So I said, very matter-of-factly, "I wish Dykstra and Daulton had died instead."

Even if I don't remember the exact circumstances of our conversation, I remember the looks on their faces when they heard— Dad's expression a mixture of scorn and disappointment, and Kevin's a look of plain disgust. Kevin—Kevin who played football and loved the Eagles and carried a Jerome Brown trading card in his wallet!—shook his head and said, "Come on, you don't wanna say that." Dad said nothing, which he did when he was especially upset. He didn't speak to me until after dinner, after he'd calmed himself. Then he administered a long lecture* about how I should

---

* These lectures were a staple of Dad's parenting. Anytime one of us performed poorly on a test, got in a fight, stayed out past curfew, etc., we knew a lecture was scheduled for that night after dinner. The lectures, in which he asked us to explain our thought process before imparting his unabridged

have more respect for human life. I nodded along with him, but still quietly harbored resentment toward those Phillies for surviving, while Jerome had not.

Three months later, the season began, and turned out not to be a story of death but one of rebirth. Randall began shilling hats that said "I'll Be Back . . . Scramblin'." I got one. It was stolen off of my head weeks later by some kids from Roxborough High. But I replaced the hat and always walked with one hand on the brim.

The team signed Herschel Walker as a free agent, giving them a legit threat at halfback for the first time since Wilbert Montgomery in the early eighties. Still known as one of the great college halfbacks of all time, Walker's professional legacy is marred by the fact that he was on the wrong end of one of the most lopsided trades in sports history, a trade that simultaneously condemned the Minnesota Vikings to years of mediocrity and enabled the Cowboys to build a dynasty. Moving to Philadelphia gave Walker the opportunity for a fresh start.

The rest of the team rallied around the memory of JB, retiring his jersey in a tearful ceremony, and dedicating the season to him with the slogan "Bring it home for Jerome!" Their team leaders— especially Reggie White,* nicknamed The Minister of Defense— were particularly religious and they really seemed to believe Jerome was out there with them, the twelfth man on the field. The ceremonies, jersey retirements, and national media coverage ensured that Jerome's premature death would make him a sporting legend in Philly, where even today people wear his jersey and speak reverently about his prodigious skills.

In August, Dad took us to training camp at West Chester University, where we watched the Eagles practice and got dozens of

---

philosophy on everything, regularly lasted for an hour or longer—a real test of endurance for a ten-year-old.

* Who, at age forty-three, became the second of three defensive starters on that team to die young. In 2007, former strong safety Andre Waters killed himself, reportedly because brain damage incurred during his football career had driven him to severe depression and maybe even dementia.

autographs. Casual fans have a hard time understanding why anyone would want to watch a team practice on a humid July afternoon, and a small percentage of training camp attendees usually walk out disappointed when they realize that they're actually just watching the team perform drills for four hours. But I was enthralled by the whole production, felt like I was getting a sneak preview of football season. I felt like I knew the team then, broiling in the heat right along with them as they fought for jobs, hearing their banter, sitting so close I could have touched them. As long as I could remember, I'd always owned Eagles clothing—every Christmas and birthday, Mom and Dad gave me kelly green T-shirts, hats, and jackets—but I'd never owned an Eagles signature, or even made eye contact with a player. Watching guys like Herschel Walker, David Archer, Roy Green, and Jeff Kemp take a Sharpie from *my* hand and scribble their name on *my* paper, I suddenly cared much more about them than ever before.

The season began with two consecutive wins, and Dad surprised us with tickets to the next game, versus the Denver Broncos. Kevin had been to one game in his life, when he was much younger, and the only memory he has of the experience is from after the game—a loss—when he bumped into some drunk and spilled his beer. The drunk grabbed Kevin by the collar and threatened him, at which point Dad—a stocky man, smaller than the drunk—shoved him and told him to back off. The drunk protested: "But he spilled my beer!" According to family legend, Dad said, "I'll spill your blood," and glared at the drunk until he backed away.*

This Broncos game marked Kevin's return to Veterans Stadium, and it would be my first experience at a live sporting event. This is what I remember from that day: pulling into the parking lot and seeing the stadium, which was huge, much bigger than I'd ever expected; weaving through the tailgating crowds in the parking lot, the smell of cheap beer and barbecue that reminded me of

---

* Everyone insists that he actually said this, which, I'm pretty sure, made him some kind of second-rate action hero. The Charles Bronson of Roxborough.

family parties; chanting "*E-A-G-L-E-S EAGLES*" in unison with thousands of strangers the length of the walk up the ramps to the infamous 700 level; straining to see the cheerleaders on the sidelines; feeling the stadium rumble when the defense was introduced; missing the first touchdown because I was in the bathroom and celebrating anyway, high-fiving dozens of strangers, and no one feeling uncomfortable hugging each other, even with their flies down; craning my neck to watch fights in the next section; and riding home, feeling like I'd just been let in on the greatest secret in the world. They'd won 30–0, beat Denver—and legendary quarterback John Elway—so badly that the Broncos had looked like a high school team. Denver gained only eighty-two yards, the lowest total allowed by the Eagles in over thirty years. At that point, I truly thought they were unbeatable. Judging by the looks on people's faces as we left, I wasn't the only one. I was too new to sports fandom to be jaded yet, too hopeful to know that in Philly, the high points exist only so that you can fall even farther.

The Eagles went on their bye week next, and had two weeks to prepare for the Dallas fucking Cowboys. If you want to know what it means to be an Eagles fan, you need to know what it means to hate Dallas. The Cowboys are success. They're boozy, coked-up headlines and swagger. They're strutting and preening and pretty and media-savvy. They're long bombs and glamour boys. They're Tom Landry and his stupid hat, Jimmy Johnson and his lacquered hair, Jerry Jones and his Botoxed face. They're totally artificial, concealing their amorality and repugnance beneath a thin veneer of good ol'-fashioned American decency. In other words, they're like everything else from Texas: overblown, gilded, and completely hollow at the core.*

Even before I paid attention to football, I knew enough to hate the Cowboys and their front-running fans. I knew you were supposed to sneer at their famous star logo every time you saw it.

---

* Full disclosure: I've only been to Texas once, for a layover in the Dallas–Fort Worth airport, when I was thirteen. I remember it as being pretty nice. They upgraded us to first-class and I got to eat pizza on an airplane.

You learn to chant *DALLAS SUCKS* by the time you're six or seven. You see "Fuck Dallas" T-shirts in the pregame parking lot, regardless of who the Eagles are playing. You learn incredible new curses as soon as Michael Irvin or Emmitt Smith appears on TV. And, if you're lucky enough, you win a mayoral election because you once hurled snowballs at Dallas' coach.*

Dallas week, it's a big deal. Especially when both teams are undefeated, as they were in '92. I watched Eagles highlights every night on the news, and begged to stay up late for *Sports Sunday* at eleven-thirty, just to hear more discussion of the Birds. Read every inch of the *Inquirer*'s sports section each day, and even checked the other boring sections, just in case they had something on the Eagles. I'd recently found a tiny, battery-powered AM radio in my grandmother's house, and now every night I tuned in to 610 WIP, the sports talk station, and listened under my sheets when I was supposed to be asleep. I listened in the evening while I did my homework, and in the morning, I clicked the radio on as soon as I woke up. I doubt they ever said much that was actually noteworthy or insightful, but it didn't matter, because all I wanted was to have the sounds of the Eagles with me, to be immersed in a steady white noise of football talk as I lay in bed.

EVEN THEN I knew, had probably always known, that I was cut out more for video game sports than for real sports. I was too out of shape, too easily flustered, and not athletic enough to compete. I had once been a good soccer goalie, but as we aged, other teams developed more skill, the shots came in much harder, from odd angles, and I couldn't keep up. So now I was a defender, and I hated it. I couldn't keep up with any of the speedy strikers or make any plays when the ball came to me. Given a chance to take a free kick, I was just as likely to hit a parent on the sidelines as I was to make a good pass to a teammate.

---

* As current Pennsylvania governor Ed Rendell did in 1991, according to local legend.

So I sulked and pouted. Apathy and lack of effort became my defense mechanisms. Dad refused to talk to me on the way home from games. He wasn't upset because I was a terrible soccer player; his own athletic legacy was equally unimpressive. He was a pretty good golfer, a sport for which I never had any patience — even playing minigolf I would fling the putter and kick obstacles until they cracked. He'd played high school football, but after one season he joined the band as a flautist, a drastic shift on the toughness continuum, which Kevin and I had always found hilarious. What upset him, he explained in a series of lectures, was that I was letting my teammates down by sleepwalking through the games. He wouldn't care if I was the worst player on the field, but it disgusted him to see his son out there not even *trying* to play well, letting strikers run free and refusing to chase after loose balls while the rest of the team hustled to cover his mistakes. I thought he was persecuting me, but I tried to appease him anyway. So I played dirty, confusing cheap shots for hard work, and then he looked even more disappointed.

But still I loved sports, diving headfirst into the video games and record books. The games allowed me to lose myself in the action, to master the players' bodies and achieve the discipline I didn't have in real life. I won championships and set records. When I lost, I threw things across the room — soda cans, sneakers, anything I could pick up. The trash can overflowed with crumpled floppy disks and broken joysticks, collateral damage from games that had crossed me.

When I played Tecmo Super Bowl on the Nintendo, I always controlled the Eagles. Now I had the opportunity not only to live vicariously through the players, but to bring them to a championship they'd never won themselves. Some Saturdays, I left my room only for meals, devoting the remaining twelve hours to video games. Thousands of hours were spent in front of that TV, controller in hand, and personal regrets pushed aside, at least temporarily. Even when I left the house, I carried games with me. On Sundays, I went to six A.M. mass with Dad — because it was the shortest service of the day — and then we went to breakfast at

Denny's afterward. I ordered a plain bagel and hot tea and he ordered a full meal. I ate quickly and played with a handheld electronic football game while I waited for him to finish. Mass, Denny's with Dad, and football—my Sunday routine for years.

Besides the video games, I also loved reading the record books. When our teachers made us go to the library, I checked out the *Guinness Record Book Sports,* reading and rereading every page, checking the same book out six weeks in a row until they forced me to get another. So I picked up *The Ultimate Sports Trivia Book.* During free time, I read old issues of *Sports Illustrated for Kids.* I had every number memorized, every date and name. I knew how many rushing yards Walter Payton had gained in his career, I knew what college Charles Barkley went to and how many points per game he scored in 1991, I knew the scores of the last fifteen Super Bowls, and I knew how many yards per game the Eagles defense had allowed during the previous five seasons.

These things didn't come up in conversation much. So I recited them to people, unsolicited. *Did you know Reggie White once had twenty-one sacks in a season, and he would have shattered the record if not for a players' strike? Did you know Wilt Chamberlain averaged almost twenty-three rebounds per game in his career? Well, I read it all in this book today.* Dad and Kevin started calling me "Stats." I took pride in my new nickname because, mocking or not, it bestowed upon me a sense of expertise; they might have smirked when they called me Stats, but they were also impressed that I could absorb so much data so quickly. They always knew they could count on me if they needed information during a game.

This is a particularly important detail because Kevin was much more like Dad than I ever was. Kevin was a born engineer, a born computer programmer, just like Dad. Even as a child, he would dismantle telephones and walkie-talkies just to see how they worked. I preferred reading and couldn't understand computers the way they could. I had no concept of spatial relations, while they analyzed the layout of a room like they were playing Tetris. They shared a coolly rational, analytical approach to problem-solving, while I was much more temperamental, less confident, prone to fits of frustrated anger, hurling shoes across my bedroom and punching uncooperative video game systems. They both loved science fiction, but I hated watching *Star Trek* with them on Saturday afternoons. Our differences always worried me, not only because Dad and Kevin got along more easily, but because I was afraid that maybe Kevin had hoarded all of the good family genes. Dad's younger brother, my Uncle Mike, was a loser who routinely passed out on his mother's couch, lit cigarettes drooping from his mouth and burning holes into the cushions. He dropped out of high school, demonstrated no particular aptitude for anything besides taking money from his mother, and was fired from a different job every week. Mom hated him. Dad was deeply disappointed in him, frustrated by his unreliability and lack of motivation. I didn't know all the details of Uncle Mike's failures, but Kevin and I both knew that in Dad's family, there was one good brother and one bad brother, a limit to the number of positive traits to be distributed between them. As far as I could tell, Kevin was the good brother, and I was bound to be the disappointment. I knew I needed to do something to stand out and fight my inevitable metamorphosis into the new Uncle Mike. When memorizing the record books offered me an opportunity to stand out, to impress Dad, I embraced it.

Books opened a door between me and Dad; I realized I could foster a deep connection with him through studying, through the accumulation of knowledge. I plowed through summer reading lists, made him take me to the library on weekends, buried myself in my studies. I wanted to know everything, especially about sports, and I wanted him to know I knew everything. Books were the currency with which I bought his admiration.

If the answer wasn't in my books, it was on *Wide World of Sports* or WIP. I wished I could call in and talk to the hosts, but I was too embarrassed to hear my own voice on the radio. Still, I dreamed about being a sports-talk host, running my own show one day, so when the idiots called with their garbled facts and goofy opinions, I could shout them down and re-educate them. From my pulpit I could crack jokes and dispense wisdom. I would be funny, but not a clown. I would be better prepared than anyone, and I would have no problem coming up with strong opinions. They had always come easily to me.

I could interview the athletes. They would talk to me like an equal, because I would know more about them and their sport than anyone they'd ever met. I would be an honorary part of the Eagles, the team's little brother. Maybe I couldn't outrun them, but I could outthink them. If I couldn't excel on the field, at least I could excel off of it. As long as I kept studying, I would always have something to talk about.

ONE YEAR after Jerome Brown's death, I faced my first family deaths. My grandmothers both died in 1993, within a couple months of each other. Dad's mother died first, after which Kevin wrote a deeply personal essay for a high school English class detailing his grief. It was really well written, I thought, and the essay was upsetting because: 1) he was moving in on my writing territory, and 2) he was much sadder than I was, which made me feel like a bad person. My sadness felt so ordinary, so run-of-the-mill, that I knew I was doing something wrong. I'd seen funerals in TV shows and movies, the garment-rending grief in response to death, but I did not feel it. So I tried harder to grieve. I tried praying to her, but that yielded no results and I felt stupid. I tried crying, but even when the tears flowed it felt artificial; I may as well have splashed my face with tap water. I dedicated my soccer season to her because I'd seen the Eagles dedicate their season to Jerome Brown, but it only made me feel worse when I played terribly; it seemed more like an insult than a tribute. I did love her, was very close to her, but I never understood how to mourn, and, at eleven, still didn't fully grasp what it meant for someone to be dead.

The death of Mom's mother—with whom I'd spent less time and wasn't as close—affected me even less. I knew I *should* be sad, I *should* be deeply pained by it, but I wasn't. At her viewing, I sat silently for a long time, wishing I could help Mom stop crying. Just before they closed the casket, an aunt asked me to fetch something from her car. I practically ran out of the building, glad to be away from that scene. When I returned, Dad was waiting for me at the door; he'd seen me run out and was worried that I'd been too upset to stay. He hugged me and told me I could talk to him about death anytime I wanted to. Of course, by the time I was really ready to talk to him about it, I was twenty-three and he was gone.

Neither death had a lingering effect on me. Neither made me worry about the inevitability of our own mortality or the fact that someday my parents would die before I was ready. Still, Mom and Dad worried, as good parents would, discussing the deaths with me and giving me pamphlets answering common kids' questions. And when my sixth-grade teacher called them to report my disruptive in-class behavior—acts completely rooted in my desire to impress the popular kids—Mom blamed it on the deaths of my grandmothers. My teacher approached me the next day, offering condolences and giving me this look of pity that I couldn't even come close to understanding. She even offered to let me retake a quiz on microscopes that I'd failed miserably. That conversation taught me one thing: if someone close to you has died, you're allowed to act out. You have an excuse for otherwise inexcusable behavior.

AFTER TWO weeks of hype, the Eagles and Cowboys finally play each other. No need to build any more suspense: the Eagles win. They whip the Cowboys so badly that you almost, *almost,* feel for them. Thirty-one to seven. At The Vet. On *Monday Night Football.* They squash superstar halfback Emmitt Smith, and Herschel runs all over Dallas, getting some measure of revenge on his former team. Randall looks great. So does Reggie. And Seth Joyner, my favorite player, is dominant. Everything is perfect. The Eagles are going to win the Super Bowl.

But one lesson you learn quickly as an Eagles fan—every time someone says the Eagles are going to win the Super Bowl, it's a guarantee that something will go wrong, and soon.

They lose two straight, and five of the next eight. One of the losses, to the San Francisco 49ers, is particularly galling even today, because the Eagles were clearly cheated by a bad call late in the game. They also lose in Dallas to the Cowboys, who are in first place in the division and have now won seven of eight. Suddenly, the Eagles might not even make the playoffs. On WIP, they want to fire everyone. They want to bring Buddy back, they say the players have no heart. In the *Philadelphia Inquirer*, they say the team is emotionally exhausted. If anyone is emotionally exhausted, it's probably the fans.

The most memorable loss of this stretch, at least for me, occurs in week eleven, when they're in Green Bay. For reasons I can't fathom or remember, I'm at my friend Dan's house playing basketball with a few other guys during the Eagles game. I want to stop and watch football, but no one else is interested, and his parents are watching some stupid movie on TV. After enough pleading, I finally get them to bring a radio outside so we can listen to the game. I barely hear the radio over the dribbling and the clanging rims. By the fourth quarter, though, we know the Eagles have blown a lead and the Packers are lining up to attempt a game-winning field goal. We gather around the radio just in time to hear Packers kicker Chris Jacke* convert the field goal. The Eagles lose, and I hurl the basketball against a fence. Dan says, "Uh-oh, Tom's gonna cry." Everyone laughs and taunts me until I actually do feel like crying. Later, I decide that I should have been mocking them for *not* wanting to cry, for not understanding.

A couple weeks later, the Eagles finally get themselves back together and they *do* make it to the playoffs. Herschel becomes their first thousand-yard rusher since '85. Randall is back in Pro Bowl form. The team finishes the season on a nice winning streak and they're undefeated at home, a stat of which Eagles fans are especially proud, as if we're partly responsible for the wins. We've got reason to believe again.

Which brings us back to the living room, where Dad sits in his

------

* Pronounced "Jackie," like the female name. In college, I was briefly involved with a girl named Jackie, and I thought of the Packers' kicker every time I said her name. This did not bode well for us.

recliner in his trademark gray Eagles sweatshirt—a Christmas gift from me and Kevin—and suspenders, while Kevin and I rock anxiously on the couch, wearing our jerseys (both number 92 for Reggie; Kevin's in white and I'm in green). The Eagles are in the New Orleans Superdome, warming up for a game against the Saints. I'm fresh off a week of serious research, during which I worked diligently to identify reasons to hate the Saints.

Their halfback, Ironhead Heyward, is too fat and slow, and he kind of annoys me, especially because he fumbles too much in our Nintendo games. Their quarterback, Bobby Hebert, has a difficult name to pronounce. The national media is picking them to win, despite the fact that they already lost to the Eagles in the first week of the season.

Worst of all, their defense calls themselves Mount Rush-No-More, which, even to a ten-year-old, is a stupid nickname. I resent that they've received more national media attention than the Eagles' superior defense. They're frauds. They get all the credit for being this hard-hitting, nasty defense, but it's the Eagles who are the meanest, most brutal group in the world, the Eagles who have been trying to behead opponents on the field since the days of Concrete Charlie, the Eagles who are responsible for the carnage now known as The Body Bag Game. Now some team has a couple good linebackers and they get the prestige? I hoped the Eagles would send every one of them off the field on stretchers.

Over the past seventeen years, I've watched replays of this game often enough to have nearly memorized every play, every comment made by the announcers, every move made by the Eagles. I'll spare you the many details. They're unnecessary anyway. Here's the point: the game begins and ends with me feeling certain that the Eagles will never lose again. In the middle there is an unbelievable touchdown by Fred Barnett, a leaping end-zone catch in double coverage. There's me dancing in the living room and spinning a football on its nose, mimicking Barnett's customary celebration. There's Reggie White getting a sack in the end zone and hopping up with hands clasped over his head as if in prayer, signaling a safety. There's me and Kevin bounding wildly from one end of the house to the other and tackling each other in the middle of the living room because we don't know what else to do. There's Eric Allen sealing the game with a defensive touchdown. There's Dad pumping his fist and smiling broadly through his beard, watching us skitter around the living room like maniacs.

Final score: 36–20, Eagles. First playoff win in twelve years. We run outside to whoop and bang pots with the neighbors. Our street feels like a community again. Someone ignites leftover New Year's Eve firecrackers, and, again, we're sure the Eagles are going to win the Super Bowl.

Then, Dallas again. Another week of hype and trash-talk. Another week of unsustainably high hopes. A crushing defeat. The Eagles score the first three points, then allow the next thirty-four. Dallas wins the conference next. Two weeks later they win one of the most lopsided Super Bowls ever, and we have to hear their insufferable "How 'bout dem Cowboys!" cheer for the next fifty years.

I leave the season a little bitter and a little jaded, but still rationalizing the losses and holding out hope for next year—a couple upgrades on the offense, a good draft, some luck, and we're right back in it. The same old lies fans tell themselves every year. After the Dallas loss, I couldn't eat, and I didn't want to talk to anyone. I picked a fight with Kevin—which I rarely did, mostly because I liked my brother and didn't understand why other brothers always fought each other—and I slouched around for days, hoping someone would ask me what's wrong so I could unload my grief on them. Once the darkest days cleared, though, the thing I remembered most was that Saints game—the uninhibited ecstatic celebration with Dad and Kevin, being allied with our neighbors just because we were also wearing Eagles green, and the certainty of knowing that everything was going to turn out right this time around. Sure, maybe the teams only get us that high and then abandon us when we come down, but, man, nothing beats those fleeting, joyful moments before you fall.

CHAPTER

SIX

WE'RE GOING TO WAR!

SWANSON AND I rushed through the crowd with a pair of stolen two-by-fours. They had once been guarded by a burly man in a green sweat suit and an Old Glory bandanna, but we'd sneaked past him when he turned his back to refill his flask. Now he would never find us; with over five thousand people swathed in green, looking for someone in that mob was a real-life version of Where's Waldo. And even if he did track us down, the evidence would soon be long gone, burned down to ashes and blown away.

We hurried back to our group, carrying the boards and a bundle of branches we'd stripped from a dead tree. Our friends smiled through the smoke and patted us on the back when we added the wood to our dying fire. The branches wouldn't last more than five minutes, but the boards would burn long and clean while we recovered our strength. Seven of us huddled around the trash can and blinked through the smoke, shielding our eyes from cinders and always wary of flames jumping through the wire mesh of the can.

It was late December 2002, around midnight, and none of us would sleep until the next afternoon, even though we'd been there since six o'clock and we'd been huddled around a trash-can fire since nine. We were camping outside The Vet, waiting for Eagles playoff tickets, and I would have waited a week if I had to—one guy did, actually, although it nearly killed him—so another ten hours was nothing. In the smoke our eyes teared up and we didn't try to hide it. Tears are contagious, like yawns and like violence, and we cried together around the fire just as we would cry together in defeat two weeks later.

EARLIER THAT day, the city of Philadelphia had declared a Code Blue weather alert, which meant the wintry conditions posed a risk of serious harm or even death to those without shelter. Philly's many homeless were being rounded up and led to safety for the night, while we stood there, bundled in four layers of clothing and cringing each time the icy air bit into our lungs. Two years ago, we'd shown up at midnight and were twelfth in line for playoff tickets. The next year we left an hour earlier, and stood about two hundredth in line. And today, we left for The Vet at six o'clock.* I was the 1,147th person in line, according to the numbered bracelet security had given me.

Ahead of us, the line stretched nearly a mile, and behind us, it stretched for two. Even with a strict limit of two per customer, there were not enough tickets to accommodate everyone. Rumors spread like smallpox from the front of the line toward the back: *Only the first one thousand with bracelets get tickets! They're gonna cancel sales if everyone without a bracelet don't get the fuck out! The bracelets don't mean nothin', it's first come, first served.* The only truth in the rumors was that we were confused and afraid. I was not going to sleep on the street in South Philly just to have some jerks cut in front of me at six A.M. and buy *my* tickets. So we waited, bouncing on our toes to stave off the cold, thumbing numbly through an issue of *Sports Illustrated,* and plotting around the fire so that we might survive the night.

---

* As with every year, Mom tried to talk me out of going, worried that I would get robbed or die of hypothermia, but I didn't listen. LauraBeth worried too, and made me a checklist of items we should bring and/or wear: extra pairs of gloves, a few bags of chips, magazines to pass the time, a first-aid kit, etc.

THE EAGLES—apparently counting on Philly fans' reputation for being congenial, polite, and orderly—had assigned only six security guards to The Vet. On one of my wood-scouting runs, I'd seen two guards ducking behind a port-a-potty, sipping on coffee. I smelled the whiskey on their breath when they yelled at me for yanking branches off a tree. Another man—wearing green and white Zubaz pants and matching face paint—carried a police barrier past them, and the guards looked away. One of them checked his watch and shook his head. Listening to the low rumble of chatter and war chants surrounding The Vet, they were more afraid than we were.

I knew we couldn't count on them if trouble started. We were on the honor system, and I imagined that Eagles owner Jeffrey Lurie is the kind of guy who, on Halloween, puts a candy dish on his front step with a note saying, "Please take just *one,*" and then is shocked to see the bowl empty five minutes later. Asked to please stand in a single-file line, wait our turn, take our two tickets, and then exit to our cars, we were willing to obey, at least until the pretense of authority had disappeared.

There were four of us—me, Swanson, Big Kev, and Ian. Swanson and I had done this twice before, but the other two had not. Not that our previous experience had adequately prepared us. We'd faced some adversity the past two years, but nothing serious: boredom, cold weather, a guy cutting in front of us in line. Each problem was solved relatively quickly, and, because the crowds were small, everyone was cordial, bonding together to make it through the night. By 2002, we were pretty confident about the whole process. We thought we were experts.

But there were a few important differences this year. First, it was much colder than we'd ever imagined. I used to think there was no real difference between twenty degrees and two degrees; once you dropped below freezing, cold was cold no matter what number you attached to it, a theory which proved to be painfully false. That night, the windchill hovered just below zero and we felt like a single flick to the ear would crack us into a hundred pieces like icy cartoon characters.

Second, there was much more at stake. Two years ago, they were a young team making their first playoff appearance in several years; the fact that they even won a single playoff game then was a surprise to many. They lost their next game, but the 2001 season amplified the hysteria when they got to the NFC Championship. And now here we were in 2002, the Eagles having won the division for the second consecutive year, one of the top two seeds in the conference, a clear route to the Super Bowl mapped out. We hadn't known what to expect in 2000, but now we demanded victory and championship glory. We would do whatever it took to be there when they won.

These heightened expectations had caused the crowd to swell exponentially. The magnitude of the mob made everything that much more explosive; the bigger the crowd becomes, the less people matter, and the less people matter, the more likely you are to do something regrettable and ugly, as we would learn overnight.

The final difference between those two playoff ticket endeavors was also the most significant—I had not promised Dad a ticket this time. Swanson, Ian, and Big Kev had all invited their fathers, and I had offered to bring Dad, but he'd declined. Scheduled for chemo and radiation treatments the week of the game, he would be far too weak to sit outside in sub-zero temperatures for three hours. Games drained you of your energy, and Dad had little to spare. I didn't know it then, but Dad and I had already attended our last Eagles game together: in the 2001 playoffs, the second time we saw the Eagles play the Tampa Bay Bucs in the first round. That time, I'd given him the ticket willingly, no lies, no tricks or broken promises, and we'd celebrated together as the Eagles rolled to an easy win. Now he was unable to attend games with me, and before the start of next season he would be gone. We would never tailgate together, never share a beer in the parking lot or own season tickets together, wouldn't even drive home angry from a loss listening to the callers on WIP ranting about how they hated the coaches. We only attended four games together. I don't know how many would have been enough, but four was too few.

STANDING IN line, the four of us chatted with our neighbors, mostly about the methods others had devised for dealing with the cold: hunting gear, space heaters, gallons of hot chocolate, liquor. Concealed beneath countless layers of clothing, everybody wobbled when they walked, puffy and misshapen like an army of Michelin Men.

The fires hadn't started yet. The remaining daylight seemed to keep people on their best behavior. When the sun is out, you can't help but feel like there's something good in the world, but when it ducks behind the horizon and leaves you to bitter winds and dreary skies, suddenly you lose faith in everything. By seven o'clock, we were slurring our speech through numbed lips and we felt like we would never see the sun rise again.

When we tired of talking to one another, we drifted closer to another group of guys, three of them, a couple years younger than us. One rolled a joint while the other two shivered beneath blankets. We heard cheering. The guys passed the joint around. Down the line, a thin trail of smoke snaked overhead. The guys pulled their blankets tighter. Another cheer erupted. Word spread that the Jets were blowing the Packers out. A Packers loss would guarantee the Eagles home-field advantage throughout the playoffs, which meant the road to the Super Bowl would run through Philadelphia. And it meant we'd have the chance to earn tickets to the conference championship game in a couple weeks.

A lonely kid nearby emerged from inside his tent with a golden retriever and a handheld TV. He was wearing a brand-new Eagles jersey, number 2 for kicker David Akers. Only three types of people wear the kicker's jersey: women, hipsters desperate to score irony points, and front-runners who bought the cheapest jersey they could find as soon as the team started winning. This kid was no hipster, and he was no woman, and I didn't like him. I didn't like that he'd been hiding inside a tent, or that he bragged to us about the quality of his tent without inviting us inside. And I thought it was bizarre that he'd been hiding in there with his dog. But I like dogs, and I wanted to see what happened in the Packers game, so we let him join us.

The Jets led by fourteen in the fourth quarter. Eight of us gathered around the little TV, talking about the many ways we hated Brett Favre, and joking about his alcohol problem. The tent kid, whom Big Kev had decided to call Wendell (that being the weeniest name of which he could conceive), invariably followed each of our jokes by repeating the punch line and expecting us to laugh with him. We ignored him as much as we could. Spending time with him was like watching a bad sitcom; he tried so hard, but was completely devoid of charisma.

With a couple minutes left in the game, the Jets scored again, and the win was locked up. The news swept through the line and suddenly we all were chanting *J-E-T-S JETS JETS JETS!* For at least twenty minutes, we continued. *J-E-T-S JETS JETS JETS!* The cold became an afterthought and, for a moment, we felt like we could stand out there until game day if we had to. But you can only distract yourself through chanting for so long. Eventually, the winds pick up and blow right through all of your layers, settling in your bones and chilling you from within.

A stocky guy with a gray Fu Manchu brushed past us and kicked over a trash can, dumping the contents out on the ramp. He took the can back to his group and dropped a few logs in there. Soon, a cone of flame leapt upward and the group closed ranks around it. The smoke was clean and the piney smell was pleasant. Ahead of us, another group rubbed their hands around the open flame of a charcoal grill. Trash cans clanged up and down the line. Soon, the air thickened with black smoke. Swanson and I dumped out a trash can and dragged it back to our group, while Big Kev and Ian ripped branches off a nearby tree. We found some loose newspaper pages, threw them in. The other guys added a few guitar magazines and sparked the whole thing with their lighter. It didn't take long for the can to flare up.

Unfortunately, it also didn't take long for the fire to burn out.

It's hard to make a quality fire from dead tree branches, articles on Kirk Hammett, and old Garfields. We were warmed for about five minutes before the fire reduced to smoldering embers, so Swanson and I went in one direction to scout for wood while the other guys checked their car for flammable materials. Before we left, we threw two of our magazines, a church bulletin, and a plastic shopping bag into the fire. The bag smelled like death as it melted in the can.

All of which leads us to the moment when Swanson and I pulled our heist on the guy guarding the two-by-fours. I felt like I'd snuck behind enemy lines. Guerrilla warfare at The Vet. We hoisted the boards on our shoulders and soldiered through the crowd. Apparently, we'd wandered pretty far from our base camp; our wristbands said we belonged in the 1140s, and the people we passed were in the 1900s or beyond—we even entered the no-man's-land where nobody had bands at all. A few people asked what the wristbands were for, and we shrugged. We had a pretty good idea—what else could they be for but to identify our places in line?—but thought it better to play dumb, act like we'd gotten lucky.

The people in the back of the line were drinking much more heavily than in our section; crushed cans dotted the walkway like a minefield. Urine flowed like rivers down the ramp, diverting around our feet and ponding near sleeping bags. Dressed up in jerseys, faces painted, people danced around the fires and chanted, while above them, the flags of the various military branches whipped loudly in the wind. It was a reverse chronology of human history—the 1900s, 2000s, and beyond were the least civilized and most savage, while those in the 100s and 200s were relatively sane and cordial. People pawed at our boards and yelled at us to stop and share the wealth. We picked up the pace. I didn't fear for my safety exactly, but I was afraid of losing our spoils.

Back in our places, we stood wind-lashed and smoke-blinded, palms down over the fire as if trying to hold it down inside the can. The Eagles had chosen not to turn on the lights in their parking lot, making it oppressively dark. For the rest of the night, we relied on the lights on Broad Street and the beacons of the fires that now surrounded us.

All discussion for the next six hours revolved around the fire. *The fire is a godsend. The fire is burning out, we need more wood. The fire is out of control. The fire will save us all.*

The only one who never fetched any lumber was Wendell, who chose instead to zip himself back up inside his tent with his dog. We saw him three more times during the night—twice when he went out somewhere to pee and then tried to act chummy with us, and once when his parents came to pick up the dog and bring him a sandwich. He probably had a space heater in there too. Whatever is the opposite of roughing it, that's what he was doing.

The rest of us took turns feeding the fire. The welcome monotony of work helped pass the time, and the delirium of sleeplessness and football frenzy made it easy to forget the Code Blue weather alert, even the terror alert. My memories from overnight are vivid, if disorganized. Mostly, it's a blur of moments shrouded in darkness and framed in smoke.

WITH THE fire dying, and the scout team still out on another hunt, we get desperate. Swanson throws a pair of batteries into the fire. They burn a mesmerizing shade of green, and then explode with a frightening crack. I had thought about throwing my cell phone in, because the antenna has broken off and it doesn't work anyway, but don't want to find out what happens when you burn a bigger battery. One of the other guys comes back from his car with a pair of sweatpants and a pile of textbooks. He throws the pants in—after which he realizes he would be warmer if he'd just worn them instead—and then drops the books in one by one. As we watch the corners of chemistry texts and Norton anthologies curl and blister, he declares triumphantly, "School's over, man."

A BONY, mulleted man in camouflage sidles up next to our burning can without saying a word. He's rail-thin, but in a menacing way; all sharp angles and jagged edges. His ribs jut out as if to attack, his arms pointed like spears. We exchange nods, and he warms his hands over our fire. A plane flies overhead, and he looks up, shielding his eyes like he's staring into the sun. Then he lifts his arms as if holding a rifle, loads the imaginary gun, and fires at the plane three times. He walks away in silence.

NOT FAR from us, probably in the 1250s, someone has an axe, and he's hacking away at a tree that's taller than him.. He and his friends alternate whacking at it, cheering each chop. They're obviously drunk, and it's lucky that no one has lost an arm yet. While they chop, a pair of guys strolls past them carrying a smaller tree, roots and all. They get to their own can and shove the tree inside as if planting it. It burns from the roots up.

A POLICE cruiser enters the lot and drives directly up a ramp with lights flashing. Before he shifts into park, an empty beer bottle shatters on the hood of his car. Seconds later, another bottle crashes on the windshield. And suddenly, it's raining glass. The cop retreats and does not return. No police will return until the next morning, after tickets have sold out.

PEOPLE HAVE been cutting in line, sneaking to the front and bartering for wristbands. The line has grown steadily since midnight; people heard there was a party down by the stadium, and they went straight from the bar to the line. There are about five times more people here than tickets available, and they have to sneak past us. Our can is positioned on an overpass, so we especially have to keep an eye out for trespassers. We can summon an angry mob with a single shout. A family of four walks beneath us, taunting us with their wristbands, and I fire a loose beer bottle at them. The father runs away, leaving the mother and two children behind. We spit on them as they try to catch him. I call the man a coward, tell him he's a terrible father, his family should be ashamed of him. Dad would never have abandoned us, would never have even cut in line and endangered the family in the first place. While the family scrambles off, I do not reflect on how embarrassed Mom and Dad would be to know the person I've become overnight, do not silently apologize to them for acting shamefully. I do not wonder how LauraBeth, who abhors yelling and violence, who sometimes worries about my temper, would react to my behavior. Instead, I exult in the glory of another victory, revel in the collective bloodlust. We've defended our territory, driven out an enemy. Just as the veterans, the stadium's namesake, had bravely battled for our country, so too will we fight for what we believe is ours. We're proud tonight—a night colder, surely, than any night George Washington ever spent in Valley Forge. The veterans staked their lives on our freedoms, and, as the night wears on, I begin to wonder why.

I INVITED Kevin to join us, but he didn't come because he had to work in the morning. Even though he wasn't there physically, I'd camped out for tickets because of him. Since Kevin had started high school, I'd envied him and his friends. They were fun and rowdy and told great stories. They all had nicknames—some cool, like Hoggie and Ratso, and some incomprehensible, like Wert. They drank and were good athletes and were popular and partied with girls. All I wanted was to have a group of friends like that, to dress like them, talk like them, get in fights like them. I wanted their stories.

By the time I reached college, I was trying desperately to emulate Kevin and his friends. I gave my friends nicknames, but none of them stuck. I tried to re-create the scenarios from Kevin's high school days, and I told his stories like they were my own. One of the main reasons I camped out for the tickets was that I knew it was something Kevin would have done. I imagined impressing his friends with my own hell-raising stories.

Later, I realized that maybe I'd missed the point of some of his stories, maybe I'd been pursuing an ideal that didn't really exist. When Kevin and his friends were in high school, they were jumped by a group of local thugs while stumbling drunk through the neighborhood, and Kevin was clubbed in the head with a bat. I only cared that he'd gotten a cool scar on his head and that he and his friends had an opportunity to seek vengeance. Vigilante justice via gang fights. I was with Mom and Dad when the police called to report the incident, and I saw how distraught Mom was, how angry it had made Dad, but that didn't matter to me. They were overreacting, I thought, there was no reason to be afraid. Kevin resisted my incessant questions about the beating, and he disappointed me bitterly when I saw him applying cocoa butter to his forehead to reduce the appearance of his scar. Why would anyone abandon something so cool?

Months later, he and his friends were arrested for stealing a golf cart from a storage shed at La Salle High and joyriding through neighboring yards. Again, I was with Mom and Dad when the police called, and again, I missed the point. They'd been very upset, enough to leave him in jail overnight, but I was impressed by Kevin's daring and boldness. You were supposed to have good times like this in high school. I eavesdropped on Dad's hour-long lecture to Kevin the next day, but took nothing from it. I told the story to Swanson, who didn't seem impressed, but he didn't have an older brother, so maybe he didn't get it. As far as I was concerned, Kevin and his friends had done something admirable, committing the kind of low-impact mischief that was the essence of being a cool teenager.

So, when I hurled beer bottles at families and set stolen lumber on fire outside The Vet, I was proud of myself. As the night wore on, I lost myself more deeply in this idea that what I was doing was all good clean fun, I wasn't really hurting anyone, and boys-will-be-boys and it's all okay. But if Mom and Dad were there, they would have dragged me home and never let me out again. I'd promised Mom I would be careful and take care of myself; I'd assured her I was responsible enough to stay out of trouble, but I'd had every intention of acting crazy overnight.

If I'd told Kevin I was acting like this to impress him, he might have laughed, and he would have asked how I'd gotten the idea that it was acceptable to act like an animal over football tickets. He probably would have been disappointed, maybe even warned me that I was being reckless. Fact is, Kevin wasn't out of control as a teenager; I'd just paid more attention to the stories that made him sound like he was. I'd filtered out the details where he was the peacemaker and the voice of reason, and I spent years modeling myself after an inaccurate version of my brother, looking up to him for the wrong reasons.

If LauraBeth were there, she would have turned away and never come back—because she is, beyond anything else, a *nice* person, the kind of person who will spend ten minutes refolding a shelf full of sweaters in a department store after someone else dishevels them, who will drive an hour to your house at three A.M. to jump-start your car, who will stay up all night taking care of you when you're sick and then call the next day to apologize for not doing more—and nothing I said could have justified my behavior to her. She doesn't understand the appeal of unruliness, and she has no interest in surrounding herself with disorderly people. I knew all of this despite my rationalizations during the night, and so I never told LauraBeth most of the details of our destructiveness. And I never told her how I'd caught a fifteen-year-old Hispanic kid cutting in line, and spit in his face while yelling a racial slur. We've always had a very honest and open relationship, but I lied to her about my behavior that night, because I was afraid the truth would scare her away.

JUST BEFORE sunrise, the security guards make another appearance. They silently push through the crowd, stopping only to kick our trash cans over and extinguish the fires. As they walk away, we huddle around the smoldering remains. Big Kev and Ian decide to scour the area for some good hot chocolate. They'll be back soon, they say, and leave us to wait for the sunrise. With no fire between us, Swanson and I drift away from the other guys. We won't ever talk to them again. Wendell is sleeping soundly inside his tent. As daylight slowly spreads, we feel the collective hangover of the city. People are awakening, stretching, remembering where they are, what they've done.

Tents and ash dot the landscape. In the sunlight, we can't hide ourselves or our pasts. In the darkness around Veterans Stadium, we had burned and pillaged our own land, committed shameful acts for the sake of a football game. Yawning and shaking the cold from our fingers, we joke about the night. Nobody mentions the violence or the rage; instead, we focus on the fire, reminiscing about how we managed to steal two police barriers, with sawhorses, or how cool it was to see a beer can burn.

Imagine, for a moment, that you're Dad. It's about six A.M. now. You've just woken up from a fitful sleep, while we've been up for about twenty-four hours straight. You're swirling your Cheerios in the bowl when you turn on the news. You see some fake-tanned reporter taping a fluff piece on those wacky fans and their crazy devotion. She's talking to someone near the front of the line, asking how long they've been there. It's all very boring. But in the background, you see movement. Then you see fear on the reporter's face and confusion in the fan's eyes.

Suddenly, you see it all—a horde of people stampeding from the back of the line to the front, racing down the ramps, over sleeping bodies, fighting to get to that ticket window. You may see me and Swanson, each wielding soccer-mom chairs like samurai swords as we charge through the crowd. You worry that we'll get trampled. You think about driving to the stadium to drag us out of the crowd and bring us home, but there's nothing you can do. The mob is too thick, you're too sick, and we're on our own now whether you like it or not. You try calling my cell phone, but the antenna snapped off weeks ago and I can't receive any calls. If you could get through, you would tell us to just leave right now, because no ticket is worth this kind of trouble. But we continue scrambling toward the ticket window. Wendell trails us, his tent, fully constructed, hoisted above his head as he runs.

The reporter stops a man with wild eyes and green paint

smeared across his cheeks. She asks him what's going on. He looks behind him, balls his fists, and screams, "We're going to WAR!" He howls some sort of battle cry and launches himself back into the fray. It's *The Day of the Locust* in real life. The world has lost its mind. The report cuts away quickly and now the news anchor is talking about a fire somewhere in the city. You turn off the TV, and we're left to fend for ourselves.

Which we do, kind of. Nobody knows who started the stampede, but we're all pretty sure it was the latecomers, the idiots who showed up at four A.M. and decided *Fuck the wristbands, I'm getting me a ticket.* They started running past us, and even though we had the magic bracelets, we didn't trust them, so we ran too. As we run, we realize the people in the front of the line are still asleep. I kick a man in the shoulder to wake him up so that he won't be trampled. If I weren't in the middle of the damn thing, I would be laughing at the absurdity of the whole crowd, screaming, charging like conquistadors into battle. But I'm there and I am afraid.

We finally reach the ticket window, which is closed. In fact, it's not supposed to open for another hour, which makes the charge even more confusing. So we're standing here, shoulder to shoulder with irate, frustrated people. Sleep-deprived, confused people who are still drunk from last night. Everyone's fists are balled and those of us with bracelets are screaming curses at the assholes who cut in line. We're outnumbered now, but we're not willing to give up the tickets we've worked so hard to earn. I'm on my toes, ready to swing my chair. Everyone knows it's only going to take one punch, maybe even one shove, for the whole thing to go up in flames. So fuck them, and fuck this whole thing. If it has to be a brawl, then it's time for a brawl. This is the only logical conclusion, right?

But this is not a logical day, hasn't been from the start. When it seems least likely, law and order are established again. Two security guards appear, and are soon reluctantly joined by the other four. They're yelling something, but we can't hear them. It sounds like they're telling us to go home, so we curse them too. They motion for us to calm down, and we do, just a bit. Still, we're yelling at them—we want our tickets, and we want people arrested. We want the guards fired, and we're ready to tell Jeff Lurie everything he did wrong, to tell him how his screwups turned a patch of concrete in the middle of Philly into the island from *Lord of the Flies*.

We're breathing heavily, worn out from the run and from our outrage, our icy breath clouding all around us. Swanson spots Big Kev, who, being 6' 10", stands out in any crowd. We yell for him, and he and Ian wade through the crowd toward us. They hand us our once-hot chocolate. In all the commotion, I've forgotten how cold I am.

The crowd begins to settle into an uneasy truce, now focused mostly on staying warm and thinking about going home. More guards appear, reinforcements, and even though they're outnumbered, they move purposefully. They surround us, hands resting on their clubs. If this had happened overnight, their presence wouldn't have mattered, but it's morning now, tickets are on sale in thirty minutes. Everyone is just rational enough to know that a riot will render the whole night worthless. We look to the guards for order, and now we're sitting on our chairs rather than wielding them like weapons. There will be no bloodbath today, no riots or tear gas. Everyone is too tired to fight. And maybe we're all trying to make penance for the way we acted overnight.

Security lines us up in numerical order, a comic but surprisingly efficient production. People without wristbands are told to leave, and most of them do so without a word, maybe realizing that they have no justification at all for acting the way they did. Before long, we're shambling back to the car, tickets in hand.

MEANWHILE, AS we near-rioted over football tickets, our government was in the early stages of planning a new war. We didn't know this exactly, but we all felt it; weapons inspections in Iraq were under way, which meant Colin Powell was drafting his career-defining failure of a speech to the UN. It meant our President was concocting reasons to bomb another country down to rubble, and to sacrifice thousands of citizens in an endless war. On the eve of our new Shock-and-Awe era, our six-week war that's lasted seven years, we were mostly oblivious, and we'd spent the night trying to maim one another over the right to pay sixty-five dollars to watch a football game. We can proselytize all we want on the beauties of America, the freedoms, the American spirit. But it's difficult to justify abusing those freedoms like this, turning against one another over a football game. We can pat ourselves on the back for being so erudite, so civilized, but the truth is, all people are capable of turning into animals in the right circumstances, just as we had overnight.

I'm sure many of the people in the crowd still believe in that old idyllic John Philip Sousa–Norman Rockwell vision of America, but it's clear that that's not our reality here. We scan the crowd, warily awaiting the first thrown punch, then the scrambling, the blood, the pepper spray, getting dragged out of the rabble by our feet, and never getting a ticket. We look for Big Kev and Ian. All we see is a pack of tired, unhappy people, dressed in full fan uniform and waiting. And I realize that *this* is America. This is the original capital of the United States, these are its people. America is not some bullshit flag-waving you see on the news, or the patrician back-patting you see during the State of the Union. America is not parades and cotton candy, liberty and justice for all. America is desperation. It's normal, otherwise sane people losing themselves in their obsessions, pained by a constant desire not to get ahead but to *catch up,* or, failing that, to live vicariously through someone else's successes. It is people like me, scrambling to fill a void whose existence they won't admit, and trying to complete themselves, or at least forget themselves, through any means possible: alcohol, sugar and fat, violence, football.

As it turns out, the tickets we bought at dawn gave us admission to the final win in the history of Veterans Stadium. The Eagles beat the Atlanta Falcons on a bitterly cold day and hosted the NFC Championship Game the next week. They closed The Vet down with an embarrassing loss, and then moved into Lincoln Financial Field, now known as The Linc, to start the next season. I attended their second game ever at the Linc, a blowout loss to the New England Patriots at which we picked a fight with a couple Patriots fans. Although we'd begun the process of tearing down The Vet that night we camped out for tickets, the Phillies still used it until September, and then it stood in South Philly for six months, abandoned, an empty shell.

In March 2004, they completed the demolition with a record-setting sixty-two-second implosion. Every serious sports fan in the city watched the video of The Vet slowly crumbling in South Philly, plumes of dust swirling upward and floating over the city. The dust hung in the air for days, resting on cars and windows, choking pedestrians. Spreading the ashes of the stadium over its home.

The Vet was an objectively terrible stadium: hideous, dangerous, filthy. And yet, everyone misses it. And yet, people lined up on the roadside to watch it go down, attending The Vet's funeral. And yet, I wanted to drive to South Philly to watch it. But I didn't have a car at the time. LauraBeth offered me hers, but her mother was in the hospital, and I didn't feel right keeping her from visiting, especially because I was unable to articulate why I needed to witness the implosion. So Sunday morning, I watched it live on TV, and was surprised to feel a profound sense of loss. Dad and I had been there together, it had housed our memories, hopes, scorn, outrage, and disappointment. It had been the centerpiece of our Sunday afternoons, the symbol for the team we'd loved. Dad had never seen The Linc completed, never seen the Eagles play there, and so The Vet was one of the few remaining physical connections I had with him. A lifetime of memories blown away in clouds of dust, then paved over. A parking lot. A new era of Eagles football beginning without any memory of Dad, without any mention of him.

AFTER WE buy our tickets, a scalper offers Swanson two hundred dollars for his pair, and Swanson pretends to hand them to him. When the scalper reaches for them, Swanson pulls back, says

"Fuck you, I'm not selling my fucking tickets." The scalper offers more money, and Swanson becomes even more combative. Scalpers violate two of the basic principles in which Swanson deeply believes: hard work and the law. Their existence, especially now while he's exhausted, annoys him, and their aggressiveness triggers his outrage. He tells the scalper to get a real job. Now we learn that scalpers are particularly sensitive to that line of criticism. Four indignant scalpers close in on us as we drag ourselves toward the car. Swanson wants to stay and fight, but the rest of us want to go. We pull him away and lead him to the car while the scalpers shout threats at us. It's mostly racial stuff, and we don't care enough to react.

Finally, we get Swanson in the car, and someone suggests stopping at a diner for breakfast. Nobody responds. We're all too tired and we just want to get away from this place. The property behind us is a wasteland, and we'd rather not look back. Still in the shadow of The Vet, we drive away unsatisfied, knowing we should feel victorious, but feeling nothing at all. This is the problem with sacrificing your principles for victory, I realize—even if you win, you end up feeling like you've lost something much greater in the process.

SEVEN

FOR WHO? FOR WHAT?

THE SECOND Eagles game I ever attended was unremarkable, except for the aftermath. The 1995 season opener—the Eagles lost a dull game to the Tampa Bay Bucs, and their new halfback, Ricky Watters, played dreadfully. We had primed ourselves to grant Watters, known as much for his ego as for his ample skills, a hero's welcome. Although we claim to love the blue-collar types in Philly, we really want the glamour boys, the wide receivers and the superstars. We want people to look at our team and envy us. We want them to be in *awe* of us. But Watters didn't make a single good play all day. His only memorable moment came in the fourth quarter, when he refused to catch a pass because he was afraid to get hit by a pair of nearby defenders. It was one of the more cowardly plays any of us had ever seen. I sulked in the back of the minivan on the ride home, while Dad and Kevin listened to the radio. Dad said the same thing he always did after tough losses: he agreed it was disappointing, then added, "But it's just a game. Did anybody die? Is the world going to end?" I shook my head glumly and admitted that the world would, in fact, continue to exist. It didn't comfort me at all, really, but it kept me quiet for a while.

On the radio, they aired Watters' post-game press conference. A reporter questioned him about his alligator arms, and Watters asked why he should bother taking a big hit late in a meaningless game. "I'm not going to trip up there and get knocked out," he said. "For who? For what?" he said, his voice cracking like a teenager's. I, along with most Eagles fans, was incensed. I wanted him cut. I demanded a public apology. I insisted that the coaches give him an extra beating in practice to teach him a lesson. I had never been more disappointed in an athlete.*

What right did he have to protect himself? He was an Eagle now. He owed it to Philadelphia to sacrifice himself, even if the play didn't matter. What good was his body if it wasn't being put to use?

For who? For what? For me. For us. Because we can't do it and you can.

I WAS always a little lazy, a little bit of a binge eater, but I never realized how fat I'd gotten until freshman-year soccer tryouts. The coaches started practice by sending us on a long open-ended run, complete with intermittent sprints. Ten minutes in, I faked an ankle injury and limped to the sideline. During a drill that involved racing up hills, I told them I couldn't go because I had a cramp. Later, they forced me to join the team for a series of full field sprints. Afterward, I collapsed on the grass behind the goal and fell asleep.

When I woke, the coaches were picking teams for a shirts vs. skins scrimmage, and of course I was on the skins team. Only when I took my shirt off did I realize how out of place I was. I couldn't fake it now, as tanned, toned kids sprinted past me to score on my goal. I couldn't pretend to be one of them when I was so conscious of how my belly folded over my waistband and my chest jiggled with every step. The other kids, and even a couple coaches, snickered at my pale skin, lumpy back covered in acne. They dribbled around me and performed tricks I'd never seen before; when I tried to imitate them, I turned my ankle and fell in a heap on the ball, fresh cut grass sticking to my sweaty skin.

On the way home, I told Dad I never wanted to go back again,

---

* Watters would later go on to prove his toughness repeatedly and become one of my favorite players. Most Philadelphians haven't been so forgiving; he's still reviled by a large segment of fans who can't forget that famous line.

and he said one bad day wasn't enough to justify breaking my commitment to the team, which is exactly the response I'd expected. The next morning, I pretended to be sick, but he wasn't buying it; he forced me to go to practice. The only way for me to get out of this would be to injure myself, but I was too afraid to do it. As Dad drove me to practice, I stared out the window of his minivan and refused to talk. He turned the radio up to fill the silence until we reached the field. Before he let me out of the car, he told me things would get better if I worked harder, and I said I would try.

The next day I was cut from the team, which was a relief. But I convinced myself that I had time to get in shape and show them all up before next season. I had begun the previous two school years by vowing to get in shape, lose weight and pack on muscle, so that come summer I could stroll the beach confidently. Every year, that determination died quickly. It was hard to go out and run every day, to cut out the donuts and the soda and the string cheese. And it was too frustrating to keep tripping over the ball, especially when other people could see me failing. I lived across the street from a public track, but ran no more than three miles all year. Dad saw me getting fatter and when he tried to push me, I ignored him and holed myself up in my room. Dad was always fat—diabetic, high blood pressure, the whole package—so it was especially important to him that his sons avoid the same fate. He prodded me constantly, reminding me that I was wasting both my opportunities and my abilities. Sometimes he pushed me enough that I did actually go to the track, but when I got there I sat on a bench for a half hour before spraying myself with water to simulate sweat and limping home as if I'd run myself into the ground.

I spent the next year stuck in the same rut: homework, TV, late-night cookie binges, and marathon sessions chatting on AOL. I was always a bit of a recluse, but when I discovered Internet communities, I nearly disappeared from the real world. Dad tried to limit my time online, but I set my alarm for two A.M. and sneaked on in the middle of the night, hoping to chat with friends about anything at all. I juggled seven different instant message windows at the same time. I wasn't yet much of a talker in real life—I couldn't handle the unpredictability of conversation, not when I had no idea what I wanted to say—but online I felt like I could say anything, and I didn't have to worry about awkwardness or inappropriateness because I had time to mull over every comment before making it. The anonymity of the Internet gave me a voice. I tried to meet girls in chat rooms, and compulsively checked the profiles of girls I thought I loved. At some point, I got a computer in my room, feeding my addiction. I met my first girlfriend online, sending flirtatious instant messages to a female friend of Anthony's—a girl to whom I never would have actually spoken, not then—and soon we were chatting deep into the night. Some nights, I fell asleep at the desk, IM window still open and flashing. I was a slave to the computer; it seemed to open infinite possibilities, although it also closed me off from countless real opportunities.*

By the time soccer tryouts began again, I was in worse shape than ever before. Three days in, I was cut again. But the new coach, Jeff, took great pride in his acerbic Northeast Philly attitude, and he liked me because he thought I was a real city boy too. I was the only kid at tryouts who had ever lived in a row home—in fact, some of the kids had never even heard of row homes before— and I think he saw me as kind of a protégé or mascot or something. So he asked me to stay on as the manager. Being the manager basically meant that everyone on the team disliked me and I wasn't allowed to play in games, but I still got to do all the dirty work in practice and run until I felt like I was going to die. It wasn't much of a deal, but I took it, because I didn't know what else to do, and I didn't want to have to explain another failure to Mom and Dad.

I attended every practice and I never faked an injury again, because Jeff didn't buy my excuses. If I told him my leg hurt, it meant

---

* Around this time, I discovered AOL's football message boards. I never posted then, but while I waited for friends to sign online, I skimmed the boards for rumors and to supplement the discussions I'd heard on sports radio.

I had to do push-ups for the duration of the run. If I said I had cramps, then I had to walk with my hands over my head, like a prisoner, and catch up with everyone when I felt better. So I ran every day, even while the team laughed at me for always finishing last. I chased loose balls on the sidelines during games, massaged the players' calves when they cramped up, gave them water when they stepped off the field. By November, the smell of fresh-cut grass was enough to make me feel ill. But I was losing weight. I passed teammates on our runs. I didn't lose my breath walking up the stairs. When I chased the loose balls, I had to hold my pants up with one hand and scoop the ball with the other. In the last game, Jeff rewarded me with playing time and asked me to try again next year.

For the first time in my life, I stuck to my vow to get in shape. I worked out maniacally, feverishly. Six days a week, I ran sprints, scaled hills, and replicated drills from our practices. I did sit-ups in the mud, sprinted up icy stairs, gasped through laps in the soupy summer air. Some days, I ran with Kevin, who had tried to help me train in the past, after undergoing his own fitness transformation as a high school junior. The weight disappeared so dramatically that Mom thought I was bulimic. But I didn't cheat for this; I earned it. By fall, I still wasn't a very good player, but I was the fastest guy on the field. When others crumpled to their knees, vomiting, after a run, I walked it off, barely winded. Sixty pounds lighter, now probably underweight, I had, for the first time in my life, accomplished something difficult.

During the summer, Dad tracked down Jeff's phone number and thanked him for the change he'd made in my life, for waking me from my lifelong stupor. He spoke reverently about Jeff and the effect he'd had on me; I think Dad may have admired him even more than I did. Dad watched me confidently now, looking at me not as a boy with a well of untapped potential, but as a man capable of overcoming obstacles. Post-game drives home, once silent, were now enjoyable, as we discussed the game itself rather than thinking about how I'd let us both down. My metamorphosis represented a turning point in our relationship: he'd always loved me, but now he respected me. Not so much because I was an average high school soccer player, but because I had finally decided to control my own body, something he'd never accomplished himself. I hadn't just achieved a simple goal; I had taken ownership of my life.

Dealing with failure seemed to be the epitome of manhood, the pinnacle of success. I needed to know success just once to know what it meant to fail, just like I needed to know life to really know what it meant to die. Now I knew success and I knew what it meant to push myself. But, years later, when the time came for me to truly deal with death, I still wasn't capable of handling it. By the time Dad died, I still didn't know myself, or what it meant to be alive.

I'VE ALWAYS told people one of the best moments of my life occurred during the second Eagles–Giants game in 2001. LauraBeth is not necessarily appreciative of this, but it's true.* We were at the game: me, Swanson, Big Kev, Anthony, and a few others. It was late December and we'd been out in the parking lot downing Jameson, ostensibly to stay warm but also to fuel our rowdiness. The Eagles and Giants were playing for the division title, which would be the Eagles' first in five years, and only their second since we'd started really following the team. Adding to the excitement was the fact that the Giants are our biggest non-Cowboys rival. We hate the Giants just like we hate everything else about New York. Their history of success, their city that gets all the attention, their damn loudmouthed fans who are just like us but act like they're superior because they live in a bigger city.

We were in the stadium studying our complimentary team pictures (it was fan appreciation day) when the guy in front of us turned to boast about how he'd snuck beers into the game: they were strapped across his chest in a bandolier like ammo. We were

---

* And I should add that she does make the Greatest Moments of My Life list. Quite a few times, in fact. She just has to share space on there with the Eagles.

sitting behind the Rambo of drinking. I thought this was one of the coolest things I'd ever seen.

In the front of the section, a hulking guy with a bushy Viking beard walked past. We barely noticed his wild hair and painted face; instead, we focused on his cheap fur coat and the train of battered hats that trailed down his back. He'd bought, then destroyed, a hat for every team the Eagles had beaten, and wore them on his back like scalps. He paused and lifted his spread arms toward us, as if opening the trunk of a car, and we screamed an Eagles chant at him. *E-A-G-L-E-S EAGLES!*

The game itself was fantastic—intense and loaded with big plays, it turned out to be one of the finest games McNabb would ever play, and it was also one of the best games of journeyman wide receiver James Thrash's life. The Eagles had held a couple leads, but the Giants took them back, and with only three minutes left, the Eagles were down by a touchdown.

We were sitting next to a father-son pair of Giants fans. The father wore neutral colors and was afraid to cheer when something went right. The son, maybe ten years old, didn't yet understand what it meant to be an opposing fan at The Vet. When the Giants scored, he taunted us; when the Eagles scored, he gave us the finger and cursed at us. We cursed right back at him and told him his favorite players had chlamydia. The father never made eye contact or said a word, even as his son provoked us.

When the Giants took the late lead, the kid danced in front of us with both middle fingers extended. He said "The Eagles fucking suck," and I told him his mother didn't love him. He spit at us, and one of us spit right back. He took Swanson's team photo and ripped it up, flung the pieces in his face. Swanson grabbed the kid by his collar, spewed a stream of curses, and threw him on the ground. The kid's hat fell off but his dad didn't pick it up. Swanson stood over the kid, fists balled, ready to fall on him. Anthony, the only sober one of us, stepped between them and led Swanson away. I stomped on the kid's hat and kicked it down the stairs to a lower level. The father watched while his son cried.

I should stress here that when I refer to this game as one of the greatest moments in my life, I'm not talking about the time we beat up the ten-year-old. I'm talking about the aftermath of that incident.

We were so caught up in the fight that we almost missed the Eagles tying the game. Fifty seconds after the Giants had pulled ahead by seven, the Eagles had scored their own touchdown, and now we were looking at overtime. But then the Giants bungled their way through another possession and punted with less than a minute on the clock.

The Eagles charged back down the field. With eleven seconds left, they took a three-point lead on a field goal, completing an improbable comeback in their most pressure-packed game of the season. We wanted to celebrate the division title, but were still wary. Giants–Eagles games have a way of ending strangely, and we knew this one wasn't in the bag until the final seconds ticked off. Besides, we've learned repeatedly over the years to cringe when things are going well. We're like dogs trying to cross over one of those invisible electric fences; the closer we get to freedom, the more painful and frightening it is.

When the Giants got the ball, they had time to run one more play. They threw a short pass over the middle to Tiki Barber, who was smothered by an Eagles linebacker. As soon as Barber got hit, we thought the game was over. But he didn't have the ball. He'd pitched it to a teammate, Ron Dixon, who was racing untouched down the sideline. The play had fooled the Eagles too; many of them were already rushing off the field jubilantly, as if they'd won the game. This was the disaster we had been waiting for. Not only would they lose, but it would be in the most staggeringly heart-breaking fashion possible. We shouted for them to turn around and follow the ball, stop celebrating, the game's not over yet.

Eagles safety Damon Moore was there, closing the gap. He was slower than Dixon but had a perfect angle, and they were in a footrace to the goal line. Finally, at the Eagles' four yard line, Moore caught him and wrestled him down. We took a moment to confirm that Dixon still had the ball, and then, then we had the greatest moment of my life.

Or maybe, more accurately, it was the greatest *feeling* of my life. To call it orgasmic, or even poly-orgasmic, wouldn't do it justice. I shoved Big Kev and he shoved Swanson, who shoved Anthony, and so on, like a row of dominoes. The eight of us swarmed so wildly that we must have looked like sharks in a feeding frenzy.

Everyone screamed so loudly that we were completely enveloped in the white noise of joy. I charged down the concourse high-fiving everybody I saw, embracing strangers. I jumped into the arms of a man who seemed like he'd been waiting his whole life for someone to hug him. Everyone buzzed through the concourse like electrons, pinging from wall to wall. Suddenly, we were all friends. The giddy mixture of relief, euphoria, expectation, hope—it was as potent as anything I've ever felt. We were bathing in endorphins. This must be what it feels like to see god.

The celebration continued as we paraded down the ramps to the street level, joining every Eagles chant, singing the fight song,* anticipating the playoffs. Swanson, still drunk, walked proudly, arms raised like the heavyweight champion, repeatedly shouting, "Playoff bound!"

Before we got to the car, he vomited a bellyful of liquor and hot dogs.

On the ride home, we slouched in the seats, some of us drifting off to sleep. My shoulders and back were already sore just from cheering; I felt like I'd played in the game myself. And as we rode quietly, I thought about what would have happened if I *had* played in that game. What if I were Damon Moore? And what if I had missed the tackle?

When I daydreamed about sports, I had the standard fantasies about winning Super Bowls and hitting game-winning free throws. But I often pretended at being a failure, missing the

---

* Lyrics: *Fly Eagles fly, on the road to victory. Fight Eagles fight, score a touchdown one, two, three. Hit 'em low, hit 'em high, and we'll watch our Eagles fly. Fly Eagles fly, on the road to victory!* This is followed by another iteration of the Eagles chant. If you go to a game, you had better be prepared to do a lot of very loud spelling.

game-winning field goal, fumbling on the goal line. I imagined myself at the press conference and practiced how I would handle my public shaming. Now I thought about being Damon Moore, having missed the tackle, and facing the media in the locker room. I would take it like a man, admit it was my fault, apologize to the fans. I would promise never to let it happen again, but everyone would see the haunted look in my eyes and know I was irreversibly damaged.

For a whole generation of Philadelphians, this is what being a fan is—you dream of dropping the Super Bowl–winning pass in the end zone, then admitting your mistake and holding your head up high. True success is so foreign to you that you learn the only real measure of your character is how close you can get, and how you cope with your loss afterward. Loss is inevitable; it's up to you to handle it stoically, like a man.

In Philadelphia, we've had some champions and some winners. But the greatest heroes of my lifetime have been guys who *almost* won, guys who were good, but not quite good enough. The city's greatest sporting hero, even though he is fictional, is Rocky Balboa, who, before becoming a cartoon character, was revered for almost beating Apollo Creed. The '93 Phillies got to the World Series and, despite losing, may be the most beloved Philly team of my lifetime. Mitch Williams, who gave up the home run to lose that Series, is a respected TV analyst now. Buddy Ryan's Eagles, who were entertaining but never even won a playoff game. The 2001 Sixers, who gave the Lakers all they could handle, at least for a day. Joe Frazier, who was great, but not quite The Greatest. Our trophy case may be nearly empty, but our moral victory case is overflowing.

In other cities, the children dream about winning championships. In Philly, we dream about losing them, but doing so with dignity.*

---

* The 2008 Phillies are the lone exception to this rule. Since they won the World Series, some have suggested that everything's fine in Philly now, the pall has been lifted. And while it's true that the championship—the first

---

THREE WEEKS later, the Eagles flew to Chicago. They had beaten the Bucs in the first round of the playoffs, and now were heavy underdogs to the Bears, who had lost only three games all season. The national media agreed that the Eagles were bound for a decisive loss. I knew they were wrong, and I spent large portions of my day wandering around campus hoping to run into anyone who would listen to my analysis.

Unfortunately, the NFL scheduled the game for Saturday afternoon at four-thirty. Because of the short notice, and the fact that *everyone* requested off that day, I was stuck at D'Alessandro's until five o'clock.

The shop was hectic. By ten-thirty, we'd already taken a dozen phone orders, some for twenty or more sandwiches. As I set up my workstation—arranging twelve open ketchup bottles in two rows behind me, frying two and a half buckets of onions, arranging my rolls so they were all facing the same direction and splayed like wings—the crowd gathered outside, most wearing Eagles green. I started making plain cheesesteaks in advance. Customers paced on the sidewalk, checking their watches, sucking down cigarettes. They plunged their hands into their pockets and bounced on their toes. Snow flurries swirled past them, the tail end of a storm that had dumped several inches on the city overnight. Plows were grinding down the road, pushing the snow into the giant mounds that were already accumulating on roadsides and in parking lots, those discolored lumps that grow so large by mid-February that you begin to wonder whether they'll ever disappear. Then the doors opened and customers charged in, shouting or-

---

I've ever witnessed—was a relief and a joyous occasion in the city, a single championship cannot possibly alter the fundamental character of an entire city. One win cannot undo generations of conditioning to losing. One great, anomalous moment—one victory among ten thousand losses—is not enough. Even the Washington Generals win sometimes. We've felt inadequate for so long that it's part of who we are, whether we like it or not. Who knows how many championships it will take for us to reinvent ourselves. There probably aren't enough sports.

ders, telling us they were in a rush, as if that would somehow compel us to work harder.

The customers were rude in the way that all large groups of people are rude, but they were also somewhat pleasant. When the Eagles were in the playoffs, everyone was a little nicer to one another, a little more hopeful. Everyone wanted to talk about the game, and time always passes quickly when I talk about the Eagles.

Most Saturdays, we hit a lull around three o'clock, which gave us an opportunity to regroup, restock the fridge, and otherwise prepare for the early dinner rush. But business only increased as we approached kickoff. The lull today would come around five-fifteen, deep into the game's first half. Then the night crew would have to deal with halftime and post-game rushes, which could be particularly ugly if the Eagles were losing. By four o'clock, I was manufacturing reasons to run down to the basement, where I'd tuned Mrs. Pinto's radio to the pregame show. When she came to work later, she wouldn't be happy to find that I'd replaced god with football. We weren't allowed a portable TV or even a radio upstairs near the griddle, so I cranked the radio in the basement loud enough for the hoagie girl to hear, hoping she would relay updates to me.

At 4:45, I called home and Dad told me the Eagles were winning by three. He was watching with Mom and Kevin. I heard cheering as I hung up. I saw my replacement parking his car at four fifty-nine. I yanked my apron off. By the time he walked through the door, I was wearing my Dawkins jersey and jangling my car keys. Before running to my car, I grabbed a bag of sandwiches that I'd made in advance and hidden beneath my jacket; although we were only allowed one sandwich per shift, I was sneaking four home for the family. Outside, the cold shocked me, freezing the sweat in my hair while winds whipped the fallen snow as if summoning it back up into the clouds.

The car's antenna had broken months ago, so the radio broadcast crackled and hissed at me. I turned the volume high enough to hear iconic announcer Merrill Reese through the static. Still leading by three, the Eagles were driving, and I was ten minutes from home. Seven minutes if I drove recklessly.

Which I did. I bypassed a stop sign because no one was around. At the top of a hill, I blew through a red light, rationalizing that I didn't want my car to get stuck in the snow. The safe route would have been to go down Ridge Avenue, one of two major roads in Roxborough, but that was also the slow route because everyone else was on it and the road was plagued by stoplights. So I sped through the hilly back roads. The Eagles kicked a field goal when I reached the top of my street. I pounded on the steering wheel, tapping the horn to celebrate. I pressed on the gas, racing down the hill, and then I lost control of the car.

Yanking at the wheel and stomping on the brake, I skidded ten feet off course and crashed into a mound of fresh-plowed snow. I shifted into park and checked to make sure I hadn't swallowed my tongue. My ears were ringing and my heart nearly exploded, but everything was fine.* The engine continued churning, I continued breathing, and Merrill's voice continued crackling. I backed out of the snow mound and then drove, slowly, toward home.

By the time I got inside, the second quarter had begun. I distributed the sandwiches to my family. I hadn't told them I'd be delivering food. Dad asked if I was allowed to take that many sandwiches in one shift and I lied to him. The Bears snapped the ball again and we stopped talking. We would save our conversation for the commercials and for halftime. Dad and Kevin were much better than me at analyzing the line play, the missed blocking assignments, the stunts and zone blitzes. I saw a mess of bodies ramming into one another, but they could break it down for me, detailing everyone's responsibilities and evaluating their performances. My job was to know the stats and the stories behind them, the narratives of the game. I knew McNabb would be motivated to play well in his hometown of Chicago. Former Eagle Stanley Pritchett was now a backup for the Bears. The EMB was rife with unfounded rumors about an off-season trade of Tra

---

* This was the second time I'd crashed a car while celebrating an Eagles score. The first incident occurred while driving through a rainstorm to Kevin's house for the 2000 season opener. Again, I emerged unscathed.

Thomas for Bears linebacker Brian Urlacher. Eagles fullback Cecil Martin had once been homeless, which made his second-quarter touchdown even more gratifying.

The Bears took the lead on a defensive touchdown, but the Eagles were clearly outplaying them, bullying them all over the field. The Eagles played angrily while the Bears played like they were entitled to a win. They kept pushing, and we knew it was only a matter of time before the Bears cracked. The game's defining moment occurred in the second quarter, when Bears quarterback Jim Miller threw an interception and, during the return, Hugh Douglas delivered a devastating block on Miller, separating his shoulder. Miller got hurt because he had been wandering aimlessly through the play as if he were immune to physical contact; if he'd been more alert, he could have braced himself for the hit and bounced back to his feet. Instead, his season was over, and he would never throw another pass for the Bears again.*

The Eagles took the lead before halftime and never relinquished it. They rolled to a 33–19 win, but if we could revise the score to reflect the game's reality, it would be something like 45–3. One of the most impressive Eagles performances of the decade, it catapulted them into their first conference championship game since 1981.

When the game ended, Kevin and I stormed outside and tackled each other in the yard. We burrowed deep into the snow mounds and tossed handfuls into the air, like Scrooge McDuck bathing himself in his riches. Celebratory car horns honked throughout the neighborhood. I underhanded a snowball to Dad, who caught it and then spiked it as if he'd just scored a touchdown.

Post-celebration, Kevin drove back to his house, and I gath-

---

* Years later, in my second semester as a TA at the University of Iowa, I would get into a heated in-class argument with a student who was a Bears season ticket holder. He insisted that the Bears would have won if not for this "cheap shot." I told him the Bears sucked and Miller was an awful quarterback, and Bears fans should accept that they'd gotten their asses kicked. When I concluded my rant, the classroom was silent and I ended class, too agitated to continue.

ered my things for the return trip to school. As I pawed through my book bag, Dad asked how classes were going. I had recently switched my major from Communications to English, and Dad seemed more interested in my work than ever. I showed him the syllabi from my English classes. He asked to borrow some of my books when I finished them. He especially liked to read my copies, he said, because the notes I'd scrawled in the margin fascinated him and made him feel like he was in a conversation with me. He respected my opinions and insights, which he discussed with me on Fridays after work.

Then he asked if I was doing any writing at school. I said I was, which was somewhat true. I had written a couple two-page stories over the past few months. Dad said he'd like to see them sometime. Although I had no intention of showing them to anyone—they were terrible—I said I'd bring them home next weekend.

I said good-bye to Mom, and Dad drove me back to school, as he did every week. Stopped in front of my apartment building, Dad reminded me to send Mom an e-mail sometime during the week, to check in and let her know how I was doing; even though I was only a few miles away, she missed me. I should make a better effort to stay in touch with her, he said. I promised I would. He clapped me on the shoulder and thanked me for staying for the game. This was the first Saturday all year when I hadn't rushed back to campus to see LauraBeth. He didn't ask me where I would watch the game next weekend, probably because he knew I would be at school with my friends. A week after attending my final game with him, I had just watched my last playoff game ever with Dad. At the time, I gave it no thought, assuming we'd have plenty more opportunities to see games together, to celebrate championships. If I'd realized how soon we'd be losing him, I would have been home with him every Sunday. When you're nineteen, you don't think long-term, and you don't ever expect anyone to die, not until it's convenient for all parties. When you're nineteen, you don't realize how quickly you can lose your Dad, and you don't realize how deeply it will hurt you when it happens. When you're nineteen and you've just seen your favorite football team play one of its best games ever, death is the furthest thing from your mind, you think the whole world belongs to you, and you think time is meaningless.

LAURABETH AND I met in college.* Although we both lived in the Honors dorm, we didn't speak until after Christmas break freshman year. Our first conversation occurred in the hallway outside my dorm room; we were the first two students in our building back from break, and we chatted awkwardly for a minute about how we were the first two people back from break. I didn't even know her name then. But the next day, I told my roommates I kinda liked that tall girl[†] who lived on the first floor. A week later, I was still talking about her while I sat in a friend's dorm furtively drinking from a bottle of vodka we'd snuck past the RA. Two of the other guys in the room knew her better than I did. One guy, named Jason, told me his girlfriend and LauraBeth were friends, so he'd try to hook us up. Another told me he liked LauraBeth too, and suggested we bet ten dollars on who hooked up with her first. I did not make the bet. Besides the fact that I felt sleazy even talking about it, and besides the fact that she seemed like a nice girl who wouldn't appreciate being wagered on like a horse, I've seen enough sitcoms to know that such plans always backfire in the wackiest way possible. LauraBeth now knows about this conversation, and she has joked that I should have taken the bet, because I could have used the ten bucks back then.

---

* I went to La Salle University, which, given my griping about La Salle High, was obviously a bit ironic, but La Salle met my two most important criteria. First, they'd awarded me a significant scholarship, a nice prospect for someone with no particular aspirations or earning potential. Second, located in North Philly, it was far enough away from home that I could feel like I was out on my own, but close enough that I could sleep in my old bed whenever I wanted.

† She is about two inches taller than me, a discrepancy that appears even greater because of her exceptionally long legs. She has the body, posture, and grace of a dancer, all earned during twelve years of ballet.

LauraBeth and I didn't speak for a couple weeks after our first conversation. She was too shy to talk to me and I was too awkward to approach her. Eventually, Jason and his girlfriend forced LauraBeth to come to my room—they stood behind her when she knocked, as if to prevent her from running off—and invite me to join her at an African drumming lesson. Her Literature professor required that each student attend one "multi-cultural event" on campus, and she didn't want to go by herself.

We each got one drum—they looked like canvas tambourines without the metal jingles, and came with a single stick. We spent half the time learning how to hit the thing in order to make the loudest possible sound, and then they taught us a very basic rhythm. The lesson ended with everyone in the room standing and dancing in some kind of conga line while the instructors sang the chorus of James Brown's "Doing It to Death," and I stayed behind LauraBeth so she wouldn't see that I can't dance, but twice she leaned back and brushed against me, which was nice. After the lesson, I walked her back to her room. Before I left, she hugged me, and halfway through that hug I wished she would never let go.

We officially started dating in early February, a week before my birthday, and about a month before Spring Break. That year, I was enrolled in a course on the religious history of Ireland, which entailed a Spring Break trip to Ireland. LauraBeth and I did not engage in big, tearful good-byes before I left, because we hadn't been together for long and things still weren't very serious. Sure, we saw each other nearly every day, but we didn't even know each other's phone number and many of the other students in the Honors program didn't know we were together. Plus, she'd been in a few bad relationships and was reluctant to trust anyone immediately, especially not me, who had developed a reputation as some kind of party animal in the Honors program, mainly due to my association with a group of heavy-drinking, pot-smoking non-Honors kids, including my two roommates. Relative to the rest of the University, I was tame and dull, but to some of the freshman Honors kids, I was wild.

Before I left for Ireland, I got her home phone number* from a
friend. On the second night of the trip, I went out to the Dublin
pubs with a group of classmates. At eighteen, I was thrilled to be
legally drinking, regardless of price or content. Within a couple
hours, I was broke and nearly blind from whiskey. Somehow, I got
separated from the group and I panicked. I jogged through the
streets yelling friends' names, panicking more when I got no response. After an Odyssean journey through the streets of Dublin,†
the final half of which I'd spent convinced that I was destined to
live the rest of my life as some kind of Irish gypsy, I found a classmate who loaded me into a taxi and sent me back to the hotel.

Back in my room, I walked straight to the phone and dialed
LauraBeth's number. The conversation was brief—I was using a
calling card with limited minutes and she was in the middle of
dinner—and we said nothing substantial. But she has since said
that my surprise phone call had a profound impact on her; it was
then, she says, that she knew she could trust me and that we could
have a serious relationship.

I would call her from Ireland again three years later, when another travel-study course took me and Big Kev there over Spring
Break of senior year. During this call, she told me the Eagles had
signed free agent Jevon Kearse to a massive contract, and they
were close to trading for Terrell Owens. The Owens news was particularly exciting because everyone knew the wideouts were the
problem with the team, and Owens was *the* ideal solution. The Ea-

---

* Which I remembered the same way I've always memorized phone numbers: by employing a mnemonic by which I assigned a different Eagle's jersey number to each pair of digits. Her (since disconnected) number went
like this: Jeff Sydner–Raleigh McKenzie–Izel Jenkins–Damon Moore–Wes
Hopkins.

† The two most memorable incidents of the night: 1. I befriended a weird,
balding Austrian named Herbert, who decided to commemorate our friendship by knifing (or attempting to knife) the bouncer at a club, an act that resulted in his arrest and my being slammed against a wall and frisked by Irish
police. 2. I tried calling Dad from a pay phone, to beg him to come pick me
up and save me. Fortunately, I didn't have enough cash for the call.

gles, who tend not to make bold headline-grabbing moves, had just endured their third consecutive conference championship loss, and, if LauraBeth was to be believed, then they'd made the boldest, most aggressive possible moves to start the off-season. I rushed off the phone to double-check her info, paying five Irish pounds for ten minutes of Internet access at a kiosk in the hotel lobby. When I confirmed she was right, I e-mailed her to thank her for the news, then hurried to meet my classmates for dinner. I relayed the information to Big Kev; we passed it around the table and gloated about our team. A Giants fan in our group hung his head while Big Kev and I spent the entire dinner discussing the upcoming season, which wouldn't begin for six months. Even though I was three thousand miles from Philly, I felt like I was at home.

LauraBeth had given me this information because she knew I would want it, and she knew I hated missing the opening of free agency. By then, there was very little she didn't know about me. But I never would have asked her about football during that first phone call.

When we started dating, I made a conscious effort to conceal the depths of my fandom. It would have been impossible for her to miss the fact that I was an Eagles fan—the posters on my wall, my clothing, and the desktop wallpaper on my computer all made this very clear—but I thought if I came on too strong with my fanaticism, if I showed her how devoted I was, she might not give me a real chance. Plus, what if she was one of those girls who hated sports? What if she refused to talk to me during football season or made me choose between her and the Eagles?

It was fairly easy to keep that part of myself hidden at the beginning of our relationship, since we started dating after football season had ended. Instead of sports, I talked about writing frequently, far more often than I actually did any writing. I thought being a writer was mostly something you did to impress girls, the type of vocation that seems deep and personal and sensitive, and allows you to excuse your anger as some sort of existential brooding. She rarely saw my writing, because I didn't want anyone to see my work before it was finished, and very few things ever got finished, save a single terrible poem I'd written for her.

Near the end of freshman year, I teamed up with a couple friends, including one of my co-conspirators on *The Scourge,* to found a new campus literary magazine, *Notes from the Underground.* Mostly, we did this because the current literary magazine was terrible, almost exclusively featuring the work of its editors. Besides, I'd never been comfortable with the idea of working my way up from the bottom, or dealing with editors. That's why I didn't write for the high school newspaper, and why I wrote only two columns in four years for the college newspaper.

We met with the University funding board several times, recruited a staff, solicited submissions, and ended the semester brimming with excitement over our new venture. We never published an issue. The only one of us who had any relevant experience was LauraBeth, who had edited her high school newspaper. She compiled the few submissions we received, arranged a layout, organized all of our materials. When I went home to work on weekends, she labored over my literary magazine for me. By midsemester, I'd already given up on it. By December, we all agreed that *Notes from the Underground* was a failure. LauraBeth held on to the materials, just in case we changed our minds, but she knew the project was dead. Given how artistic I was supposed to be, given how passionate I had been just months earlier, she was plainly disappointed by my apathy. But it was hard work, and there was no glory in it, and that hardly seemed worth the time. Not until junior year would I begin to view creative writing as a legitimate career choice; my Fiction Writing professor was an accomplished author who had gone to a famous writing school in Iowa, and his success suddenly made writing seem like a real possibility. His influence and encouragement would drive me to apply to graduate schools for Creative Writing, but none of this was a consideration at the time.

Another factor in the demise of our project: we'd begun the process in Spring, but now it was Fall, which meant football. I've always been less productive during football season, because I spend hours every day reading about football, and Sundays require that my full attention be directed to the TV. I made no time for the magazine: weekends were spent working at D'Alessandro's, going to parties on Saturday night, and watching football all day Sunday.

Over the summer I had finally come clean to LauraBeth, told her I was, in fact, a serious Eagles fan, and I was going to sleep out for regular-season tickets with Swanson. She'd shrugged and said that sounded like fun. I'd reiterated that she should know I'm a pretty big fan, you know, I kind of really get into it. "I have two brothers," she'd said. "I know how it is."

Despite her assurances, I didn't feel comfortable watching football with her when the season started. When my roommates and I watched the first game in our campus apartment, I didn't invite her. She asked what I was doing for the second game, and I told her she could watch with me, "but, you know, there aren't gonna be any other girls there, so maybe you won't feel that comfortable." She did not join us. I went to the third game—an easy Sunday night win over the Cowboys, before which we'd peed on the car of a Cowboys fan and dumped all of our tailgating trash on the hood—with Swanson and the rest of my friends.

Before the fourth game of the season, I found myself alone in my apartment. My roommates had gone home for the weekend and my friends on campus were otherwise indisposed,* so I invited LauraBeth to my apartment. We watched the Eagles play the Cardinals together. I had prepared myself to answer a litany of inane questions—*What's a first down? Why did they just kick the ball away? How many points do they get for making a touchdown?*—because that's what's supposed to happen when you watch football with your girlfriend. She asked none of these questions; it turns out, she understood the game fairly well, and really had been watching football with her father and brothers for years. She'd watched the games by herself the first few weeks and was excited to join me. A few times

---

* Big Kev was unavailable because he worked security at the stadium—with full access to the players and the locker rooms—which I thought was pretty much the coolest job ever.

during the game I pumped my fist or stood to cheer a big play, but mostly I remained seated and restrained. In the closing minutes, I stopped talking and pulled the couch closer to the TV. The Cardinals—the terrible, awful Cardinals—moved downfield easily on their final drive of the game, and with nine seconds left, some joker named MarTay Jenkins scored a touchdown to take a one-point lead. I hurled a soda can across the room and cursed at the screen. I punched a pillow, but that was unsatisfying, so I kicked our TV stand three, maybe four times. Then I flopped onto the couch. LauraBeth sat in silence while I continued cursing. She put a hand on my shoulder to comfort me, and I slid away from her. Ten minutes later, I mumbled to LauraBeth that I might have broken my toe. She said, "Well, that was stupid, wasn't it?"

"It was stupid how they lost," I said.

"Well, it's a good thing you broke your toe, then. That probably made it better," she said.

I knew she was right, so I didn't say anything. Her point made, she went into the kitchen for a bag of ice, which she held to my foot. Later, I apologized for acting like that and assured her I wasn't really that kind of guy. She nodded and looked like she wanted to believe me. We watched most of the remaining games together, and I lost my temper several more times, but she stuck with me. It was probably fortunate for our relationship that the Eagles had only five losses that season.

SOMETIME IN early May 2001, about three months into my relationship with LauraBeth, I was at an after-party for Central High's senior prom. My date—a friend who needed me as a last-minute substitute, due to her boyfriend's suspension from school—was nestled into a corner with her boyfriend, who had been waiting for her. I'd spent the last hour stepping over entwined couples and talking to a group of dateless guys, all of whom had taken ecstasy, and all of whom continually begged me to rub their forearms so that they could feel something. Everything about this party was desperate and lonely and sad: the generic, bass-thumping party music droning through the room; the lip-smacking, unzipping sounds of awkward makeouts on the floor; the overeager laughter and intense chattering of high schoolers racing to get drunk; the pair of single girls in the kitchen shouting the lyrics to "I Will Survive," using a half-empty bottle of tequila as a microphone; the doped-up single guys in dire need of human contact. I missed LauraBeth. She'd had no problem with me escorting my friend to the prom—had encouraged me to go, in fact—but I knew she was alone at school and I wished I could be sleeping next to her, instead of on the floor of some stranger's basement. I drank a couple beers, hoping it would help me loosen up and enjoy the party, but that only made me feel lonelier. I found a computer in an empty bedroom upstairs and logged on to AOL, hoping to send LauraBeth an instant message. She wasn't online, so instead I e-mailed her, told her for the first time that I loved her, and I was sorry I'd never said it before, I'd just been acting like one of those guys who are stereotypically afraid of commitment, but all I wanted was to be with her because everything else is sadder, bleaker, emptier without her. I had not planned on writing any of this, didn't even know I was thinking it until I saw it on the screen, but once written I did not doubt the words at all.

Having realized that maybe this was serious, maybe it wasn't some college fling, I invested myself more deeply in the relationship over the next several months, focused harder, essentially, on trying to impress her. Prior to this moment, I had gone out of my way to compartmentalize my life. I saw her a few times per week, but made sure to spend a greater or equal amount of time with friends. I consciously avoided talking about her when she wasn't around, because I didn't want to seem like I was losing part of myself. But post–e-mail, I dropped the pretense of holding her at arm's length and instead embraced everything about being in a committed relationship—we saw each other every day, I slept in her room most nights, I left loving notes on her door. This is the period during which I wrote her the aforementioned awful poem. This is also the period during which I spent a thousand dollars to surprise her with a four-day trip to Portland, Maine.

She has always spoken dreamily about traveling—everywhere, anywhere, as often as possible—and she had specifically talked about visiting the New England coast. So, in February '02, while shopping for a first-anniversary present, I eschewed the standard gift bags of shampoos and lotions and candles, and instead decided the moment called for a grand gesture. I called Dad and asked if he thought the surprise vacation was a bad idea. Initially, he seemed shocked, presumably due to the fact that I'd never asked him for relationship advice in my life, and I couldn't say exactly why I'd done so this time, although it should be noted that Dad was a good gift-giver and he rarely spent money on anything except when it came to presents for Mom. When it came to her, he had no budget, routinely spending thousands of dollars on beautiful necklaces, bracelets, and earrings. So probably I called him because I knew he would support my idea and give me the necessary push to commit to the plan. He told me it sounded like a big expense, but then paraphrased Robert Heinlein, saying one should always leave room in the budget for luxury.

When I showed LauraBeth the plane tickets, I promised this would be the beginning of a lifetime of travel together. I did not anticipate then that our travels would lead us to Iowa City, but of course I was caught off guard by many things over the next several years. All I knew then was that wherever I went, I wanted Laura-Beth with me, and she felt the same way.

IN DECEMBER 2001, two months before I surprised LauraBeth with the trip to Maine, Dad was diagnosed with cancer. In April, LauraBeth's mother was diagnosed with ovarian cancer, the same illness that had claimed her grandmother. LauraBeth did not joke about it like I did about Dad. Already, her life had changed dramatically; while I had Mom at home to take care of Dad and worry about him and watch him suffering, LauraBeth was the one who had to endure these things with her mother. Her mother deteriorated more quickly and more noticeably than Dad did, and LauraBeth had a front row seat for the whole depressing show.

Her sadness was exacerbated by my moving off campus junior year. Big Kev, Anthony, and I moved into a house in Manayunk with an old friend named Bill. Although Manayunk was only fifteen minutes away, the distance seemed daunting. We'd become accustomed to seeing each other every day and sleeping in each other's rooms nearly every night. Now, it seems stupid that we worried about maintaining a long-distance relationship of five miles, but we were in love. I did not understand why she cared for me so deeply. I did not question it.

After moving, I slept in LauraBeth's apartment several times a week, often while Bill threw parties in our house. The last time I had attended one of his parties, he had inexplicably blamed me for a bet he'd lost on the Eagles, and then fired a full beer can at my head, cutting me above the eye. I'd shoved him out of his chair, and, later, he kicked my bedroom door down while I was asleep. Thankfully, someone grabbed him before he pounced on me. I slept in my car on the street that night,[*] and hadn't talked to him since. Prior to this incident, our friendship had been on tenuous ground already, thanks mainly to my distaste for his girlfriend—who was practically our fifth roommate, and who was literally unable to walk and chew gum at the same time, gum routinely tumbling out of her mouth and being ground into our carpet. I never liked her, and Bill had heard me railing against her for her inability to understand even the simplest of concepts.[†]

I was sleeping in LauraBeth's room while Bill's friends robbed our house. They stole DVDs, CDs, and video games. They took Eagles memorabilia. They smashed my keyboard for some reason and dripped blood on my desk. They ransacked my dresser and found the wad of cash I'd stuffed into my sock drawer—over $1,200, because D'Alessandro's paid under the table and I was too

---

[*] I thought about calling Dad, but didn't want him to know I was drunk, and besides, it seemed like part of growing up was learning not to call on your parents every time you made a mistake.

[†] Once, Big Kev spent thirty minutes trying to explain to her, a college student, that the number 1 is actually larger than 0.9.

lazy to go to the bank. Soon after, we kicked Bill out of the house, and he left without paying us back.

The Eagles called about a month after the theft. They wanted to sell me season tickets for the inaugural season at the new stadium. I'd been on the waiting list for a few years, and now finally had my chance to get into every game, to buy playoff tickets without camping out, to be as close to the Eagles as possible every Sunday.

But I couldn't afford the tickets, because Bill had stopped paying his rent two months ago, because we'd been robbed, and because we each had to pay extra rent until we found a new roommate. Had I gotten the call a couple months earlier, I would have had my tickets, and I would still have my tickets today. Instead, they pushed me to the bottom of the waiting list and I haven't heard from them since. Now they make sporadic announcements that the list is ludicrously long, longer than a thirty-year wait for the people on the bottom, and I wonder whether I'm willing to wait until I'm sixty. Sometimes I think, as long as I'm alive I'll be there. At other times, I'm sure there's no way I'll still be waiting when the call comes; I will have moved on to something else, something more fulfilling, something that rewards and reciprocates my adoration. At least, I hope I will have moved on by then.

SATURDAY AFTERNOON and I'm at D'Alessandro's again. It's early spring in '03, and I'm working extra hours to try to reclaim some of the cash I lost in the robbery. Customers started lining up fifteen minutes before we opened the doors, and it's been hectic since. There's a full schedule of youth football games across the street, so we're going to be packed all day. Some parents bring their kids, still in full uniform, into the shop and reward their exercise with a cheesesteak.* Other parents sneak away during their

---

* They're not the only football players we ever served. A handful of lesser-known Eagles ate my cheesesteaks over the years. Indianapolis Colts wide receiver Marvin Harrison, a Roman alum, is a semi-regular. And I used to

kids' games. One couple has downed three forty-ounce bottles of Bud while their son is playing, and I'm starting to wonder whether they're ever going to go back and get him.

Mark the Butcher stomps upstairs from the basement. While Mrs. Pinto haunts that basement at night, Mark runs it during the day, as he routinely puts in ten-hour shifts. He bums a cigarette off of the manager and squats in the back room. Two of his fingers are duct-taped—he says the glue in the tape has healing properties, so he uses that instead of Band-Aids when he cuts himself—and he's wearing the same clothes as yesterday. I say hi to him and he ignores me. He's hated me as long as anyone here can remember. He's told Fitz, who makes the schedule, never to put us on the grill together, and he hasn't said a friendly word to me in years.

As far as I can tell, the animosity is rooted in the fact that once, in 1998, I gave Eagles tickets to Fitz without asking Mark first. Dad and I were supposed to have gone to that game, but the Eagles were winding down the worst season of my lifetime, and it was too cold to justify sitting in the stands to watch such an atrocious team.* I had begged Dad for three years to buy the tickets; I'd been eager to forget the bitter aftertaste of the season opener in '95. Dad had bought the tickets from a co-worker—he didn't say how much he'd paid, but I'm sure it was greater than face value—at the start of the '98 season. By December, however, the Eagles looked like they had quit; they were the worst team in football and nothing seemed appealing about the prospect of sitting

---

fantasize about Bucs defensive tackle Warren Sapp, then my most hated player, ordering a sandwich from me, so I could load it up with extra oil, cheese I'd picked up off the floor, spoiled mayo, and every other revolting thing in the shop. I never saw him, which is probably good for both of us.

* An aside about this team: one of their best players, Irving Fryar, had suddenly declined, and he blamed an injury called turf toe. Sitting in the car with Dad, I mocked Fryar for succumbing to a stupid toe injury. Dad pulled over and lectured me for twenty minutes about the importance of the big toe, stressing that I had no right to judge someone's toughness based on something I didn't understand.

in freezing temperatures to witness an execution. I didn't want to go, but also didn't want to admit it; a real fan goes no matter how bad the team is, right? But Dad suggested we stay home, and I agreed. Even then, it seemed stupid to shiver through a pointless game just to prove you were a real fan.

So, I walked into work on Saturday and handed the tickets to the first taker, assuming this generosity would curry favor with my co-workers. Instead, Fitz took the tickets, insulted me for giving up on the team, and never thanked me. When Mark the Butcher learned he'd missed out on Eagles tickets, he spent the entire night grumbling about how he was the biggest fan in the place, how he hadn't been to an Eagles game in years, and how he *could* have gone to the game if it weren't for me. From that point, our relationship progressed in the way these things generally do—I found out he didn't like me, so I decided I didn't like him and started making jokes about his drinking problem, which made him dislike me even more, and so on.

All the tension mounted last night, when I was finishing my shift and Nicole, our manager, told me Mark had been kicked out of his apartment. I laughed. He didn't have any money, because he'd blown it all on booze and pills, and he'd already taken an advance on his pay for the next two weeks. "Could he stay with you tonight?" she asked.

He was drinking next door, at the bar where all of our co-workers drank. I was the only one who'd never been in there, and also the only one who'd never been invited. I asked why she couldn't take him in, and she told me it wouldn't work. I asked why none of his friends at the bar could take care of him, and she shrugged. I told her I didn't want him in my house. I insisted that I didn't owe him anything after the way he'd treated me. Besides, I'd already been robbed once and I wasn't going to let any more drunks near my stuff. As I spoke, he had walked in the shop and heard me. He stared at me through bloodshot eyes and assumed his best George Thorogood voice. "I know, everybody funny," he said. "Now you funny too." He pushed past me to make himself a cheesesteak, then stalked out into the night.

Now it's Saturday afternoon, the shop is bustling, the kid who's working with me isn't getting the job done, and I'm not sure we're ever going to see an end to the rush. My face is glazed in sweat and grease, and I feel like my entire head is a giant pimple waiting to be popped. The kid is struggling to finish a feed and I'm out of meat. I ask Mark if he has a minute to help us catch up, and he laughs. He stabs his cigarette out and trots downstairs. I stare out at the crowd helplessly. The couple at the counter finishes their forty-ounce and they leave to pick up their son, who I imagine is hoping some nice person will come and kidnap him and take him away from this place forever.

ABOUT TWO weeks before Dad died, LauraBeth and I visited him in the hospital. He was mostly coherent, but had a hard time staying awake. During his intermittent bouts of consciousness, we talked mostly about school. I told him about the projects I was working on, the stories I had to write, the finals for which I was studying. It looked like I would be getting my first 4.0 in college. He gave me a toothless smile and said he was proud of me.

He sat up in bed and said he wanted to show me something. LauraBeth helped him move the blanket off of his legs, and he told me to touch his calf. I did not want to. I was afraid to hurt him, and, even though I knew there was nothing contagious about cancer, I felt uncomfortable touching someone who was so sick. The intimacy of it made me feel especially awkward, which is odd because Dad and I had hugged many times before; it's not like we were one of those father-son pairs who only shook hands and never shared a kind word. Maybe I was just afraid to touch him because then the whole thing would feel too real.

LauraBeth pressed a finger down on his calf, so I followed. We both left deep indents in the skin; it was like pressing down into an angel food cake. The flesh did not spring back, and our fingerprints took a long time to disappear.

"See how you leave that indent?" he said. "That just confirms the theory I've had for a long time." He took a deep breath. "I've always retained a lot of water. That's why I have so much trouble with my weight. And now it's worse because I'm laying in bed all day." His eyes fell shut.

He was, LauraBeth later explained, technically not retaining water. The problem was that he wasn't urinating at all, and there was a backup of toxins building up in his body. What we touched in his calves, that was the stuff that was slowly killing him. If I had only known that, I would have lifted his leg and wrung it out, squeezing every ounce of that shit from his body.

Dad's eyes opened again, and he continued as if he'd never drifted off. "You have the same problem. It's really easy for you to put on weight. You really need to be careful," he said. "Have you been running at all?" *No, but I have been eating more.*

I made some excuse about having a lot of schoolwork, and he faded away again. LauraBeth said we should let him sleep. I didn't want to go, because I was afraid his last words would be telling me I was fat. He was right, I realized—I had put on a lot of weight since starting college. The Freshman Fifty. When I got home, I stood on a scale for the first time in years, then threw it out because I was sure it was broken. I got a new scale and it told me the same thing: my weight had climbed back over two hundred pounds. Last time I'd been that heavy, I was in high school, I was a terrible athlete, and Dad was openly, vocally disappointed in me. He'd been so proud when I'd lost all the weight for soccer and now I worried that his last memory of me would be as a failure for having fallen back into my old gluttonous habits so quickly. I scrutinized recent pictures of myself. I was a slob, squeezing into clothes that didn't fit, my belly hanging over my waist, my face swollen with excess. LauraBeth had been too kind to tell me how fat I'd gotten, but there was no ignoring Dad.

If these did turn out to be his last words, then he was using his dying breaths to implore me to start taking care of myself again. Even though I knew he was right, I couldn't motivate myself to actually do it. Why bother taking care of my body, preserving my own health? What was the point? For who? For what?

———

DAD'S DEATH was not sudden or surprising, which did not make it any less sad. It had been a week since the doctors stopped talking about getting him home and instead focused on making him more comfortable.* Mom, a longtime oncology nurse, never expected him home, had known the whole time how this thing would progress, although she hadn't told us, and had allowed me to maintain my naive belief that Dad would eventually return home, completely cured. Given what she knew from experience, her steadfastness during that period has always seemed particularly heroic to me.

We spent Dad's final week watching him helplessly. The only thing I could think to do was make jokes and pretend like we weren't all waiting to hear his final breath. I brought books with me and sat by his bedside, skimming over the same page a hundred times.

Only Mom was there when he died. She called Kevin with the news and Kevin called me at two A.M. on a Friday. I asked him, "What happens now?" He didn't know. But he told me that Mom had told him to make sure I didn't break anything. Although I would later go on my rampage in the bar bathroom in Toronto,† I did not break anything then. He told me to meet him at Mom's house, and then hung up.

LauraBeth, who was staying at my house while we waited for Dad's death, sat quietly next to me, her hand resting on my shoul-

---

* Maybe the most patronizing euphemism I've ever heard. A lot of words could have described Dad then, but "comfortable" was not even close.

† An event that, I realize, seems to demand greater detail but which is as simple as it sounds: during the summer of '03, we went to Toronto (which locals referred to as T.O., selling shirts that said "I [heart] T.O." Had we gone there a year later, after the Eagles had acquired Terrell Owens, I would have bought several) for a concert, and it was only a few months after Dad died, and even though I'd felt fine most of the night, I found myself standing alone in the bathroom and suddenly felt abandoned and miserable in the most frightening way, like I was going to collapse and never stand back up again, and I thought maybe the best thing to do about it was to break as much stuff as possible as quickly as possible. It did not make me feel any better.

der. I walked to the computer and passed the news to Swanson via instant message. He called me two minutes later, sobbing, asking me why I wasn't crying too. "I don't know," I said, and I assured him I was okay. He told me I wasn't okay, and I shouldn't be okay. He said I should let myself cry. He said my Dad was a great man, and it wasn't fair for us to lose him already. He asked for details on the funeral, but I had none. He asked what he could do for me, but I had no idea. I had no answers, no jokes, nothing. I was empty. I told him I had to go, and I drove to Mom's house. Everything there was still exactly the same. His books were still scattered next to his recliner, his clothes still hanging in the closets, his computer still turned on. There was still a hole punched into his bedroom door from some ancient time when he'd lost his temper. There was still a note by the door asking deliverymen to knock loudly because he was working* in the basement. It didn't feel like he was gone; it felt like he was just working late and he would be back soon, heating up leftovers and falling asleep on the recliner with the TV blaring. No one sat in his seat, just in case.

At night, lying in my old bedroom, I tried to convince myself he was still there, but I couldn't hear him snoring down the hall. How odd it must be for Mom, I thought, to have to relearn how to sleep without the dissonance of Dad's snoring echoing in the bedroom.

Three days later, we were standing next to the casket in a funeral home and shaking a hundred different hands. Kevin and I used to joke with Dad that he had only one friend, besides Mom, but the funeral debunked this notion. Dozens of heartbroken people shuffled past his casket, crossing themselves and mumbling forgettable platitudes while their weary gaits and sad eyes told me all I needed to know, which was this: *Your father was a good man, and the world was better when he was here.* Even though I had nothing to do with Dad's fundamental goodness or likability, I took pride in it. He was my Dad, and he *was* a good man—reliable, honest, intelligent. This seemed indisputable. The real question

---

* Even though he was too sick to leave the house, he'd insisted on working regular hours from home.

was whether I was a good man. It's only natural at these things to measure yourself against the virtues of the deceased (i.e., *He was the hardest-working man I've ever met, and yet I'm skipping classes and whining about my twenty-hour workweek*) and to use their vices as a lens through which to critique yourself (i.e., *Sure, he should have taken better care of himself, but I haven't exercised in two years*). No matter who's in the casket, everyone always makes the funeral about themselves in some way.

Bill arrived early in the viewing. He knelt in front of the casket, said his prayer, and then shook all of our hands sincerely and sorrowfully. His girlfriend hugged me. I thanked Bill for coming and he said nothing. They left, and, as they were walking out the door, his girlfriend's gum tumbled out of her mouth. Next, I saw Mark the Butcher. He looked heartbroken when he passed the casket, as if he were mourning his own father. He hugged Mom and then shook my hand. I thanked him for coming, and he offered to cover my shifts for the next week. At the moment, it seemed like what I really needed was something to keep me busy. I told him I didn't need any time off. Although my co-workers had all been well aware of Dad's illness, Mark was the only one to pay his respects. I had talked about Dad's cancer incessantly at work. On one shift, about two weeks before Dad died, a customer interrupted to reassure me that everything would be fine, his dad had had the same problem but he'd pulled through and now they were a big happy family again. Everything will be fine, he repeated before leaving. This was also my co-workers' refrain, even if none of them believed it.

The stream of mourners continued. The handshakes, the empty conversations, the people who comment on *how good he looks,* as if we'd embalmed him ourselves. I barely spoke to anyone. Later, I would give the eulogy because everyone knew Dad loved my writing and when you call yourself a writer, people expect you to always have something interesting or relevant to say, even when you haven't got a single pertinent word to share.*

---

* I decided to reread the letter I'd failed to read to him in the hospital. It went as well as something like that can go, I suppose, with no tears or stut-

But you've been to funerals and viewings and you know all the different ways that they're awful, and you know the grief of seeing that casket close for the first time while people you don't know offer you halfhearted condolences and you can't even remember a word anyone said because nothing seems to matter, and it just seems so stupid to stand there and worry about the future, or even to think deeply about the past, and the best thing that could happen with a day like that is for it to end as quickly as possible. When everyone left, the funeral director gave us a minute alone to say our final good-byes to Dad. No one said anything while we stood in front of the casket, heads bowed. Mom placed a rosary in Dad's hands. Near his feet, we laid a folded Eagles T-shirt. Then they closed the lid and sucked all the air out of the room. All life's pain is compressed within that one brief moment when the casket shuts in front of you and you know that it's officially over.

A MONTH later, I was unemployed. On consecutive weekends, I'd gotten stuck working from open to close on both Friday and Saturday, because everyone else was allegedly out of town. I worked alongside our worst employees, the new kids and the malcontents, and by the end I thought it might be nicer to collapse face-first on the griddle than to finish my shift. During the final shift of my second exhausting weekend, several of our allegedly vacationing co-workers came in and placed a big order, not bothering to explain why they couldn't work, or why I had to be stuck there all day while they were clearly in town and not doing anything. I gave my two weeks' notice at the end of the night. I returned for a couple shifts, then told them I wasn't going to bother

---

tering, but it was kind of a hollow victory. A sample passage from the letter/speech, the writing of which isn't so great, but is pretty representative of the overall tone: "Besides, even though I'm becoming a writer, I still don't think there are words powerful enough to convey the feeling I'm trying to express. Sometimes writing just doesn't get it done, and it's something you have to feel. I feel the love from you, and I hope you feel the same bond with me."

with the two weeks. I was done. They asked me to be a team player while they hired and trained a new guy, but I had no interest in helping them anymore. I didn't go back to the place for two years. Dad, I knew, would not have approved of any aspect of this decision, especially not my shirking the two weeks' notice.

I was low on cash, but figured I'd saved enough to get through summer without working. I also had inherited Dad's minivan, which enabled me to sell off my junky old car. I got $200, which I immediately spent. Someone on the EMB had posted a link to an online memorabilia auction, and I dived into the bidding. Got myself a framed, autographed Chuck Bednarik jersey; $239 plus shipping. Hauled it up to my bedroom and propped it against a wall. This was an essential for any true Eagles fan, a remnant of Philly I could always carry with me. Now I owned a prized piece of Eagles history—a relic from the last great champion in team history, the patriarch of modern Eagles football.

Three weeks later, my rent check bounced. Then I got a letter from the bank telling me that I was running a negative balance. I punched a hole in my still-broken bedroom door and tore through my drawers looking for extra cash. I had none. LauraBeth looked at the mess I'd made and said that breaking things wouldn't solve any problems. I slumped on the edge of my bed and told her my hand hurt. She sat behind me and rubbed my shoulders, but I shrugged her away. Eventually, I realized the only way out was to sell Dad's van. In one month, I'd lost so much, and now I was scrambling just to keep from drowning. I sulked in my room, penniless, carless, fatherless. With another year left in college, I had no particular direction or plan. LauraBeth and Chuck Bednarik were in the room with me still, but LauraBeth had been around for so long that I took her for granted. Years later, Bednarik would fail me too, but for now, it seemed like he was all I had.

CHAPTER
EIGHT

LONG-DISTANCE RELATIONSHIPS

WHEN THE Eagles lose, people all over the country think about me. I do not say this out of arrogance or self-absorption; dozens of people have confirmed this fact. From Tallahassee to Seattle, Madison to Austin, L.A. to Boston, there are people who think about me every time they see the Eagles on TV. They worry about me. They care.

This is no trivial matter. It means something that they e-mail me for my take on the latest quarterback controversy, that they call or send text messages after blocked punts and long touchdown runs. They talk to each other about me, wonder how I'm handling a tough loss.

All of this is flattering in a way—it's always nice to have people thinking about you—but it's also depressing. To most of the people I've ever met, I've been reduced—reduced myself, maybe—to a caricature of Eagles fandom, a one-dimensional cartoon of The Philly Guy who loves cheesesteaks, cream cheese, football, and hurling batteries at people. My identity is so wrapped up in the team that most people can't separate me from the Eagles. A friend from grad school recently found a picture of me online, posing inside the stadium in full Eagles gear, and sent an e-mail that said, "Holy shit, of course you're at an Eagles game!" My response: "Hey, if I weren't at an Eagles game, how would people recognize me?" That was supposed to have been a joke.

IN AUGUST 2004, I loaded a U-Haul and embarked, with help from Swanson and Ian, on a nineteen-hour drive to Iowa City that took us past mostly nothing at all for hundreds of miles. Mom never said so, but she was unhappy to see me go. When Kevin had moved to Maryland for a year after college, Mom had missed him, but Dad and I were still there with her. Now she lived alone in the house for the first time ever. Remembering Dad's advice during college, I promised to e-mail and call her regularly. I also left LauraBeth behind, two days after her birthday. I'd asked her to move with me, but knew she couldn't. Her mother was dying, and her sickly grandfather had recently moved into her house. Laura-Beth did not want me to go, and I didn't want to go either. But I'd been accepted at a well-known Creative Writing program* and didn't know what else to do with myself. If I'd stayed, I would have lived with Mom and worked in some sterile office, editing memos or filing documents or whatever English majors do for a living. If I moved to Iowa, there was, if nothing else, the promise of a two-year delay before I had to start working a real grown-up job.

What I'm saying is this: the choice to move was not really a choice at all. I pretended I was excited to leave, ready for a wild cross-country escapade; artsy types are supposed to be adventurous and free-spirited, ready to travel anywhere at a moment's notice. I tried to convince everyone that moving to Iowa City was

---

* Obligatory background information on the program: the writing-related question I find myself answering most often (besides, "Hey, wanna know a good story you should write?") is "Why would anyone *want* to move to Iowa?" The answer, which I usually mumble or gloss over too quickly, for fear of seeming obnoxious, is that the Iowa Writers' Workshop was the first graduate Creative Writing program in the country, and therefore has developed a very strong reputation, having been home to numerous great authors. Out of about eight hundred applicants to the fiction program every year, they accept only twenty-five. Once accepted, very few people turn them down. All of which made it particularly shocking when I was accepted, since I'd been rejected by the seven other schools to which I'd applied. One program even shirked the form letter and went out of its way to tell me that my application was "not competitive." I thought about throwing Iowa's response in the trash without checking it, but, luckily, LauraBeth and Mom made me open the envelope.

exciting and essential to my vocation; I even convinced myself, mostly. I was a writer, right? Writers need stories to tell, so moving was part of the job.

Prior to moving to Iowa, I had never been outside of Philly for more than twelve consecutive days, and I had never lived with less than three people at one time. Then, suddenly, I was supposed to live by myself for two years in Tornado Alley. Swanson and Ian rode home the day after moving me, and it wasn't until my first night alone that I realized quite how anxious I was. I had nothing to do, no one to talk to, and no idea how to take care of myself. I did not sleep. I lay in bed and stared at the ceiling, thinking of reasons to justify moving back home. I sent LauraBeth a text message telling her I was nervous and I missed her. Had she begged me to come back then, I might have listened. Instead, she reassured me that everything would be fine once classes began, it was normal to be nervous. She never asked me to quit or move home, because she knew, long before I did, that I had to be there, that it was important that I mature and become self-sufficient.

Not that she was particularly happy about the arrangement; while I prolonged my college life for another two years, she would be stuck living the life of a forty-year-old woman, running a house and working while two people depended on her for their well-being.

Because things were so hectic at home, she wouldn't be able to visit me for a while. So, once Swanson and Ian boarded the Greyhound to head back to Philly, I was officially on my own. Out of options, I actually focused on writing. I spent the next two days planning, writing, and perfecting a short story about a family that held weekly barbecues at a pet cemetery to honor their dog's memory.* One draft, about ten hours of real work. I felt great about it. I congratulated myself on being so smart, so far ahead of

---

*An idea I'd gotten from a newspaper article about a New Jersey pet cemetery that was excavating and returning the pets of all the people who hadn't paid their debts. Presumably, they also ran a side business in nightmare manufacturing.

the game. A former teacher read it and said he enjoyed it. I sent it, unsolicited, to a couple of college friends, who offered bland praise. They all were trying to be supportive, but none of them gave me honest critiques. What I needed was the type of read Dad would have given me. He would have noted the inconsistent plot, the overwrought prose, the rambling exposition. The first true critic of my work, Dad always pushed me to improve; without his input, I settled for a deeply flawed first draft.

Still bored, I began another story. And in the middle of that one, I got a call inviting me to a Welcome-to-the-Writers'- Workshop barbecue. I was ambivalent about the invitation. I know that I make awful first impressions; due to a mixture of shyness and awkwardness, I've always struggled with meeting people and making introductory small talk.* When I told LauraBeth I was going to skip the party, she insisted that I go. She knew I would fall apart if I didn't find some social outlet soon, because as much as I dread meeting new people and tap-dancing through conversational minefields, I also love talking. Telling stories, complaining, thinking out loud, whatever. When I'm alone, I talk to my dogs. When they're not around, I talk to the TV, or myself. Even as I write, I'm giving myself verbal feedback on my progress. And I often talk out loud to myself in public, which has attracted many confused looks from strangers.†

I arrived late to the barbecue, even though it was being held at a park two minutes from my apartment. I somehow ended up at a

---

* These conversations ("So, where are you from?" "Who are your favorite writers?" "How do you like Iowa?") are exhausting. I find them unbearably dull and formulaic, and I'm terrible at feigning interest. I usually contribute little and reveal nothing of myself, besides a lack of enthusiasm, which leaves people thinking that I'm either a) dull and lifeless or b) rude.

† Until I was twelve or thirteen, I was so shy that I hid behind my parents when meeting people, and so quiet that some relatives never heard me speak. Supposedly, I used to greet people by barking at them. My teachers worried I was autistic, but Dad explained that I was perfectly fine; I just didn't like people. Now I talk so frequently and so rapidly that I even annoy myself sometimes. The old joke in the family is that I'm making up for lost time after having been silent for so long as a child.

different park a mile away, and wandered back toward the actual site red-faced and annoyed. When I moved, I'd seen it as an opportunity to reinvent myself, to leave my negative characteristics behind. Chief among these was my notoriously poor sense of direction, which still got me lost driving the two miles from Mom's house to Swanson's, even after fifteen years of friendship. This was the first of many moments over the next two years when I realized I couldn't get away from myself, no matter where I went.

About thirty people were there, drinking cheap beer and standing in awkward small-talk circles. I felt nauseous. I thought about running away before anyone saw me. Someone waved to me. It was Chris, whom I'd met earlier in the week at a teaching orientation; our financial aid packages required us both to teach three classes in the Rhetoric department during the academic year, even though neither of us had any teaching experience, or training in education, at all.* Now that he'd spotted me, I was stuck at the party. I wandered into the group and hesitantly opened my first beer. It was about six o'clock.

I skulked around the perimeter for a while, contributing nothing but occasional laughter, and feeling like a creepy conversation voyeur. Instead of talking, I drank. Borrowing one of Dad's old tricks, I carried two beers; in case I got caught in a terrible conversation, I could hold up the second beer and claim I had to deliver it to someone. And if no one stopped me, well, then I could just drink more.

By seven-thirty, I was drunk.

By eight-thirty, I had met almost everyone at the party.

By nine, I was talking about the Eagles.

I'd been drowning in a conversation about books, one of the first real literary conversations I'd ever had in my life, and also the point at which I realized I was in over my head. I had no idea what

---

* I cannot overstate how horrifying this prospect was to me—standing in front of a full classroom of undergrads for fifty minutes, *four days a week,* seemed like torture. I'd hoped for some kind of crash course in how to be a great professor, but our three half-days of orientation consisted mostly of tips on syllabus-writing and warnings not to have sex with our students.

these people were talking about. They made obscure literary references and inside jokes about George Saunders and *Anna Karenina*. They discussed structure, tone, voice: terms I'd heard before, but which I didn't actually understand. Someone asked me what I thought about *Stop-Time* by Frank Conroy, and I said I thought it was a pretty good book. When they asked me to explain myself, I said, "I don't know . . . it was an interesting story." They laughed, but I think they thought I was being ironic, mocking the ignorant people who don't really read or understand literature. So I played along and added a few more dumbly obvious comments, because at least they were talking to me. I made mental notes to read the books they discussed, to study the terms they used, but, by the end of the night, I'd forgotten them all.

I overheard someone behind me mention the name James Thrash. Thrash had been a mediocre receiver for the Eagles for the past four seasons, a hardworking guy, but also an obscure player. Only an Eagles fan, or a truly dedicated NFL fan, could really be talking about James Thrash in the middle of Iowa City. I followed the voices and found two older guys standing off to the side, talking football.

I pointed to my hooded sweatshirt—black, with an Eagles logo centered between the words "Property of Eagles"—and introduced myself as a huge fan, still desperately searching for a good place to watch this season's games. Lee, the taller and more athletically built of the two, introduced himself as an Eagles fan from Jersey—the best news I'd heard since I'd moved to Iowa City. The other football fan was Steve, a husky guy with white hair and a perpetual mischievous grin. He was a Redskins season ticket holder who subscribed to the NFL satellite package, and who had played football at a relatively high level in college. I hadn't had a good football talk since moving, and I quickly engaged them in discussion of the upcoming season.

The next hour was a monument to our football fandom, a conversation about everything NFL-related, especially the nuances casual fans don't understand: line play, special teams, Cover-2 defenses, SAM linebackers. A few non-fans lurked near us and tried to dissect our football jargon, but I saw on their faces the same helpless expression I'd borne when listening to the writerly discussions of point of view, voice, and pedagogy. Every football thought I'd ever had spilled out of me, filling all conversational gaps, fighting off even the smallest silences that threatened to derail our discussion. Eventually, sadly, we were interrupted. We were out of booze, and the whole group was moving on to the bars downtown.

Details beyond this point are a little hazy, but three episodes from the night stand out. First, we're sitting in a booth, sharing our backgrounds, and I rush through mine. *I'm from Philly, went to La Salle, was an English major, enjoyed my creative writing classes, thought it would be easier to come here than to get a real job.* The guy next to me explains that he's already published over a hundred poems but wants to try his hand at fiction writing, see where it takes him. The guy across from me has been published in a few major journals, including *The Paris Review,* and has spent the last couple years teaching English at Purdue. The woman next to him is an experienced journalist with a degree from Yale.

Later, I'm repeating my story to someone at the bar, telling him I'm really nervous, I don't think I belong here, this isn't the place for me. And he's trying to comfort me, telling me I wouldn't have gotten in if I wasn't good,* and, besides, you're here now so why not make the best of it? I tell him I wish this place was more like home.

Second memory: I'm meeting dozens of new people, forgetting their names instantly. I steer most of our conversations

---

* A few months later, I heard from two second-year students that my application had been rejected during the initial screening process, but had then been un-rejected by Workshop director Frank Conroy. Frank always read every applicant's writing samples, and it was well known that he was in the habit of salvaging rejected manuscripts. Although I cannot confirm that I was among those fished out of the reject pile by Frank—and, I should note, the guys who told me this story were drunk at the time—I found it easy to believe. I never felt that I belonged there in the first place, and this story reinforced the idea that I'd somehow snuck in through the back door.

toward football, and if someone reveals they're a fan of some team besides the Eagles, I follow up with one of two jokes: *Seahawks fan? Sorry to hear it,* or *A Giants fan? Well, we can't be friends.* I see a guy who I think is Lee, and I say, "Here's my Eagles fan," slapping him on the back. The guy turns and says, "Fuck that, I like the Broncos, remember?" I don't remember, actually, and I'm not even sure who this guy is or if he's in the Workshop, but I take his word for it, and wonder if I'd just imagined that whole conversation with Lee.

Final memory: I get hopelessly lost walking back to my apartment. While wandering through the nearby back roads, I stop to vomit in the grass, and hope no one is watching.

A WEEK later, classes started. I was in a class with Frank Conroy, who, besides being the longtime director of the Workshop, was an Iowa legend to be feared and respected, emphasis on "fear." I'd been warned repeatedly that he was a literary bully, an ogre who'd reduced people to tears, destroyed their confidence, and even once caused someone to faint because his criticism was so harsh. Naturally, everyone wanted to be the one student who blew him away. My creative writing teacher at La Salle had described Frank as a "scary father figure," a description he meant in the best possible way. The reason Frank was so brutal in Workshop, we would learn, was not because he was an insecure jerk, but because he cared so much about the language and was so invested in our writing that bad stories legitimately upset him.

There were eleven other people in the class, all older and more accomplished than me. Several already had Master's degrees, and one had a PhD from Harvard. At least one of them used to be a lawyer, and they'd all been published before. One guy wasn't necessarily accomplished, but was so ostentatious about his few successes that I thought he was much better off than he actually was. Lee was there too, and now I learned that maybe our Eagles fandom was the end of our similarities. It seemed like he knew everyone there, and he had this passionate way of talking about writing that could entrance people, sometimes even Frank. Also, he edited his own literary journal, and he had already published a book with a very impressive-sounding title.* The median age in the class was about thirty-two, and the average education quality was Ivy or better. The problem wasn't that I didn't fit in; it was that I so obviously didn't fit in that everyone knew it immediately.

I decided the only way to ingratiate myself with the group was to blow them away with my story about the pet cemetery, which I hadn't revised except for running spell-check. So I volunteered my story for discussion in the first workshop of the semester, which would be held a week later.

Over the course of the week, I convinced myself that not only was my story good, but it was great, and I vaguely expected Frank to lay the story on the table, smiling, and say, *No need to discuss this one. It's going straight to* The New Yorker. *Bang-up job, son.* Then they would all hoist me up on their shoulders and carry me triumphantly from the room.

Obviously, this is all just a big setup for a spectacular failure. In our weekly workshops, we would discuss two stories written by people in the class. Each story would get at least an hour of attention, during which everyone in the class had to detail the aspects of the story they liked, and, especially, those they didn't like. During this process, the writer was not allowed to speak. We started the first workshop of the year with my story. An hour and fifteen minutes later, my entire writing life, such as it was, had crumbled around me. My classmates were relentless, yanking on every loose thread in the story. Frank went through the first seven pages, detailing the flaws with every sentence. This was a public execution, not of the clean, efficient firing squad variety, but more like a stoning. I spent the last half hour thinking about dropping out, and how I would explain myself to Mom and LauraBeth when I came home two years too early. LauraBeth would be so happy to see me she wouldn't care that I was a coward. Mom would welcome me home, the prodigal son. We could all pretend none of

---

* *Incidents of Egotourism in the Temporary World.*

this had ever happened. But we would all know I was a quitter. We would all know that Dad would be disappointed in me. I don't pretend I feel his spirit guiding me or that his ghost is reading over my shoulder while I type, but sometimes you can't help thinking he knows, somehow, that you're letting him down. When I thought about dropping out, the prospect of Dad's disapproval paralyzed me.

Before we began the day's second story, Frank looked me in the eye and paused as if to deliver some fatherly wisdom. The difference between these two stories, he said, is that one deserves a second draft, and yours does not. I was silent for most of the remaining class time. I did try to give some input on the second story—I thought it shouldn't have been written in present tense—and Frank promptly disagreed with me. After class, I was forced to go out to dinner with the group and eat Indian food for the first time. It tasted like failure.*

After dinner, I followed the crowd out to the Fox Head, which was generally considered the writers' bar. During the walk, I drifted behind the crowd and Lee fell back to meet me. He told me he thought one part of my story was really cool, reciting one of the lines from memory, and gave suggestions on how to build on this strength. He shared some advice he'd gotten from an old writing teacher about killing dogs in stories† and he bought the first round at the bar. His generosity on that walk may be what ultimately stopped me from running away; I wasn't exactly relieved, but I felt slightly less terrible.

In the bar, I drank PBR off the tap and sat near the TV so I could see the *SportsCenter* highlights. When people asked how my workshop had gone, I either ignored them or made jokes about it.

---

* They say taste aversion is the most potent form of classical conditioning. Usually, it only takes one trial, one association between a specific food and poisoning/sickness to drive you away forever. So it seems relevant to mention that I still can't eat Indian food, and the smell makes me vaguely nauseous.

† The advice: don't do it.

I WAS in Philly for the start of the 2004 season, watching the game at Kevin's house. Even though I'd just started classes at Iowa, I had flown home for LauraBeth's mother's funeral.

Post-funeral, LauraBeth and I had plans to spend most of the week together. We hadn't been separated for very long, but it was a relief to see her again; when she hugged me in the airport, I realized how long it had been since I'd been touched by another human being. But on Sunday, I wasn't with her; I was in my brother's living room, watching the Eagles dismantle the Giants in their season opener. Terrell Owens, the team's big new acquisition, scored twice and was even better than we'd dreamed. Donovan McNabb made one of the best throws I've ever seen in my life. Even Jerome fucking McDougle made the most memorable play of his career—a heart-stopping, fumble-forcing hit on Giants rookie Eli Manning.

It would have been a perfect Sunday if everything else wasn't going wrong. LauraBeth's mother had been buried the day before, and she and her brothers were slogging through post-mortem phone calls and paperwork while I gorged on cheesesteaks and Yuengling. Although none of us discussed it, her mother's death reminded us of Dad and we regretted that he wouldn't be around to enjoy what we all *knew* would be the best season in Eagles history. There was an empty space on the couch where he should have been sitting, and Kevin's wife was pregnant with a daughter who would never know her grandfather. And next week, I would not be there either. While the Eagles steamrolled through the NFL, I would be stuck halfway across the country in an empty apartment, wishing I could find a good stromboli anywhere in the Midwest.

At the end of the week, I had to go back to Iowa. Leaving LauraBeth was more difficult this time, because I knew we wouldn't see each other again until Christmas break, and because she wasn't yet ready to be alone. In the immediate aftermath of the death, she'd been too busy to properly mourn, but now that the funeral was over, the paperwork and phone calls completed, the loneliness was beginning to weigh her down. The first week after Dad's funeral wasn't nearly as bad for me as the second, and that wasn't as bad as the third. My grief was parabolic, gradually increasing the greater my distance from Dad, until at some point, somewhere in the future, it would begin to decline at the same rate. I warned LauraBeth she hadn't faced the worst of it yet. She asked me to stop talking about it, and we agreed to enjoy the week while I was home.

And it turned out to be a good week, all things considered, as we'd crammed a month's worth of dating into five days. We spent a day at the Jersey shore, eating fudge and walking hand in hand on the boardwalk. We went to the movies. We watched TV together until we fell asleep on the couch, waking up curled around each other at four A.M. We barely left each other's side, unwilling to waste even a minute of our time together. We marked off the days on her calendar until I could come home again. We tried to forget about Dad and her mother. We tried to forget I was miserable at school.

She cried for most of the ride to the airport, and didn't want to let go when she hugged me at the entrance. I had come home to comfort her, but there was nothing I could do to help her now. I promised to call as soon as I landed, and then we parted. We wouldn't see each other again until Christmas. The only good thing about leaving was knowing that eventually I could come home again.

MEANWHILE, BACK in Iowa City: two friends, Mike and Chris, had covered my classes for me while I was out of town. They, along with Lee, were my best friends in the city, and for a while they were probably my only friends. Chris was the first person I met out there, and I quickly learned he was even more sarcastic than me, which meant that people may not have liked us very much, but we sure did like ourselves. He was my age but carried himself like he was fifty-five—we passed plenty of afternoons sitting on his porch sipping whiskey and listening to John Lee

Hooker while Chris puffed on a cigar. Mike was the second guy I'd met in the city. He was only a couple years older than me, but looked like he was forty-five—my first bald friend. People tended to like him better than me or Chris, because he was more congenial and charitable; while Chris and I were quick to judge and label, Mike was more apt to give people second and third chances. He had similar tastes to us, but his demeanor balanced the group a bit, which was probably good for all of us.

Mike picked me up at the airport and we drove immediately to a bar to meet Chris. We made the hazardous discovery that on any given night in Iowa City, you can find someone who is selling one-dollar pitchers of beer all night. At those prices, there was really no reason to ever stop drinking. Go out with five bucks and two friends, and you can still come home loaded.

All of which is a roundabout way of saying that most nights I was at the bar, and most nights I was not writing or reading anything, except on the EMB, which I read every night when I got home. I got in the habit of drunken typing, and even got pretty good at it. Even if the thoughts weren't very clear, every word was typed clearly and correctly, a talent in which I took quite a bit of pride. Many mornings, I sat at the computer and found a window open to the EMB, a half-composed post on the screen, and notes to myself about how to fix it in the morning. And, one morning, I checked the computer and realized I'd sent an e-mail to my Dad.

The problem with living a mile from the bars is that when you're walking up the hill to get home, you have nothing to do but think. On my late-night walks, I often called LauraBeth, even though it was three A.M. on the East Coast and she had to be at work by six. I gave her the rundown on the night's events, the gossip on people she hadn't met, complaints about people I didn't like. She listened patiently. I asked her how her day had gone, and she insisted everything was fine, even though it was all a transparent lie. This period was exceedingly difficult for her. She was trying to cope without her mother, taking care of her grandfather and the dogs, adjusting to a new career as a nurse. I had abandoned her during the most difficult time of her life. She was lonely. Her brothers were away at school, and none of her friends truly understood how she felt. Most days, she had nothing to look forward to. Her grandfather was demanding and didn't trust her; she overheard him calling friends and telling them, loudly, that LauraBeth was neglecting him and chasing after his life insurance money. She worked twelve-hour shifts and spent her free time driving him to doctors' appointments, bingo halls, and diners, but he barely spoke to her. Her home had never been so dreary. When these topics arose, I changed the subject. Instead of addressing her sadness, or comforting her, I rambled about how much fun I was having, because I was afraid to face the first real challenge our relationship had encountered.

Sometimes she said I was drinking too much, or asked if I was getting my work done, to which I usually replied with silence or lies. She yawned as I huffed toward my apartment. When I got there, I said good night, then logged on to the EMB.

Sometimes she was asleep and didn't answer, and it was on these nights that I realized how depressed I was. The Midwest has a way of exacerbating your loneliness, the whipping winds and cold, open spaces a constant reminder of how far away you are from everybody. The horizon looks like it's in another world. The empty spaces, the darkness, the bitter cold—when you're alone, you feel like you're on the moon. So one night I found myself walking up the hill in tears, wishing I had never moved here. I tried talking out loud to Dad, maybe a kind of prayer, but doubted he could hear me, just as I'd always doubted the effectiveness of prayer.

When I entered my apartment, I decided the best way to reach him would be through e-mail. He'd worked with computers for twenty years, and I was never a good speaker anyway, so an e-mail would make everything easier. Initially, it was supposed to be a friendly hello, telling him I missed him, but I couldn't stop my fingers from skittering across the keyboard. I meticulously re-typed words and rewrote sentences so he wouldn't know I was drunk, and when I was done I had a two-page e-mail, in which I told him I loved him, apologized for being a bad son, explained why I never visited him in the hospital, and begged him to forgive me for wasting my talent. I was acutely aware of the fact that I was frittering away any abilities I did have, but that awareness paralyzed me more than it motivated me. He would have expected me to be writing great stories, and I was writing nothing, besides e-mails and message board posts. I told Dad I was scared, and I knew I was a disappointment, but I really loved him and wished he would just come back, even if only for a day, because it wasn't fair the way he left us before we were ready.

Yes, the e-mail did mention the Eagles, briefly. I had to tell him how good they were, and how much he would have loved watching them. But mostly, the e-mail was about me. I sent it to his old AOL address and went to bed, feeling sick.

In the morning, I remembered the e-mail and realized Mom would probably be able to read it, because she'd gotten access to his account after his death. She's never said anything about it, but still I feel guilty for having laid all of that baggage on her. Maybe she forwarded it on to Dad, if only she knew how.

I was disappointed, because overnight I'd been sure that the e-mail would be some kind of catharsis that would allow me to move on, but in the morning I still felt miserable. This was the third time I'd tried to cure myself through writing to or about Dad, but I learned that no matter how many times you try to heal yourself, you never feel better, at least not completely. It's a terrible idea, really, to think that you could write a short story and make it all go away. It's supposed to be therapeutic, but it's more like picking at the scabs of your old wounds—the more you pick, the more obvious the scar will be when it finally does heal over.

I DON'T mean to imply that I thought about my Dad every day. In fact, I've always found the familiar "I think about him every moment" sentiments to be hyperbolic and false. The truth is, there were long stretches where I didn't think about him at all, stretches during which I did all kinds of things that would have embarrassed him—like unwittingly having a drunken conversation with my own reflection at a poet's birthday party—and then, in specific, unpredictable moments, I remembered that he was dead and never coming back again.

When I walked to classes, my ankles ached, and I thought of him; he'd always had problems with his ankles and was rejected by the Army during Vietnam because of an abnormality with the bone structure in his feet. At twenty-three, I knew I owed my chronically painful feet to him.

When I gorged on wings and pizza on Sundays, I thought of him, how he always overate on weekends and spent most of the day lying in his recliner with an upset stomach, while Mom sat annoyed across the room. I thought about how he'd always been fat, how he'd bought a treadmill and then piled boxes on top of it, how his obesity was a constant. And I worried that I was getting fat again, that I would end up diabetic and unathletic and cancerous just like him. When I drank, I swallowed hard to keep the booze from settling in my throat and forming into a tumor that would choke me from the inside. About once a month, I decided it was time to get serious about my health, did a few push-ups and sit-ups, drank a half gallon of water, then ate a platter of pepperoni and cheddar for dinner.

When I lectured my students about the importance of taking responsibility, of knowing the consequences of your actions, I heard Dad's voice repeating the mantra he'd invoked a thousand times when I was a kid. And when they protested, didn't hand papers in because they had a cold, or their printer didn't work, or their roommate was annoying, or their great-uncle had broken his leg, or this paper was too hard, I blew up in class. I snapped at them, hissing that my Dad was dying for most of my junior year, but I still did all my work, still finished a ninety-page research project on the Holocaust, still wrote several stories for my fiction class, and still pulled a 4.0 while carrying a full course load. *I did this all,* I told them, *while shuttling back and forth to the hospital, and knowing my Dad was about to die, and I didn't once complain to any fucking teachers. So don't come to me and give me shit about your dog getting hit by a car or your best friend getting pregnant, because it doesn't fucking matter.* Their stunned silence shamed me. Ostensibly, it was all true, but I did exaggerate how much I'd visited him, and realized that now I was using him as an excuse for being an asshole, and that it was particularly hypocritical for me to give that speech, since I was now making the same kinds of excuses about my own work.

When LauraBeth talked about how she missed her mother, when I felt how devastated she was, and in some ways still is, by the loss, I felt guilty for not being equally haunted. I tried forcing myself to cry, but I couldn't match her grief. I was an open wound then, but still I didn't think about Dad every day. This all caused me to feel worse about myself and wonder if I wasn't sad enough. When I felt like this, the easiest solution was to head downtown and meet someone for a beer.

My Iowa friends and I had established an informal fandom exchange program during football season. If they watched the Eagles with me and Lee on Sundays, then we agreed to watch the Redskins with Steve, Notre Dame with Chris, and Florida State with Mike. By the end of my time in Iowa, I think they'd become partial Eagles fans, while I'd become a partial fan of their teams. We weren't just exchanging our time; we were exchanging obsessions.

TV service in Iowa City is unreliable at best, so we had to watch the games at the bar. The first phone call I made in Iowa City had been to a bar called Sports Column, to ask whether they had all the NFL games on the satellite package. The guy told me they did, and I explained, "That's awesome, because I'm from Philly and I need to watch my Eagles—" and he hung up on me. I don't know why I needed him to know where I was from. Furthermore, I don't know why he told me they had the satellite package when they very clearly did not, and didn't even have enough TVs to show every NFL game. When I asked them about it on a Sunday afternoon, the bartender mocked my Philly accent and walked away. I did not spend much time in that bar.

Luckily, there was another bar that did show every game, and I staked out my seats an hour in advance every week. Most Sundays, I was buzzed by two o'clock, and decided to stick around for the later games. Most Saturdays, I was drunk by the end of lunch.* What do you do with yourself when you're drunk before sunset? It's too early to go to bed, but there's no way you'll be able to get any reading or writing done if you stop drinking now. All that happens is you sit there and feel yourself sobering up, an uncomfortable process better saved for overnight. So, we stayed out, watched more football, and ate a couple meals at the bar. During the NFL playoffs, we parked ourselves near the biggest TV an hour in advance and ate two or three meals during the games. After the games, we stumbled to the Fox Head around midnight and met up with the writers who didn't like sports.

The writers who didn't like sports were divided unevenly into two camps: those who loathed the sport industry, and those who were indifferent but could fake an interest if they had to. Only a handful truly detested sports, and I never got along with them. They talked about David Sedaris and I wanted to talk about David Akers. They were concerned about myopic politicians and I was worried about nearsighted refs. I didn't mock the things they cared about, but they hated the things I loved. And they thought less of me for being so passionately involved in sports. No one ever told me so explicitly, but it was clear in their condescending eye-rolls and grins when I talked about sports, their patronizing questions about football,† and their frequent explanations that "football just seems like such a waste of time." Maybe it was, maybe it is. One thing was for sure: it was definitely a waste of time to hold those conversations.

The other group of non–sports fans was friendly enough with me, and at least willing to engage in real conversation. When something big happened in the sports world, they knew I was the guy to talk to. When Ricky Williams retired from football be-

---

* I generally drink less, or not at all, during Eagles games, because I want to remember the details.

† E.g., "Do the Eagles have some kind of game or something this weekend?" and "Does everything you own have an Eagles logo on it?"

cause he preferred smoking pot, people wanted my opinion. When the Pacers and Pistons got in a brawl with their fans during a game, people wanted my input on their punishments. When the Red Sox won the World Series, everyone wanted to know how it felt to watch another tortured fan base get its reward. In short, people were interested in what I had to say. A good feeling, especially when my opinions on almost everything else garnered no respect. In class, I was silent unless forced to speak. When I suggested that one student change her story from present tense to past, nobody even acknowledged it. After class, I saw the writer in the bar and sat next to her, tried to follow up on my suggestion. Before I finished my second sentence, she stood without explanation, walked away, and sat inside a phone booth, arms folded across her chest, until I left.

Over the course of the year, I'd heard plenty of scuttlebutt about how I didn't belong in the Workshop. One second-year student told people that I shouldn't be there because I was too immature, and maybe I should reapply after I grew up. Another complained that his Workshop experience was being ruined by ignorant college kids—I was the only person in his class under twenty-seven—who didn't know how to write. Instead of talking about real writing issues, he said, they wasted their time discussing the basics of grammar and revision. At least one other person had openly wondered at a party how I'd even gotten into the school if I couldn't write a single clear sentence. If you hear enough negativity about yourself, you can't help believing in it a little bit. Through much of my first semester at Iowa, the only feedback I'd heard was that I wasn't good enough.

When it was my turn to be workshopped again, I cranked out another story that was less reprehensible than the first one, but still not well received. While I further detached myself from the classes, the Eagles rolled to the best start in franchise history.

By mid-semester, everyone in the program knew three things about me: I was from Philly, I loved the Eagles, and I was the go-to guy for sports talk. So when they needed to quench their thirst for a little old-fashioned guy-talk or satisfy their intellectual curiosity about what makes serious sports fans tick,* they found me. It was a symbiotic relationship: they indulged their own passions or satisfied their curiosity, and I got to meet someone new. But, often, when the subject progressed beyond sports, we found we had nothing else to talk about. Everyone in the program was better educated and better read than I was, and rather than playing catch-up, I further embraced sports, at least maintaining my authority in one area. Roderic, a second-year student, told me he thought people faked an interest in sports when around me, or exaggerated their own fandom in order to try to match mine. I think he saw this as a bad thing, but I took it as a tribute to my sports expertise. At least I had *something* over these people, even if it meant they thought I was one-dimensional and our interaction was built on false pretenses.

Most of these conversations occurred over a pitcher, and I forget many of the details. Sometimes it felt like a revolving door of new faces, all seeking some kind of information or insight. At these times, I felt, however briefly, that I'd found my niche, that I belonged.

By the time I left Iowa in '06, I'd connected with dozens of intelligent, well-read people who cared about my obsessions. Maybe they hadn't been concerned about sports initially, but eventually they were concerned enough that many of them took a mild rooting interest in the Eagles. I felt like an Eagles evangelist, spreading the word of the beauty of football; they saw how much it meant to me, and they wanted to know if they could feel the same thing. So even if they didn't understand it, or didn't watch the games, they made sure to take note of what happened and to pass along their condolences when something went terribly wrong. After the Eagles lost the Super Bowl, people gave me tender, pitying looks, as if someone had just died. Their concern was

---

* Some people just couldn't understand how someone could be simultaneously intelligent and passionate about sports. I felt like the subject of an anthropological study.

honest and real. And this was enough to pull me out of my depression after a particularly bad game.

Now when I get word from friends on the West Coast asking about the Eagles, or soliciting my take on some big sports news, I'm grateful. For all the negatives my obsession has wrought, and for all the ugliness it's caused in me, I know that it's sown some positives too. Football is my icebreaker; it's helped me make connections to many people with whom I would otherwise never have connected. It's made them care about me, and it's been core to the development of my identity, my voice. Sports in general, and football specifically, have always been the glue that's bonded my relationships, for better or for worse.

CHAPTER

NINE

GIVE ME SOME RESPECT RIGHT NOW

WHOEVER I was before I left for Iowa, I was twice that guy by the start of my second year, and triple that by the time I left. In my desperation to fit in, I'd degenerated into an inescapable caricature of myself.

Chris often introduced me to his college friends as "the ultimate Philly guy." Even then, I knew he was lying to them. I wouldn't be welcome in half the homes in Philly. I was a little too educated, a little too pompous, a little too *artsy* for the average Philly guy to like me. Chris's friends didn't care about any of that; as long as I did my little tap dance and talked about the Eagles, I was in.

It gave me something to talk about, and besides, it's a lot easier to reveal yourself to a new group when it's a partly fabricated version you're exposing. So then I became an "alpha male," as a classmate once called me; I became one of the manly men, not because I was all that masculine, but because I was doing everything I could to fit that stereotype and I was surrounded by people who weren't at all interested in football, or boxing, or basketball.* Not that any of this was necessarily a conscious decision; it just hap-

---

* I should note that classmates had organized a few intramural football games during my second year, and I never played in any of them, giving vague excuses for my absence (i.e., "Busy working on this story, you know?"). In reality, I avoided these games because I was afraid to out myself as a poor athlete and a bit of a pushover. Had I played, I worried I would be exposed as a fraud. Then what would I have?

pened. The first friends I made were sports friends, and it never seemed worth the trouble to look beyond them. As I further insulated myself from the rest of the program, it became easier for me to fall into the delusion that I *was* the ultimate Philly guy.

WINTER 2005, LauraBeth's first night in Iowa City: we're at a party, and I'm giving her the gossip on everyone in the room. She flew out for a long weekend after working a series of twelve-hour shifts at the hospital. She was supposed to have arrived on Thursday afternoon, but her flight was delayed several times. After a few false starts—she boarded the plane twice, but they didn't take off—I drove to the Cedar Rapids airport and waited for her. We spent the night in different airports, her half sleeping in an O'Hare terminal, and me slumped in a chair across from a massive sculpture of Herky, Iowa's mascot—a menacing humanoid-hawk hybrid in a yellow sweater. We were only two hundred miles apart now, but it felt farther than ever.

She arrived early the next morning, but I had to leave her immediately to teach, despite having spent exactly zero minutes preparing for class. I let her sleep most of the day, then dragged her out to this dull party, which, like most of our parties, consisted of a lot of mildly unstable, poorly nourished people standing in circles and swigging cheap beer while one-upping one another with obscure literary references. Sometimes, a couple guys sneak into the bathroom to do lines off the sink. Nothing wild or exciting happens, despite what I've promised her. LauraBeth stands with me deep into the night, but her boredom is evident. I reassure her that usually these things are more fun, but the only difference is that usually I'm much drunker. We leave the party early, and I decide to spend the rest of the visit with LauraBeth alone. I take her on a comprehensive tour of Iowa City (which, given the size of the city, is complete in about ninety minutes), take her to a couple nice restaurants, walk with her down by the Iowa River. I show her the best the city has to offer, just in case she agrees to stay with me. She can't do that, of course, and I probably don't do a great job of selling the city, about which I am still ambivalent. She leaves on Monday morning. I cancel class to take her to the airport and see her off, and when she's gone, I wish I'd left with her.

THROUGHOUT ALL of my time in Iowa, the Eagles were still there, in the midst of the greatest season in team history. Through the first seven weeks, they looked unbeatable—we always knew from the first play who was going to win. Lee and I watched in awe, a dumb post-coital glaze over our eyes. In week two, Minnesota went down on Monday night. Week three, Detroit didn't have a chance. In week four, they played the Bears in Chicago, where I just happened to be for the weekend, road-tripping with Chris.

We met Chris's Chicago friends on Friday. We would spend the night in the city, then drive to South Bend in the morning for a Notre Dame game and the requisite after-parties. Chris introduced me as the biggest Eagles fan in the world, and I pointed to my green hooded sweatshirt and matching hat. One friend said he wished he'd known an Eagles fan was coming, because he'd just turned down free tickets from his boss.

I hadn't even thought about going to the game. For some reason it had never occurred to me that I could attend an Eagles game outside of Philly. I was disappointed that he hadn't accepted the tickets, but I was even more disappointed in myself for not having thought about buying tickets in the first place.

A couple hours later, we were out on the town. The first bar we walked into was so green it looked like it was St. Patrick's Day. Hundreds of Eagles fans had flooded the place, and thousands had swarmed the city. We were there only five minutes before I heard my first Eagles chant of the night. Chris and his friends were swapping stories about the old days, so I offered to go up and buy the next round. I didn't find my way back to our table for an hour, because I wandered through the horde of Eagles fans, talking to all of them, exaggerating the Philly accent I'd been

working to conceal in Iowa City. I looked everywhere for familiar faces. I joined in the fight song. I even sang the stupid T.O. song.*
I felt, however briefly, like I was home again.

Early the next morning, we embarked for South Bend, where we drank for about twelve hours straight. On Sunday morning, I woke up at eight o'clock, slammed doors and ran faucets until everyone else was awake. I waited by the front door, packed bags in hand and Dawkins jersey on my back. I had to be home in time to watch the Eagles game.

The Eagles won an ugly one in bad weather. And they kept winning.

Next, it was a 30–8 win at home against Carolina, vengeance for the '03 playoff loss to the Panthers. It was around this time that I began to notice Sheldon Brown. As a rookie in '02, he'd made a splash against the Cowboys with two of the most violent hits we'd ever seen, but he'd been relatively quiet since then. Meanwhile, his counterpart at cornerback, Lito Sheppard, garnered plenty of attention. He put the exclamation point on the Panthers game with a graceful, weaving sixty-four-yard interception return for a touchdown. Through the rest of the season, he would emerge as the big-play guy in the secondary, the guy who could turn a game around in one instant. He would be named to the Pro Bowl and All-Pro teams. Meanwhile, Sheldon was quietly never, ever getting beat. He may not have made big plays, but he didn't make mistakes, and was as reliable and unassuming as any player on the team. After the Panthers game, everyone raved about Lito, but, as I told Lee repeatedly over the next two years, Sheldon was my guy, he was the one who deserved the praise. His approach reminded me of Dad in the sense that he operated with a quiet professionalism that went unheralded by most, but which made all the spectacular stuff possible. If it weren't for his steady play, quarterbacks wouldn't have thrown at Lito, and Lito never would have had the opportunity to become a star.

---

* For Terrell Owens. The song is pretty simple—the letters T.O. sung to the tune of "Olé Olé Olé."

A week later, they won a shoot-out against the Browns, 34–31 in overtime. When Brian Dawkins was called for a late hit on Browns quarterback Jeff Garcia—a slight man with a lisp, often rumored to be gay—I leapt out of my seat and yelled something about the league wasting too much time protecting fags. Lee pulled me back to the table and told me to calm down.

Next game, versus the Ravens, was a grudge match, due to a whole series of legal and verbal disputes between the Eagles, Terrell Owens, and the Ravens. T.O. scored the game-winning touchdown, and at this point I was sure he was the greatest thing to ever happen to Philadelphia. Lee and I couldn't even conceive of a way that the team could possibly lose. Quinn called me from The Linc just so I could hear the cheers; after the crowd finished the fight song and the Eagles chant, he hung up. As I did every week, I called Kevin afterward to evaluate the Eagles' performance and discuss the upcoming opponent.

Through the first eight weeks of the season, the Eagles were undefeated. In week nine, the Steelers blew them out, completely outclassed them. Any other year, this is the point at which they would have collapsed, lost four straight, sustained a couple key injuries, and otherwise made me feel ill. But, instead, they bounced back immediately and looked unbeatable for the next four weeks, culminating in maybe the most perfect thirty minutes of football in history, when they scored thirty-five first-half points on the Green Bay Packers. The Packers were supposed to be the second-best team in the conference, but they didn't even belong on the field with the Eagles. I watched that one alone in my apartment,* eating most of a pizza and cranking the volume on the TV. After big plays, I called Quinn and Swanson and Big Kev. At halftime, I checked the EMB to see what everyone else thought about the game, and to join in the frenzy of giddy posting. It didn't matter what I posted then; everybody loved everybody else, and it was enough just to be invited to the party. I made my weekly halftime phone call to Kevin, this time to talk Super Bowl. We'd all had

---

* The game was being locally broadcast, because Iowans love Brett Favre.

plenty of faith up to this point, but now the Eagles looked like champions. Not one of those *if everything goes right and we catch a few breaks* kind of teams, or a *they have a shot, but they need all of their guys to step up at the right time* kind of teams, but a legit, for-real Super Bowl team. Like most Eagles fans, I felt like I'd just found a winning lottery ticket on the street.

If you've been paying attention, you already know what's coming next. Bad news. Next week, the Eagles barely beat the Redskins. Then I flew home for Christmas break, and I was able to watch the Cowboys game with my family. We were at Kevin's house when Terrell Owens broke his leg. He limped off the field badly, nearly in tears, and I felt like I was going to vomit. My friend Paul sent a text message; he was at his college graduation, but he'd heard there was something wrong with T.O. I confirmed the news, and he responded: "Fuck!" Kevin's house fell silent. All that hope had just died right in front of us. In Kevin's house, we'd witnessed the amazing start to the season and also, we thought, the painful end.

When I got home, I had e-mails from four Iowa friends, all asking some variation of "Are you going to be okay?" I told them I wasn't sure. I couldn't eat the rest of the day, and in the morning, I felt like I'd been in a car accident. My neck was stiff, my legs sore. I shuffled downstairs to have breakfast and check the paper to see if maybe the whole injury was a false alarm. I couldn't finish my breakfast, as I parked myself in front of the TV, holding an ESPN vigil, hoping for any information on the condition of T.O.'s leg. I sat in Dad's recliner, which creaked when I shifted, as if it were rejecting me. I pressed my weight into the chair, hoping to make it fit my shape. While I watched *SportsCenter,* I thought about how Dad would not have panicked in this situation. He would have said exactly what Andy Reid did, which is that you move on and play the next guy in line. That's why you have backups, right? One of his favorite axioms when things went wrong: *You'll have this,* accompanied by a half shrug. He may not have convinced me anyway, but without Dad's reassurance, I had lost all faith.

Owens had broken his fibula, and was already rushing to have screws implanted in the bone. Recovery time: six to eight weeks, minimum. The Super Bowl was in seven weeks. Not that that would matter, because without him, they wouldn't be able to get through the playoffs anyway. T.O. was built like Superman and moved with the grace of a ballroom dancer. He had a ten-million-dollar smile and an infectious enthusiasm that had reinvigorated both the team and the city. But one awkward tackle had broken him, and suddenly there wasn't much to believe in anymore.

Reading the EMB was like going to a wake. Everyone was so numb they couldn't even muster any emotion yet. We were broken. I thought about T.O.'s leg every day for weeks, and I read every article I could about orthopedic surgery and leg injuries, seeking some hope for his return. By the time their first playoff game rolled around, three weeks later, I'd convinced myself that they could do it without him, but even then I needed to see proof of it on the field.

I had to fly back to school before the playoffs started. I had made sure to pack a sweater I'd left at home when I'd moved in August. It was a V-neck Eagles sweater, in the old kelly green and silver colors of the teams from the seventies and eighties. On the breast was the old logo. Both the waist and the cuffs were lined with alternating silver/green stripes. Hanging loosely on me, it looked hideous. It had belonged to Dad; maybe even to his dad before that. I don't remember Dad ever wearing it, although I have seen him wearing it in decades-old photos. I don't know if he stopped wearing it because he'd gained too much weight, or because it was too ugly. I'd found it before the '03 season, when we were clearing his clothes out of the house. The sweater lay on top of a donation box, but I saved it and made sure to wear it during the playoffs that year. It hadn't exactly brought the team good luck, but Dad had owned it the last time the Eagles played in the Super Bowl. It seemed only right to continue the tradition, and I wanted Dad to be with me on Sundays. The sweater had to be there when they finally won the whole damn thing.

So I was wearing Dad's sweater when the Eagles played the Vikings in round two of the playoffs. I watched that game in my apartment, with Lee, Mike, Chris, and Nam, my Australian friend to whom I wanted to introduce the joys of American football. I'd awoken around seven-thirty, spent the morning pacing my living room and calling home to talk about the keys to the game. I read and reread the EMB for injury updates and last-minute strategy sessions. I cleaned. I made several cheese-based dips and wandered around the streets to burn off some energy. I did not read anything for classes. I did not write.

The game started at noon, and the Eagles controlled it from the start. They were ahead 14–7 in the second quarter when McNabb completed a pass to L. J. Smith, who was streaking toward the end zone. He got hit from behind and fumbled, the ball arcing like a rainbow over the goal line. It fell directly into the hands of Freddie Mitchell—touchdown Eagles. One of the luckiest plays anyone had ever seen. This was the sign we'd all been waiting for; this was our proof that everything was going to be okay and the team was destined to be champions. They rolled to an easy win, and then we all suddenly became medical experts, calculating T.O.'s recovery time, and researching the merits of his famous hyperbaric chamber.* He would be back in time for the Super Bowl. No way he would miss it.

There was still the matter of the NFC Championship Game, but that was a foregone conclusion, at least to me. Of course, the previous two conference championship games had been locks for the Eagles too, and they'd blown both at home. But things were different this year. This time, they were a team of destiny.

The game started at 2:00 P.M. CST. I couldn't sleep past eight, and by eleven I'd already talked to everyone at home and read every article I could find on the game. I called Mike and told him I was going to the bar early, asked if he'd come with me. We were there by eleven-thirty, and ordering our first pitcher. At noon, we ordered lunch and our second pitcher.

---

* As if he wasn't already enough of a superhero, now he slept in a specially designed healing pod that preserved his body by bombarding him with oxygen. I wished I had a hyperbaric chamber.

I slowed my drinking because I wanted to be able to focus on the game, but still, by kickoff we'd been through at least three pitchers, and I was ordering a plate of fried something. Four more guys had arrived, and I got the sense that they were all watching me as much as they were watching the game. If the Eagles blew this one, they knew, I might throw myself in front of a bus.

But they did not blow it. The game was never really in doubt. Many times, Dad had told me and Kevin about the 1980 NFC Championship win over Dallas. He'd always stressed that he *knew* the team was going to win. When he woke up that day, he felt confident rather than anxious. And when he looked at the Cowboys on TV, he saw in their eyes that they weren't ready to play, saw that the Eagles had already won the game before it started. When the Eagles played the Falcons, I finally understood what Dad was talking about. This game belonged to us from the start.

Falcons quarterback and then—media darling—and also one of my most hated players—Michael Vick looked terrible and helpless. He took a hit from Hollis Thomas that was less of a tackle and more of an engulfment; Vick didn't go down, he was swallowed up by a black hole. After the game, Sheldon Brown was asked how they were able to stop Vick, who was better known and more hyped than all of his teammates combined. His response: "If you want it to be a one-man show, play golf." That response made it official: Sheldon Brown was my favorite player.

Back to the game. Brian Dawkins delivered one of the most memorable hits in Eagles history when tight end Alge Crumpler, at least two inches taller and fifty pounds heavier than him, was running full speed across the middle of the field and Dawkins, from a nearly stationary position, launched himself recklessly into Crumpler. Crumpler collapsed as if he'd been shot, while Dawkins stayed on his feet. It seemed physically impossible, but this is why we love Dawkins: he lets us believe in the impossible.

The Eagles sealed the win when McNabb found Chad Lewis for a fourth-quarter touchdown. Up seventeen points with about three minutes left, they couldn't lose. I jumped out of my seat and spiked my hat on the barroom floor. Steve bought me a shot of

Crown Royal. And the celebration was over. I didn't feel any different. I felt exactly like I do on birthdays when people ask if you feel any older. The answer is always *No, I feel like me, why would anything change?* I watched the next game, ordered more food, and wondered what was missing.

Meanwhile, the streets in Philly overflowed with delirious fans. People rushed outside to hug their neighbors, bars gave out free booze, strangers became best friends. Nobody cared that it was bitterly cold, or that the murder rate was still climbing. Nobody cared that the city was crumbling from the inside out, or that it was more segregated than ever. The only thing that mattered was that the Eagles had won.

Swanson called to let me hear the cheers. He told me he'd never seen anything like it, at least not since the Phils went to the Series in '93. I knew then that I had to fly home for the Super Bowl.

I **WAS** also teaching during this time, although I wasn't doing a very good job of it. After one week of training, I was expected, as a twenty-two-year-old who looked sixteen, to teach Rhetoric at the University. I didn't even know what the word "rhetoric" meant until about two weeks into the semester. I did the job because it was part of my financial aid package, but I put as little effort into it as possible. Before I'd left for Iowa, my old creative writing teacher from La Salle had told me to forget about teaching and write my ass off. For the first two semesters at Iowa, I used this line as justification for all of my procrastination. Teaching four days a week, I spent no more than ten minutes per day preparing for class. I spent more time counting down how many hours and days I had left to teach, and manufacturing excuses to cancel classes. It was a terrible course. There was no plan, no pedagogy—another word I'd never heard until Iowa. The anthology we used was awful and I had no idea how to actually fix anyone's writing. It had always come naturally to me; how do you convey that ability to someone who can't even write a complete sentence?

They knew I wasn't prepared or skilled, and they knew I was terrified. Since starting high school, my two lowest grades have both been in public speaking courses, thanks mainly to my anxiety. But here I was in Iowa, somehow expected to teach writing *and* public speaking, never planning lectures and hoping to skate by with cheap jokes and the occasional profanity. Undergrads love it when you curse.

My students learned nothing that semester, I'm sure of that. I don't even remember most of what I did, besides showing them as many movies as I could, and always holding open discussion, hoping they'd done the reading and had something insightful to say. By the end of the semester, I started every class five minutes late and ended ten minutes early. Usually, class devolved into a recess atmosphere, where we broke into groups and chatted or gossiped. I gravitated toward three football players—Rasheed, one of the best students I've ever had; Andre, who was from Camden, New Jersey; and Rodney, whose writing and reading skills were at about a fourth-grade level. Rodney knew Deion Sanders, and his half brother was a big-time college star. He had the phone numbers of several Dallas Cowboys, and he was a major prospect himself. Rasheed and Andre were legitimate prospects too, both offensive linemen at a school known for turning linemen into pros. All three of these guys could have conceivably gone on to play in the NFL,[*] and it was the closest I ever expected to get to a real star athlete.

These three were my only black students. I had two white football players—one of whom was the backup placekicker, possibly the least impressive position in any sport—in my classes too, but I never really saw them as being star athletes. The other three guys, though, I was sure I'd be watching them on Sundays, and I never even gave a second thought to my own skewed racial expectations.

One day, they were reviewing one another's rough drafts, and I interrupted their work to talk to Rasheed about the Eagles. The

---

[*] And, in fact, one of them was recently drafted by an NFL team.

other students listened in, and class effectively ended, although we still had twenty minutes left. One girl called her boyfriend on her cell phone. When I told her to hang up, she turned away and continued talking quietly. Two other girls decided they were hungry and asked if they could leave to get a pizza. I said, "Well, I guess you can do whatever you want, but it doesn't mean you *should*." They got up and left the room. Another pair followed, and then they all drifted out without a word to me. Ten minutes remained in the class period, and I sat alone in the middle of the room.

ON MY first-ever day of teaching, I asked my students to introduce themselves to the class. After a couple of mostly forgettable introductions, we met Hamad, whose abridged life story goes like this: he received a Master's in engineering in Egypt before moving, with his extended family, to New York City; in New York they told him his foreign degree was worthless, so he drove cabs; the city was too dangerous, so he moved to the Midwest; he decided to pursue another degree at the U. of Iowa; now he delivered pizzas six days a week. Many of my students had clearly never met a non-American before and had only seen Arabs on TV post-9/11. They stared at him as if he'd just stepped out of a sarcophagus, as if they couldn't believe Egyptians walked just like us. I probably stared at him too. I was shocked by how good-natured he was about the outrage his life had become. He was better educated than all of us, including his teacher, and he was subjected to delivering pizzas on a college campus. How could he endure the whole schooling process again? How could he bear delivering pizzas to overprivileged college students who probably all assumed he was an illiterate moron or a terrorist? I asked no follow-ups, because I was afraid to offend him, and I felt like he deserved better than to answer my inane questions in our inane composition course.

Now seems like the appropriate time for me to admit two things. First, seeing Hamad in class reminded me of Dad, who returned to school when he was fifty and had been working toward his Associate's degree when he died. I wondered how he would have reacted to a teacher like me, a class like mine. I knew he would have been disappointed. Unprepared and unfocused, I approached a difficult job the same way I had approached challenges as a young athlete: I stopped trying. I showed up hungover several times a week, and I was so desperate for the students' approval that I had no authority over them. My first batch of teaching evaluations, received after this semester, was largely positive, but that was only because they had fun in class and they thought I "kept it real," whatever that meant. But no one learned anything, and they didn't respect me, because I was disorganized and distracted. Some thought I'd graded unfairly, favoring the football players, since I paid disproportionate amounts of attention to them and their work. Although I did grade as fairly as possible, I can't blame the students for thinking otherwise. Several others noted that I should be better prepared for class, and one wrote: "Relax more. Don't be so nervous!" Maybe the most telling evaluations, though, suggested that I learn how to stay on topic. One student wrote: "Try not to talk about sports . . . not everybody wants to talk about football every day." In the end, the only reason my evals looked reasonably good is that the students thought I was nice, and they knew I couldn't afford to lose my job, so they softened their critiques enough to protect me.

Given this atmosphere, it's no surprise that Hamad, along with two other students, dropped my class almost immediately. Dad would have dropped that class too, and he would have called me into the kitchen for another lecture on the importance of taking pride in your work. I wouldn't admit to him how terribly I was failing as a writer or how every day at Iowa made me feel worse about myself. I didn't admit these things to anyone, not directly, although I tried to joke about them with LauraBeth; she never laughed.

Each day I walked into the classroom, I felt like a failure; I knew I was doing my job poorly and I didn't know how to fix it. I felt, once again, like my Uncle Mike, the lesser brother. Kevin was married, had a suburban house and a wife and a child and a good job and a plan and the respect of others and self-respect. I had none of these things. I did have LauraBeth, but how long would that last if I continued bungling at work, if I never accomplished anything? If I couldn't respect myself, how could she respect me? If the rule is that there is one good brother and one bad brother, then I was definitively the bad brother, and the thought of Dad seeing this truth nearly crippled me. During that time, I felt a steady pulsing dread that I was on the verge of losing everything. Kevin was building his loving family and I was destined to sleep on Mom's couch until the day she died. I leaned even more heavily on the Eagles then; the less successful I became, the more I needed them to do something remarkable. I needed them to redeem me.

Second admission related to Hamad, the pizza-delivering Egyptian: his story made me angry, because his extended family included his grandmother, which seemed impossible, as she had to have been in her nineties, at least. Is it wrong for me to say it annoys me when other people's parents and grandparents live deep into old age? When fifty-year-old men still watch football games with their fathers? When families have the gall to walk with their octogenarian relatives in public, flaunting their resiliency and good fortune in front of all of us who have lost loved ones too soon?

It's not that I wish death or harm on old people; I just can't help wondering what gives them the right to live when Dad, who was the most decent and respectable man I've ever known, couldn't? It seems ridiculous to me when people refer to the death of a parent as "tragic,"* because that's the natural order of things;

---

* A famous example: when Brett Favre's father died in 2003, sportswriters across the country referred to the death as a tragedy, even though Favre was in his mid-thirties and it's pretty common for people that age to lose their parents. You've probably heard the legend by now: Favre's dad died the night before a Packers game. Favre went out and played "with a heavy heart" as millions of articles have said, and had one of the best games of his life — 399 yards passing, four touchdowns, a dominant win. Peppered with questions about his dad, he gave the standard *I know he's watching me* answers. A great game to watch, and a wonderful story, really. But the media have since tainted it by mythologizing it so egregiously that the story is unbearable to

your parents are *supposed* to die first, and you're supposed to live with it, and then die before your children. But that doesn't make you feel any less despondent when it happens, and no matter how many good years you spent together, you always find yourself wishing you could have had one more minute.

IN THE spring semester, I focused my syllabus on the rhetoric of pro sports. Now we could talk about sports whether they liked it or not, and I could put my obsessions to good use. I still had no idea how to be a good teacher, but I was more prepared this semester anyway. Uninterested as I was in teaching then, I had some pride and didn't want to embarrass myself again. Besides, I had a job to keep.

A week before the Super Bowl, I wore Dad's sweater to class. Some of the girls laughed at me, but I pretended not to hear them. I showed my students a video about the Eagles. About fifty minutes long, it detailed the history of the team, the devotion of the fans, and the connection between city and team. During some replays, I got chills in the back of the classroom. When they showed Reggie getting his safety against the Saints in the playoffs, I pumped my fist quietly under the desk. Near the end of the film, sportswriter Ray Didinger perfectly encapsulated everything I wanted my students to understand about sports and about me. He said:

> The Eagles are precious to the people in this town. They're a family heirloom handed down from generation to generation. That's

---

hear. In the end, it all boils down to this: a guy went to work the day after his dad died, and he did a good job at work. As cool as it was to watch, and as emotional a game as it was, the fact is, thousands of people do the same damn thing every day. The fawning hero worship continues even now. Last semester, I was teaching a class about gender, and asked my students who they think is the ultimate male, and why. One guy wrote, "Brett Favre: good at football & his dad died." My written response: "I guess if that's all it takes to be a real man, then I'm halfway there."

why the people stay with them, year after year, through the bad times, through the losing seasons . . . The Eagles are part of your family. They're part of who you are . . . It's been a long time since this team won a championship, and yet, every year, they have the hope that this is going to be the year. And they show up, year after year, waiting for it to happen. Now that's the definition of loving football, and that's the definition of loving a football team.

When the video ended, I asked my students why we had just watched it. One raised his hand and said, "Is it because you're from Philly?" Another said, "Because you like the Eagles?" I laughed and told them that those things were nice, but not really why we watched it. But, yeah, that's why we watched it. I just wanted to see them, I think. I couldn't admit it to my students, but we watched that film because I needed to feel like I was at home, and it's not because I like the Eagles; it's because I *love* the Eagles.

During the two-week break between the Falcons game and the Super Bowl, the Eagles dominated my life so thoroughly that I rarely thought about anything else. I read every article written about the game—in the national outlets, the Philly papers, the Boston papers, even the papers in Jacksonville, the Super Bowl's host city. The first two to three hours of each day were spent scanning and posting on the EMB, and I was sure to check it again before bed. Over those two weeks, I consumed equal parts oxygen and Eagles news.

The biggest story—at least among those not related to the players and coaches directly involved in the game—focused on Chuck Bednarik, who had publicly declared his support for the Patriots, saying, "I can't wait until the Super Bowl is over . . . I hope the 1960 team remains the last one to win. I hope it stays that way." Some lucky reporter had called him to collect a few platitudes about how it's great to see the team back on top again, how he's rooting for the boys in green, and so on. Instead, they got one of the franchise's cornerstones openly rooting against the team in the Super Bowl.

In retirement, Bednarik feels marginalized. Like many retired players, he thinks the NFL is neglecting its disabled veterans, and he's physically broken down, his hands gnarled into claws like something you would see on a mythical beast that lives in the forest. He thinks the modern players are grossly overpaid and he resents having become a forgotten relic. Most young fans have no idea who he is, especially outside of Philadelphia, and he thinks they're ignorant savages. He has publicly feuded with Jeffrey Lurie, who refused to buy hundreds of copies of Bednarik's autobiography to distribute to team employees. Nowadays, he's Cantankerous Charlie.*

When I read his comments, I was more disappointed in Bednarik—then hanging above the TV in my living room–than I was angry; one of my heroes had let me down. How could he be so petty when we needed him? Some fans haven't forgiven him for it still, and even booed him when he was honored at halftime of a 2007 game. He's one of the few champions we've seen in this town, and we needed all the winner's karma we could muster in a game against the Patriots. When he stepped away, he left a void we couldn't fill.

Of course, this had no actual bearing on the game. But they did lose by only three points, and maybe the vocal support of their greatest leader would have been enough to push them over the top. He'd forsaken us, and it took some of the joy out of the experience for me. This was a game being played not just for me and my brother, not just for our friends and neighbors, but for our parents and grandparents, who'd had the pleasure of seeing the last championship. A perfect bookend to the story of their fandom, an opportunity for some kind of closure. But *the* representative of the older generation wanted nothing to do with us, and I couldn't help wondering how we'd let him down.

---

* It's hard not to see his connection to our city. His life is a story of small gains and huge losses, triumph and betrayal, talent and hair-trigger rage. He's bitter in a way that would make Don Rickles cringe, and he's convinced of his divine right to this bitterness. For everything good, there is an equal amount of bad, and twice the anger.

Aside from Bednarik's betrayal, all other Eagles talk was positive. The EMB was like a two-week block party, as we floated through the waiting period convinced that anything was possible. We were sure the Eagles would end the Patriots' dominant run. Terrell Owens was going to try to play on his broken leg, and I never had a doubt that he would excel. Just that fall we'd seen former Phillie Curt Schilling bleeding through his sock and pitching on a battered ankle to help the Red Sox overcome their own history of futility. It made perfect sense, then, that another cursed city would be saved by a one-legged man. At least, it made as much sense as anything else in sports does.

When I talked to LauraBeth on the phone, I scanned the EMB and typed as quietly as possible. The board was crowded with hundreds, maybe thousands, of new members who had joined over the past few weeks. As long as the Eagles were winning, we were glad to have more people in on the party; if something went wrong, though, we knew the front-runners would be the first to disappear, just like old Wendell hiding inside his tent while we hunted for firewood.

I laid out intricate, detailed reports on how and why the Eagles would win the Super Bowl. I convinced myself that the Patriots—defending Super Bowl champs—were overrated and just plain lucky. I imagined the feeling of being in the city the moment that final second ticked off and the Eagles won the Lombardi Trophy. The EMB kept me plugged in to the Eagles and to Philly when phone calls home didn't work.

I called Mom to tell her I was coming home to watch the Super Bowl at Swanson's house; I did not, probably could not, explain why I wasn't watching it with her and Kevin. I talked to Quinn, Swanson, Big Kev, Anthony, and Kevin regularly, but they were busy working real jobs and couldn't indulge me at all hours. If Dad were around, I would have plotted the game with him. I imagined being back home, walking down the stairs in the morning, and seeing Dad at the kitchen table with a bowl of Cheerios. The sports page would be folded neatly in my spot; he would be waiting for me to read through so we could enumerate a detailed game plan for the hundredth time that week. But I saw no one in the morning. I sat in my living room, turning up the volume on ESPN to fill the apartment, and staring up at Bednarik's jersey while I ate breakfast. I called LauraBeth about the game, but she told me the constant football talk was excessive. Even though she was a fan and she was excited too, she needed me to talk to her about anything else, or, more important, to *listen* to her while she talked. She understood how much the Super Bowl meant to me, she said, and it meant a lot to her too, but that didn't mean it had to count for *everything*. She warned me that I was getting my hopes up too high, setting myself up for disappointment. I knew she was right, but still I needed to get my fix, and so I turned to the computer. When people weren't available, the EMB was always there.

TWO DAYS after the win over Atlanta, I booked a flight home for Super Bowl weekend. LauraBeth loaned me some money, and Quinn and Swanson chipped in with twenty dollars each. It was still an expensive flight, but I couldn't imagine being in Iowa City when the Eagles won the Super Bowl. It wouldn't have been right.

Once I bought the ticket, every thought turned to my flight home. I needed to find a place to watch the game. I needed to pick the right celebration beer. And I needed to think of something memorable to scream as I streaked down the road joyfully.

I went out with Lee and badgered him with my thoughts on the Super Bowl. He was excited, but not like I was; in fact, he seemed amazed by my excitement. It was around this time when I told Lee I would cry if the Eagles won the Super Bowl, and it was around this time when I found myself sitting in a bar, slapping Lee in the chest and shouting, "The Eagles are gonna win the fucking Super Bowl!" while he laughed.

When I returned to my apartment, I downloaded fan-made videos from the EMB, basically Eagles highlight reels set either to AC/DC or intense John Williams–style classical music. On my monitor, Brian Westbrook sliced through the defense and rushed for a long touchdown against the Cowboys. Ike Reese tipped a pass and intercepted it. Jeremiah Trotter, dressed in a ridiculous fur ensemble, told us, "You might walk into The Linc, but you gonna limp out." Dawkins flexed and stomped his feet next to Michael Vick while Merrill Reese declared, "Brian Dawkins just had a quarterback for lunch." I flexed just like he did, and stomped, rattling the dishes in my sink.

I cranked the volume, and watched the videos on full screen. I turned off the lights and let the music blare through my building. It was three A.M. and the Eagles were in my apartment. There was McNabb scrambling for 14.1 seconds before hitting Mitchell in stride sixty yards downfield, in what Troy Aikman called the greatest football play he'd ever seen. There was Jevon Kearse nearly decapitating Lions quarterback Joey Harrington.

And now here is Dawkins again, standing at a podium after the Falcons game, accepting the George Halas Trophy* and dancing to a beat only he can hear. Terry Bradshaw tries to interview him, but Dawkins is lost in the mania that possesses him during games, causing him to refer to himself as "Idiot Man." He screams "*Hallelujah,*" the crowd roars, and he stares down at the trophy with an intensity that seems to make Bradshaw uncomfortable. He's in constant motion, practically vibrating; electricity runs through his veins. When Bradshaw asks how they stopped Michael Vick, Dawkins shouts that they have all the respect in the world for Vick, but nobody respected the Eagles' defense. He bounces on his toes and barks, "*Gimme some respect right now!*" The crowd unleashes a seismic cheer and I feel, however briefly, like I'm there. I watch it again, this time mouthing the words along with Dawkins, standing and screaming, "Gimme some respect right now!" just as he does. I start over and do it again several times, until I'm too tired to continue, bouncing on my toes and screaming, "Give me some respect right now!"

---

* Awarded annually to the NFC champions.

CHAPTER
TEN

IT'S JUST A GAME

IT'S TEN A.M. and I'm walking down Church Street. I have a class to teach at ten-thirty and I'm about a mile from my classroom. I usually leave earlier, but yesterday was Tuesday, and on Tuesday nights we go out to the bars after workshop. I just woke up ten minutes ago when someone banged on my door. He said he worked maintenance for the building, and then asked, "You done with your toilet?"

"For now," I said. "I mean, I guess I'm done."

"All right, then I need to take it."

"I'm probably gonna need it later," I said, rubbing my eyes. Pushing past me, he promised to bring it back today. Five minutes later, he was gone and there was a big hole in my floor where my toilet used to be. This seemed somehow ominous as I scrambled to gather my things. There was no time to shower. Standing next to the black hole in my apartment floor, I splashed water on my face and patted my hair down with wet hands. I wondered what would happen if I fell in the hole, where I would go, who would miss me. Those thoughts would have to wait until later, though; I had to get to class. Still wearing the jeans I'd slept in, I pulled last night's shirt over my head and ran out the door, book bag in hand.

So here I am, racing stiff-legged up the road, trying to wake up, wishing I had gone home at last call instead of going to Chris's place for a Jameson on the porch. My head throbs. My mouth is so dry I feel like I'm chewing on a sock. The metallic taste of PBR lingers on my tongue and I'm too drunk to be crossing the street, let alone teaching a class. I feel like I'm working very hard to walk but not getting anywhere; it's like running in a swimming pool. I'm pinballing between the curb and the grassy hill on my right.

I stop to tie my shoe, which I guess has been untied the whole walk. Kneeling, I think about how nice it would feel to tip over on my side and nap in the grass. Inhaling deeply, I prepare to stand, but something rolls down the hill and hits me in the foot. It's a newborn bunny.

At the top of the hill, a rabbit is nursing its hairless litter. One of the bunnies lost its balance and tumbled down, stopping right at my feet. It's slick with goo and barely recognizable as a living thing. It looks like a half-chewed piece of pork. Its chest heaves but it makes no sound. Neither its mother nor its siblings look down from the top of the hill. When they move on, it will be left behind. I think about scooping it up and returning it to its family, but I'm afraid to hurt it; it looks like the most fragile thing in the world, and I could so easily crush it in my palm, especially given the state I'm in. "Hey, bunny," I whisper, "get back up there." It looks like it's trying to roll over. "Go back to your family. They're up there," I say, pointing, and it looks like the bunny is trying to scrabble up the hill.

It gets nowhere. This thing is the definition of helpless, and it will starve to death when its mother moves on. Tomorrow, someone will step on it without even knowing what was there. My eyes are moist, and I think that if I weren't so dehydrated, I would be crying.

"Come on, you can do it, bunny," I say, nudging it with my toe. "Just try to get up there." Behind me, a campus bus has stopped and dropped off a load of students. They walk past me and the bunny. Most are indifferent, but a few are watching me as I kneel on the sidewalk, eyes bleary and bloodshot, urging the bunny up the hill. "That's my teacher," one of them says.

THERE'S THIS romantic notion about writers and drinking, this idea that alcohol somehow fuels creative energy. Writers drink, supposedly, because they're trying to cope with the overwhelming sadness of the world. Or maybe writers drink because it opens their minds in ways sobriety can't allow. They sacrifice their long-term health for the sake of great art, and sell their souls for the opportunity to make something beautiful and true. Surrounded by empty whiskey bottles, the writer fights through the darkness to save the world through his art.

Hemingway sold himself as the toughest, drunkest, meanest sonofabitch in the literary world, and it worked for him (at least until he lost his mind). Fitzgerald probably drank more than Hemingway did, and it ruined him even more quickly, but the theory is that without the booze maybe he couldn't have written *Gatsby* and *This Side of Paradise*. Iowa City legend says Raymond Carver used to wait outside Dirty John's Grocery every morning so he could buy another bottle of wine as soon as they opened. Faulkner and Capote. Eugene O'Neill, Cheever, Steinbeck, Poe, and so on.

In 1987, a neuropsychiatrist named Nancy Andreasen published the findings of a fifteen-year study at the Iowa Writers' Workshop, in which she concluded that thirty percent of the faculty were alcoholics, as compared to seven percent in the control group of non-writers. She also found that eighty percent of the writers—as opposed to only thirty percent of the control group—had had affective disorders (i.e., major depression, manic depression, etc.), and two of the writers studied even killed themselves.

I should stress that none of this stuff has anything to do with why I drink or why I write. I'm no Frederick Exley, driven to the bottle by a mixture of sports obsession and existential dread; in fact, my football hero (Bednarik) is the guy who nearly killed his hero (Gifford). I started drinking heavily because it made people like me. Over time, I grew to like the taste, and I drank more. By the end of my second year, I was drunk at least four nights a week, and usually more. Sometimes I tried to have only one, but it was impossible. Moderation, as usual, was not an option.

———

BY THE start of my second year at Iowa, I felt much more comfortable than I had before. I had a small circle of friends, I was teaching creative writing instead of rhetoric, and I'd had a year to adjust to the city.

I was feeling a little better about my writing too—I'd been awarded a fellowship that promised more money and less work.* Supposedly, the biggest advocate for giving me the fellowship was Frank Conroy, who was enamored by a nearly autobiographical story I'd submitted about a drunken kid hitchhiking with a crackhead stripper. I'm told that others in the room weren't as impressed as he was, but he insisted. At one point, he slapped the conference table and demanded that they reward "the story with the whore in it." When I saw him later, he told me the story was still a little rough, but interesting and *actually quite funny*.

Having spent my entire first semester reeling from his harsh critique of my initial story, and having seen firsthand how difficult it was to elicit praise from him, I took his compliments as a validation of myself as a writer. He'd eviscerated my sloppy first story, and all the work I'd done post-evisceration had been completed with a single goal in mind: to impress Frank. As much as I appreciated the support from friends and family, I knew the one thing I'd needed was harsh, direct criticism, someone who wasn't afraid to hurt my feelings and who cared deeply about the writing itself. For most of my life, this had been Dad's role; now Frank was filling this void. By the summer, Frank had died of cancer; our class was the last he ever taught. Although he was gone, I was glad to have elicited that moment of approval for my work, and I approached my writing more seriously and vigorously than ever.

Besides the fellowship, I'd also finished the rough draft of a

---

* Mom's response: "I wish your father were here to see this." I understand why she says things like this, but I do not know what to say besides "Yes, me too. I also wish he were here." Maybe that's all I'm supposed to say. Or maybe I'm supposed to keep my mouth shut and let Mom have her moment.

novel over the summer.* I holed myself up in my old bedroom in Mom's house† with several cans of Coke and typed until two or three A.M. most nights. End result: 92,000 words, 288 pages, the most prolific three months of my life. While I worked, I redis-covered my creative energy; for the first time since Dad's death, I looked forward to writing and found it to be rewarding rather than torturous and awful. This was the place where I'd discovered writing. This was the same room in which I'd written my play about dinosaurs, the same room in which I'd toiled over so many essays and short stories before printing them and rushing them downstairs to Dad for his approval. In Iowa City, it was easy to forget why I was pursuing a degree in Creative Writing, why I'd thought any of this had been a good idea in the first place. But at home, there was no overlooking the basic truth: I wanted to be a writer, because I didn't know how to be anything else and because my Dad needed something to read. So I stayed in my room and worked, reporting my weekly progress to Lee via e-mail, reading during my downtimes, and talking endlessly about my book, to the point that sometimes I even forgot about football.

While I did all of this work, I went through detox for alcohol and fried food. Most days, I was at home with Mom, or out with LauraBeth, who doesn't like crowded bars and doesn't need the pretext of drinking to spend time with me. Sometimes I won-dered what was going on at the Fox Head on a given night, but mostly I didn't even think about alcohol. I had writing to do, and I didn't need to be drunk to have fun with LauraBeth. I spent many nights sitting quietly on the couch while she, exhausted from work, fell asleep in my lap. She had driven to Mom's house to see me after her shift, because she didn't want to return to her

---

* Against Frank's advice, actually. He said it was a bad idea for someone so young to get bogged down in a book-length project, especially since I still didn't have a handle on writing short stories yet. Like most good advice I've received, I ignored it and didn't understand it until years later.

† Which, by now, had been mostly cleared of Dad's belongings. Still, pic-tures of him were everywhere. His fingerprints on doorknobs. Dust on fur-niture, maybe remnants of him. We breathed him in. We did not forget.

empty home. I watched TV and tried not to wake her, content to spend the whole night like that if necessary. When she woke up she asked me to come home with her, and I followed. I didn't care where I was, as long as I was with her. Mom never worried about me when I was with LauraBeth; she trusted her and was relieved, I think, to have someone looking out for me.

It was a good summer. Almost daily, Mom told me how happy she was to have me home, how she was proud of me. I saw Laura-Beth as often as possible, and I did real, serious work for maybe the first time in my life. Drinking rarely and avoiding bar food, I also lost weight that summer. I was healthier and happier than I'd been in years.

MEANWHILE, THE Eagles' season had begun disastrously. During the off-season, Terrell Owens had lost his mind, decided he was being underpaid and disrespected, and spent most of the summer insulting teammates before being kicked out of practice by the coaches. The whole situation reached its apex when he staged a bizarre press conference from his driveway, answering questions while doing shirtless sit-ups.

Morale only declined once the games started. Before kickoff in week one, Jeremiah Trotter was ejected for fighting. Sometime during that game, McNabb took a cheap shot from a defender and sustained a hernia, a pain through which he would play for the next eight weeks. They lost the game, as they would do frequently in 2005. They kicked Owens off the team after seven games. Then McNabb aggravated his injury in a loss to the Cowboys and had season-ending surgery. Everyone else got hurt and the backups were all terrible. The low point occurred in week thirteen, when they paid tribute to recently deceased Reggie White, and then played maybe the worst game in franchise history, losing 42–0 on *Monday Night Football*. They finished the year with a 6-10 record, their first losing season of the decade.

Still, they played two memorable games that year. I missed one, but saw the other live.

After my experience in Chicago in '04, I had made sure to check the Eagles' road schedule well in advance. The league usually releases the schedule in the second week of April. By the third week of April '05, I'd planned my road trip. The Eagles were scheduled to play in Kansas City, about two hundred miles south of Iowa City, which was a reasonable drive. The Chiefs played in historic Arrowhead Stadium, and Kansas City was supposed to have great barbecue. I couldn't think of any reason *not* to go to the game.

Chiefs tickets went on sale in June. I did not need to camp out this time; instead, I called the ticket office the afternoon they went on sale and bought four tickets with no problem at all. Convenient as this was, I hung up convinced that Chiefs fans didn't care enough about their team. How could there still be tickets available? How could they have made it so easy for an opposing team's fans to get into a game?

I followed the Eagles to Kansas City in week four. Their record was 2-1, but they had looked sluggish and unimpressive so far. The Terrell Owens mess—exacerbated by constant media attention—continued, and the team was clearly drained by the whole thing. They were the only team in the league that looked exhausted in week one. Mounting injuries also concerned us. McNabb had his hernia. David Akers, the best kicker in franchise history, had torn his hamstring, so now they had to rely on some joker named Todd France.* Even then, we felt like the season was on the brink of collapse. But we believed—or wanted to believe— the old mantra that the team repeated all season: winning cures everything.

Mike drove down to KC with me and Lee crammed into his compact car. Big Kev flew out there and met us at the hotel. We spent most of the first night in the hotel bar, where I wore my Dawkins jersey in case we ran into any Eagles fans.

We did meet a few older guys, Philly transplants living in the Midwest. I talked to them for a couple minutes, trying to deter-

---

* Whom Big Kev and I called Todd Freedom.

mine whether they were EMB users. I told them I'd been trying
to find a good tailgate group by searching on the Eagles message
board, but they didn't react. I said again I saw on the message
board that most of the Eagles fans were meeting in parking lot A.
They were glad to hear about the tailgate, but didn't mention anything about the EMB. I don't know what I was expecting exactly;
I guess I wanted to see them perk up and say, "You're on the EMB
too? Are you swamistubbs?" Then they would introduce themselves, and we would know everything we needed to know about
one another. Instead, they went to bed early and left us in the bar
with a bunch of Chiefs fans.

One kid incessantly yelled, "Eagles suck!" across the bar. We
laughed the first few times, but I was getting drunk. When he
yelled it again, I responded that if the Eagles sucked, then the
Chiefs must be really terrible. He persisted, so I asked him what
his team's record was in '04. "Your shitty team couldn't even make
the playoffs," I said. "And your coach cries too much." Another
Chiefs fan walked over to our table and apologized, then ordered
us two pitchers. He shook our hands and told us to have fun tomorrow. I had no idea how to respond.

In the morning, we wandered over to lot A, dragging a trunk
full of beer behind us. I wore Dad's kelly green sweater over my
Dawkins jersey. The sharp scent of barbecue wafted over the lot,
settled into our clothes. We passed a few groups of Chiefs fans,
and they all greeted us warmly, told us to have a good time. Big
Kev gave them the finger. I laughed, but Mike and Lee did not.
The Chiefs fans looked more shocked than angry.

Lee was taking pictures of the stadium, and Mike, still half
asleep, was too concerned about finding food to notice anything
else. Big Kev and I charged ahead of them, cracking beers and
staring down Chiefs fans. We passed a group tailgating around a
modified and bejeweled hearse. Covered in sequin-y Chiefs doo-
dads and all kinds of sparkly weirdness, it was decorated like the
walls of generic American chain restaurants/food factories like
T.G.I. Friday's. Inside, there was a coffin, which had been con-
verted into a beer cooler. The Chiefs fans saw me and Big Kev

staring at the coffin, so they called us over. Lee rushed ahead to get a picture of the weirdness while they talked to us about where we were from, how we liked KC, what we thought about the T.O. situation, and so on. Halfway through the conversation, I realized I had put on my most serious Philly-guy voice, as if to authenticate my roots. One of the guys offered me a beer, and I refused it. "We got our own shit," I said. "We know how to fucking tailgate."

He shrugged. Then he warned us about the noise in the stadium. "Hope you brought your earplugs," he said, chuckling.

"It gets plenty loud in Philly," Big Kev said. He spit on the ground between us and them. "We can handle it."

Lee finished taking his pictures, so we turned to leave, telling them we had some Eagles fans to meet. They offered us sandwiches, but we told them we had plenty of food, which wasn't true; we had no food at all. Then they told us to have a good time. "Yeah, we'll have a real good time," I said, nodding at them. "You have fun watching us kick your fuckin' asses." They laughed. "Come find us after the game and we'll see who's laughing," I said. Mike pulled me away and asked me why I was trying to fight those guys. "Because," I explained, "that's just what you do." On the walk, we had a couple similar encounters: Chiefs fans were bizarrely friendly and accommodating, even when we tried to antagonize them, and that only annoyed us more. If the roles had been reversed, we wouldn't have been offering beer to the visiting fans; we would have been throwing beer cans at them.

We finally found a pocket of Eagles fans in the middle of the lot. They welcomed us into the group and we shared our beer. Somebody tapped me on the shoulder. He was built like a thumb and sported an oversized McNabb jersey. "Are you swamistubbs?" he said. I nodded and he told me he was iggle4life, a guy I'd talked to on the message board. He'd also driven down from Iowa, and found us because I'd announced on the EMB that I would be wearing my sweater and I'd be next to a seven-foot guy with a beard. He was with a few other EMB guys; we all shared our screen names and our real names. I forgot their real names immediately. We took a few pictures together and then sipped our beers through minutes of silence. Finally, someone started an Eagles chant and I threw my whole body into it, howling through the lot. Post-chant, I drifted away from the EMB guys and we did not speak again.

Two hours later, we trekked all the way up to the top of the stadium, taunting Chiefs fans the whole way. Arrowhead holds almost eighty thousand people, and it felt like we were the only ones in the stadium wearing green. The place was redder than Lenin's closet. A few Eagles fans dotted the section near us, but not many. Lee said he felt like he was in another country.

Before the game began, I noticed that former Eagles defensive coordinator Emmitt Thomas was in their ring of honor, a space reserved for the franchise's all-time greats. I was first disappointed that I'd never known he was a player, and, second, upset that I didn't know where he was now. I turned to the Chiefs fans behind me to ask what position Thomas had played. One guy shrugged. Another asked who I was talking about. And another said, "I think he played defense." Strike three, Chiefs fans. You made it too easy for me to get into your stadium, you were too accommodating in both the bar and parking lot, and you didn't even know anything about one of the great players in your team's history. Ask me about Bednarik, Van Buren, Retzlaff, McDonald, or any of the others, and I'll tell you everything you need to know. I sure as hell won't shrug.

It was hot up there and getting hotter. I left my sweater on because I was sure I'd lose it if I took it off. Even in that ugly old sweater in eighty-degree weather, I knew I looked less ridiculous than the guy in front of me, who wore a Marc Boerigter jersey. Boerigter was a bottom-of-the-roster guy who once had a fluke season in which he scored eight touchdowns on only twenty catches. Presumably, this guy then dashed out to the store to buy up the Boerigter jerseys before they sold out. Three years later, and he hadn't scored another touchdown or done a single noteworthy thing. I like obscure, unheralded players as much as anyone, but there's only one reason someone would buy the jersey of a mediocre backup like that: Boerigter was a scrappy, athletically limited white guy, and fans love slow white guys.* Maybe it's because those guys look most like the fans, or maybe it's just because some folks still aren't comfortable seeing all those powerful black men on the field. Either way, wearing the Boerigter jersey announces to everyone in the vicinity that you love white dudes, and you don't care whether they're good or not.

I told him all of this. I asked him if it was worth $250 to advertise that 1) he didn't know anything about football, and 2) he was racist. I told him it was the dumbest jersey I'd ever seen. And don't even get me started on the hat. He wore an enormous foam hat shaped like an arrowhead. If it were fastened to the end of a real arrow, it could have felled a dragon. I told him the foam hat really made him look like an adult, and asked him if it cost as much as the Boerigter jersey. I asked if they came as a package deal. I talked so quickly, I probably repeated the same insults a dozen times. I thought I was hilarious.

The Chiefs scored five minutes into the game. Their fans celebrated the touchdown with some kind of chant that sounded like "We're gonna kick the shit out of you,"† and when they got to the "you" they turned to the nearest Eagles fans and pointed, chanting, "You, you, you!" The thousands of angry fingers pointing at us—that was mildly terrifying. Maybe they'd tricked us with their nice-guy act and now that we were trapped inside they were showing their true colors. Maybe now they were going to turn ugly and violent, and send us tumbling down the stairs.

We got the same treatment a few minutes later when the Chiefs kicked a field goal. And then again early in the second quarter when the Chiefs went ahead by seventeen. Arrowhead is leg-

---

* Believe me: this is coming from a guy who used to wear a Kevin Turner jersey. I didn't consciously pick him because I was racist, but I'm positive that his whiteness was a factor in my decision.

† That did seem a little too PG-13 for that crowd, so I'm not sure if that's what they said. We asked the guys behind us what they were saying, but they shrugged. I can't imagine participating in a chant without knowing what you're actually saying. Even the Jerry Springer audience doesn't do this.

endary for reaching unfathomable decibel levels, and this was one legend that did live up to the hype—my ears were ringing for two days after the game. The stadium literally shook when the fans cheered; I felt like I was standing on the deck of an aircraft carrier.

The Eagles were bungling their way through the first half, dropping passes, fumbling kickoffs, and missing blocking assignments. And then Sheldon Brown jumped out of the shadows to grab an interception. He glided down the sideline nearest us and scored his first career touchdown. He shocked us out of our stupor and gave us hope again. I screamed myself hoarse, joining in the fight song and the Eagles chant. Most likely, things weren't going to turn around, but I'd spent hundreds of dollars on this trip, and I needed to have at least one moment where I believed.

Then the new kicker missed the extra point. And the ensuing kickoff was returned for a Chiefs touchdown. No matter how many times I see the pattern this team follows, I always forget at crucial moments.

We slumped in our seats. The guy in the foam hat jumped up and taunted us, performed the whole *you you you* routine, and we had no response.

The Eagles scored a quick touchdown before halftime—a short pass to Terrell Owens—but we only offered them sarcastic cheers before running down to the concession stands.

While Big Kev and I waited in line for beer, we bitched about the team and the guy seated in front of us. "I think we should start a fight," I said.

"If we keep playing like shit, then I'm just gonna hit that guy," he said.

I was reminded of a high school friend, a fellow Roxborough guy, who was failing out of La Salle with a 0.2 GPA; instead of leaving with his head hanging in shame, he decided he might as well go out in a blaze of glory and beat the hell out of an upperclassman he'd always hated. At least then he could leave on his own terms. He got expelled and then promptly enrolled at Roman. Similarly, our whole trip had been a failure, but at least we could bring a little bit of Philly to Arrowhead if we had to.

When we got back to our seats, the PA announcer explained that the Chiefs were honoring a few of their all-time greats during halftime. As they introduced the players, Big Kev and I booed. Then he shouted several times, "Where's Derrick Thomas?" Derrick Thomas is Kansas City's Jerome Brown—one of the most beloved, and talented, Chiefs of all time, who died mid-career in a car accident. We were well aware of this fact. Big Kev called for him again, and I laughed theatrically. Someone threw a soda at us, but it hit the girl behind me in the back of the head, splashing ice on her whole group. Her group started bickering with the guy who threw the soda, while she kicked my seat and warned us that we'd better be careful. "Shut your fucking mouth," I said.

The second half began and we prepared ourselves for more embarrassment. But the Eagles looked a lot sharper now. They got an early field goal, cutting the Chiefs' lead to eight points. This field goal was particularly exciting, since Todd Freedom had already missed two kicks in the game and we worried that he might never make another one again.

The defense looked stout, and the team avoided all of the mental errors that had marred their first half. They moved with confidence, scoring again to end the third quarter. They'd tied the game at twenty-four, and the Eagles fans were alive again, singing that stupid T.O. song and doing our damndest to outcheer the Chiefs fans.

The Chiefs couldn't stop T.O. or McNabb. Their defense, historically terrible, couldn't stop anyone. The Eagles scored the next ten points, and then added another touchdown a few minutes later. They led by ten. Dejected Chiefs fans streamed out of the stadium. I resumed insulting Marc Boerigter—who was on the field for about eight plays the entire game—leaning forward and shouting insults directly into the guy's ear. I sang the T.O. song and smacked the foam hat off his head. Big Kev poured nacho cheese on his jersey while I clapped my hands next to his ears. Lee tried to calm me down. He told me that the guy next to him had asked how old I was. They couldn't believe I was twenty-three. "They told me you need to grow up and stop taking it so seriously," he said. Much later, Lee told me that he explained my behavior to the other fans like this: *His Dad just died, and he still has a lot of anger about it.*

When the Eagles kicked another field goal, I patted Boerigter on the back and started another rapid-fire stream of insults. Lee pushed me back into my seat, told me I was getting out of hand. Mike told me to relax before we got ejected from the stadium. The Boerigter fan shook his head and said, "It's just a game."

"Yeah," I said, "and we just kicked your ass."

The win was the biggest comeback victory in the history of Arrowhead Stadium. I was exhausted and sunburned, but we had to celebrate. In the parking lot, we found our group again, guided by a man standing on his RV, waving a giant Eagles flag as if we'd just conquered new land. A pair of Eagles fans walked by and we offered them beers. One was so drunk he thought we'd challenged him to a fight. The other said, "No thanks, if I start drinking, I'll have to do cocaine again." Then he dropped his pants. The first guy said, "Yeah, that's my brother—he thinks he can just piss anywhere."

A group of Chiefs fans stepped over the urine stream and we taunted them. They stopped and congratulated us on the win, wished us good luck for the rest of the season. "The Eagles really earned it," they said, smiling and shaking our hands before walking off. I just didn't get these people.

I TOOK another trip in October, this time back to Philly. Anthony had asked me to be the best man at his wedding. I was glad to do it, especially to have an excuse to fly home. There was one major drawback to this trip—he was getting married on a Sunday afternoon. During the Eagles–Chargers game. One week after the Eagles' bye week, during which it would have been ideal to have scheduled a Sunday wedding.

The game started at 1:00, and the wedding was supposed to start at 3:00. But we had to get there early for pictures and preparations, ushering, and other groomsmen duties. I drove up with

Mom, Ian, Swanson, and LauraBeth. On the way, we listened to the pregame and the kickoff on the radio. We were the first ones to arrive, so we got back in the car and listened to the opening minutes of the game. It sounded brutal; nobody could get anything going on offense, and the Eagles were playing as sluggishly as they had all season.

I knew I wouldn't be able to listen to much more, but I'd arranged a solution before leaving for the wedding, enlisting Big Kev to send me text message updates on the game. Through the course of the wedding, he sent me thirty-nine messages and made two phone calls during particularly important moments.

As you might expect, I wasn't the only one there who wanted to watch the Eagles. But I was the only one receiving constant updates. During the buildup to the wedding and the early stages of the reception, about a dozen guys took turns visiting me to check on the Eagles' status. Before we embarked down the aisle, the pastor leaned over to me and said, "What kind of fucking guy gets married during an Eagles game?"

It was during this event when I began to seriously consider marrying LauraBeth. Kevin had married two years earlier—two months after Dad's death—but he's nearly six years older than me, and had lived with his wife since finishing college, so their marriage wasn't exactly surprising to anyone. Because of our age difference, he'd always lived several steps ahead of me, pioneering his way through adulthood while I stayed behind and followed his example. Anthony's wedding was different. We had been friends for years, inseparable in high school, and were now only a year removed from college. For him to get married—to own a home with his wife, to fill that home with china and matching furniture sets, to worry about school districts for hypothetical children, to mingle with the neighbors at cocktail parties—was the official declaration that he was an adult, that we were all becoming adults.

Standing on the altar, I watched LauraBeth and imagined her joining me up there. Would she be happy with me? Would I be ready to make the leap into adulthood? What did I know about being a husband? Why would any woman want to marry a man who was terrible at his job, who had no prospects and hadn't demonstrated any ability to earn a living? The sheer number of questions was overwhelming. But one thing I didn't question was whether LauraBeth was the right person. No one else doubted it either. During the reception, Swanson got drunk* and insisted that we were the next ones to get married. We both shrugged and half denied it, because we hadn't yet talked about marriage ourselves. "Oh, come on, you know it's true," he said, and the rest of the table nodded. Mom was sitting next to me during this conversation. She nodded too. Later she offered me my paternal grandmother's wedding ring, in case I ever wanted to give it to someone; I shied away from the conversation and did not take her up on the offer, but now I was assured that she'd be happy to welcome LauraBeth into the family.

I wouldn't decide to propose to her until about six months later, and then I did it on a whim, waking one morning and knowing immediately that I wanted to go to the mall in Coralville, Iowa, to buy a ring. Eventually I was going to marry LauraBeth anyway, so it seemed unreasonable to fight the inevitable, especially when people close to us were dying at an unsettling rate. Dad had missed Kevin's wedding and LauraBeth's mother would miss ours, and I didn't want any more empty seats at our ceremony. Essentially, I proposed to her when I did because I was afraid another important person—Mom, LauraBeth's father, our brothers, her grandfather, whoever—might die before the wedding.

Anthony's bride was running late, as brides tend to do. So we waited in a gazebo, and I checked my phone for updates. I had to put my phone on silent before the bride walked down the aisle, so I missed the message telling me that the Eagles had fallen behind 14–10. Luckily, LauraBeth was keeping track of the score—her brother was updating her during the ceremony. She passed the word to Swanson and Ian, who used hand signals to tell me the

---

* A surprisingly difficult task, as this was a dry wedding, save for a glass of wine served with dinner.

score. I missed part of the vows because I was trying to decipher Swanson's signals. The score remained the same when the ceremony ended, and I rushed to the reception. Inside, six of us crowded around my phone every time it buzzed.

The Eagles' defense came up with a big stop, holding the Chargers to a field goal. Then Todd Freedom answered with his own field goal to bring them back within four points. Big Kev called to detail the latest scoring drive, but I had to go quickly because I was needed for photos with the bride and groom.

Time was running short, and the Eagles' offense was still struggling. It looked like the game was lost when the Chargers lined up for a field goal with about three minutes left. Then I got another phone call.

Big Kev yelled something about a blocked kick. I asked who picked it up, and he yelled, "Yeah, they blocked it!" I asked again, and he said, "They blocked the field goal!" Another try, and he shouted, "Two minutes left!" Finally, he told me Matt Ware scooped it up and ran it back sixty-five yards for an Eagles touchdown. We cheered so loudly that men throughout the reception rushed over to hear the news. The Eagles had just taken the lead on one of the most unlikely plays in football. They sealed the win a minute later when Sheldon Brown forced and recovered a fumble.

In 2003, the Eagles' season was saved by an amazing punt return, an unlikely game-winning touchdown. We convinced ourselves that the same thing would happen this year, although the Eagles had given us no reason to believe in them. I hadn't been able to watch or even listen to the game, but I felt the same high I did in Kansas City. I was quickly losing faith in the team, though; we weren't cheering a win so much as we were celebrating an escape.

I'VE BEEN conferencing with students all morning, and they can tell I'm still drunk. I laugh at jokes they can't hear. I'm wearing the same clothes as last night, radiating the odor of stale smoke. I can't even sit up straight, and feel like I might fall asleep mid-sentence. I don't have any water, so I'm stumbling dryly over my words. Twice, I stop in mid-conference to tell students how much fun I had at the bar last night. They look disappointed, or at least annoyed. I'm not fooling them, but I'm still trying desperately to fool myself.

I was out all night drinking with a semi-famous author. He was very nice, paid for our drinks on his publisher's tab, and was generally a fun guy. But I followed him around like a whimpering dog looking for scraps, prodding him to reveal the secrets of being published and semi-famous and well respected. I pretended I was slaving away on my own work, although I hadn't touched the rough draft of my novel since summer and I'd only written one story all semester. He gave me the old *keep plugging away, never give up, get used to rejection* speech I'd heard a hundred times already. Authors always emphasize how hard it is to be successful, but I always ignored them or kept asking the same questions, hoping they would reward my persistence by teaching me the shortcut to success.

I did not call LauraBeth that night because I'd driven home blind drunk—so drunk that I wouldn't remember the drive in the morning—and didn't want to admit it to her. I slept only three hours and then spent the morning rushing through my conference preparation, struggling to even see the words on the page, let alone understand them. I made a few line edits and left a couple suggestions on each, but each story had more or less the same notes—*show, don't tell; don't overwrite your dialogue; consider expanding this scene.*

Come conference time, I have little to say. A student has just asked me to explain what one of my line edits means, and I can't do it. I have no idea what the words say, or why I would have written them. I can feel her disappointment. She's taking a class with someone from the famous Iowa Writers' Workshop, and the teacher can barely lift his head up, let alone speak, write, or instruct. The teacher doesn't look like he's cut out for this life, and he looks like he knows it.

———

JULY 5, 2002—we were in Severna Park, Maryland, at my Uncle Ed's house to celebrate Independence Day by setting off explosives and gorging on steamed crabs and Michelob. Even Dad had a beer in hand. He had never been a big drinker, and his diabetes forced him to give up alcohol entirely, except for the glass of Crown Royal* he poured himself every April when he did our taxes. Now that his appetite had been ruined by a year and a half of chemo, he'd lost weight and didn't have to worry about his blood sugar anymore. He could have candy again, so he kept Life Savers stashed in his car. He could have ice cream again, so he waited eagerly at the window of the ice-cream truck several times a week. He could drink alcohol again, so he walked to the cooler in Uncle Ed's garage and picked out three bottles of Michelob, handing one each to me and Kevin. Dad was a real stickler for the law, for honesty, the kind of guy who would drive back to a restaurant to return fifty cents if he'd been given too much change. Yet, there was no discussion about me being only twenty years old, no declaration that any rules had changed. There was no acknowledgment that Dad had more or less officially declared me a man. This was the first beer I'd ever had with Dad or Kevin. I felt like a character in a John Updike story, or in a commercial for fishing rods.

Dad was not prone to impulsive action, but it didn't seem like he'd planned this. Maybe he was moved by the moment, or maybe he knew this could be his last chance to ever have a beer with his sons. He couldn't afford to wait seven months until my birthday.

Dad and Kevin sat across from me at a long picnic bench, picking at crabmeat. We started talking about the Eagles. Training camp would open in about two weeks, and Kevin and I would trek to Bethlehem, Pennsylvania, as usual, to watch the Eagles practice. Still reeling from their second consecutive NFC Championship Game loss, the heartbreaker versus the Bucs in the final game at The Vet, they appeared to have squandered their best

---

* On which Kevin and I would get grimly and royally drunk after Dad's funeral.

chance at a Super Bowl. Kevin was more optimistic and Dad more patient, as always. They argued that the Eagles still had the best defense in the conference, one of the best quarterbacks in the league, one of the best coaches in the league. This was all true, I conceded, but at some point everyone's luck runs out, doesn't it? How many chances did the Eagles need before they could finally break through? Besides, their recent draft looked like it had been a disaster.* Although their secondary was their greatest strength, they had used their first three draft picks on defensive backs. I was outraged; the players they'd drafted might not be relevant for two or three years, and by then the team would have missed its chance to win a Super Bowl. Kevin agreed the draft strategy was insane, but said he really liked their fourth pick: halfback Brian Westbrook, who would eventually turn out to be one of the best Eagles of the decade. I listed all the players I would have preferred they drafted, detailing their heights, weights, times in the forty-yard dash, and college stats. Dad was silent during much of this conversation. He didn't follow the off-season maneuvering; while I fancied myself an amateur general manager, he only cared about the games. During my ranting, he handed me another beer, and he listened intently to our debate. He interrupted only once to ask where I found all this information,† and then he called me "Stats" for the first time in years. We shared a laugh over our beers. When we asked him to come to training camp with us, he said he wasn't feeling up to sitting out in the heat all day. This is one of the difficult things about spending time with someone who's dying: even when he looks fairly healthy, even though you can almost convince yourself sometimes that Dad is back and ready to live unencumbered by illness, there are always reminders that, in fact, he's still sick and he's still dying.

Uncle Ed, carrying his own Michelob, sat next to me and

---

* It turned out to be their best draft of the decade. Three of their top four picks have played in at least one Pro Bowl, and the one non–Pro Bowler was Sheldon Brown, about whom I've said quite enough already.

† The EMB, of course. Always, the EMB.

joined our conversation. He is a Baltimore Ravens fan. This does not cause any tension between us. Although it seems like their regional proximity might make them rivals, the Eagles and Ravens barely have a history. By 2002, they had played each other only once, a brutal 10–10 tie. This is not to say that I like the Ravens; it infuriates me that they already have more Super Bowl wins than the Eagles, despite having existed about half as long as I have. They won their Super Bowl before their fans could ever know what suffering and longing truly meant. If there were any justice, they would have been barred from Super Bowl participation for a decade, at least. But I hold none of this against Uncle Ed.

As the night progressed, Uncle Ed was feeling boisterous, which is to say Uncle Ed was feeling like himself. Outside of our immediate family, he was always Dad's favorite relative. He contrived many reasons to travel to Baltimore, and, hey, as long as we're down there, why don't we stop and see Eddie? Uncle Ed was a Marine before becoming an air traffic controller. Powerful and compact, he was a clenched fist of a man—tightly packed, always appearing to be on the verge of violence. He smoked two packs a day, drank so much that beer cases were the only furniture in his first apartment, fought anyone who crossed him. He owned a racehorse and then lost a racehorse. He trusted people and, despite all of his wildness, was loved by his neighbors and his family, and everyone knew he was a good guy, just a little passionate, a little temperamental. He'd settled down since hitting middle age, which isn't to say he was tame, but he was reliable, honest, and diligent. This, I think, is why Dad liked him: beneath the surface, they were very similar in many ways, especially with respect to their core values. The difference was, Uncle Ed's hell-raising had rewarded him with better stories, all of which he loved telling. I've heard his best stories a dozen times each, but have never tired of them, especially because with each iteration they evolve a little bit. At the end of the night, when everyone's tired from drinking, he takes center stage and he never disappoints, his voice a military bark, his chest puffed up in exaggerated bravado, his face animated as he jumps out of his seat and throws props across the room for emphasis. Many of the stories involve someone yelling, "You son of a bitch!" They're all supplemented by his wife, who corrects his hyperbole and fills in the details he can't remember.* They all end in his wheezing laughter and his youthful, devilish grin sneaking through to the surface.

Dad's rapt attention during these sessions clearly revealed his admiration for Uncle Ed. He loved stories, loved being in the presence of a great storyteller. I wanted to be like Uncle Ed. I wanted to command that kind of attention, to be able to impress a whole room just by talking. I felt the same kind of passion and I wanted to be able to channel it in the same way, to make people love me.

Usually, at these parties, I didn't say anything during the story-telling hour; it seemed like adult time and I was just a kid stuck in the room. Probably inspired by my drunkenness, I talked more than usual that night, telling my own stories—in a much tamer, less exuberant way than Uncle Ed—and I had their attention, I got some laughs. I participated and found that I had a voice, that I enjoyed sitting in a quiet room and chatting over a few beers. I have spent the past eight years trying to re-create that moment, sometimes succeeding, other times failing miserably.

At night, after everyone drifted off to bed, I called LauraBeth and talked to her until she fell asleep on the phone. I barely slept, but felt completely refreshed in the morning. After breakfast, Dad pulled me aside and asked if I'd had a good time. I had, and so had he. He said he was glad to see me talking so much. "When you open up, you can be pretty charming," he said, "and actually quite funny."

AFTER ANTHONY'S wedding, after the Eagles' comeback against the Chargers, things started going right, everything went back to normal,

---

* A role LauraBeth has since adopted during my own storytelling perfor-mances.

everything we'd ever hoped for was happening. A steady ascent to excellence. It seemed impossible. Dreamlike. The Chargers game had sparked a thirteen-game winning streak, which meant the Eagles had earned their fifth consecutive division championship. They steamrolled through the playoffs, all the way back to the Super Bowl. Winning had indeed cured everything, and even T.O. had stopped wreaking havoc in the locker room. And so now it's February 2006, and I've flown home with Laura-Beth to watch the Super Bowl at her mother's house. Everyone is here. LauraBeth's younger brother spins a football between his palms, rocking in his seat while waiting for kickoff. Her older brother paces between living room and kitchen, where he's cooking a pot of chili. Her father has just changed into his jersey and now he's talking to Kevin. Kevin's wife is here too, entertaining their daughter, who is too young to understand what's happening. She plays in the middle of the floor, oblivious. LauraBeth is hugging her mother because they haven't seen each other since she moved to Iowa City. Her mother's hair has grown back to its normal length and the color has returned to her face. I'm on the couch, sitting between Mom and Dad, who is wearing his sweater. I brought it home for him, wore it on the plane before returning it. We thought we'd lost him three years ago, but nobody even talks about the cancer scare anymore.

Dad and I are so engrossed in our conversation that we almost miss the Eagles returning the opening kickoff to midfield. I'm telling him how much my classmates love my writing, how living with LauraBeth in Iowa City has helped us both to really embrace our independence, and he's telling me he has always believed in me. He's telling me he has a lot of respect for LauraBeth and he knew we would succeed. He's telling me he can't wait to come visit again.

Dad has finally earned his Associate's degree. The sickness slowed his progress, but he soldiered on, graduated with honors, and now he's expecting a promotion at work. I still don't really know what he does, besides that he works with computers, but I know he works hard, and that's what matters. He's put on a little bit of weight since The Hospital, but not too much; just enough to look like himself again. His hair has grown back, curling around his ears. His beard is full-grown again, thick, a little bit gray on the chin, and, as usual, it's catching the crumbs that drop from his mouth. He's mopping a spot of chili from his beard when he looks to the

TV. The Eagles are about to score the game's first touchdown. He slides forward on his seat, leaning forearms on knees, and peers deep into the screen as if trying to see beyond it. McNabb rolls out to his right and scrambles for a touchdown, and before he crosses the goal line, we're on our feet, both families bounding around the room, slapping one another on the back, feeling like this touchdown (and the next one, and the one after that) will heal us all. Dad's smiling and Mom's smiling and LauraBeth's smiling, and we're all smiling because of course we are, what else is there to do? Why would anyone do anything else?

NOW, HERE'S what actually happened:

I watched the rest of the '05 season unfold miserably, usually with Lee in a half-empty sports bar that cooked its burgers in the microwave and served its mozzarella sticks cold, with ketchup. Nothing ever improved, and the season unofficially ended in week nine. *Monday Night Football,* the Eagles' second game since kicking T.O. off the team—they were ahead of the Cowboys with a few minutes left, but McNabb threw a terrible interception to Roy Williams, the same guy who broke T.O.'s leg in '04. He scored the game-winning touchdown and McNabb injured himself trying to make the tackle. The Eagles lost the game and their quarterback. They lost five of the remaining seven games, a few of which were blowouts.

At the end of the season, I did what fans do: I rationalized the troubles away. I convinced myself that they needed a bad year, a palate-cleansing, to prepare for another Super Bowl chase. The rookies looked great and the team's future was brighter than ever; 2005 was just an unlucky bump in the road, but gray skies are clearing up, etc.

All platitudes remarkably similar to the ones you hear at a funeral. *Maybe it's for the best—he was suffering, after all. He's in a better place now. God just needed another angel. Maybe God needed someone to help him with his computer problems. This really puts things in perspective, doesn't it?*

I leaned heavily on these banal comforts when I thought about the death march that was the Eagles' 2005 season. When you identify yourself as a football fan first, and a real person second (maybe even third or fourth), nothing is more devastating than watching your team collapse.

Fourteen years as an Eagles fan had yielded a hundred frustrating or disappointing moments for every wonderful, transcendent moment. I never had any control over any of it, and, most of the time, I was left alone and angry, trying to understand what had just happened. Most sensible people would leave a relationship like this.

At the end of that season, I watched the Super Bowl in Iowa City, with Kevin Gonzalez, one of the Steelers fans in the Workshop. Since the Eagles weren't involved, I drank more than usual; by the final whistle, I'd had at least a dozen drinks, including a couple shots we did to celebrate Steelers touchdowns. Pittsburgh won, and Kevin celebrated by pouring an entire pitcher of beer on his head, as if giving himself the obligatory post-game Gatorade bath.

When we left the bar, some of the beer froze in his hair, but he didn't notice. He was dripping with stale Budweiser, short at least a hundred bucks, and so drunk he could barely stand. But the distant, contented look on his face told me all I needed to know; he looked like he'd just achieved Enlightenment. We spent the rest of the night in a bar, talking about the game while Kevin nodded and smiled, a dope fiend who'd just had his fix.

It occurred to me then that I could stop drinking if I wanted to, but I couldn't ever stop caring about the Eagles.

ELEVEN

RECONCILIATION

DURING THE cocktail hour following our wedding, we used a wall-mounted TV to broadcast a brief slide show, featuring photos of me and LauraBeth ranging from adorable childhood to mildly embarrassing teen years to cute couples shots. One professional photo displayed a five-year-old me clinging to a football and grinning. Of the forty slides, five somehow involved football and/or the Eagles.

Early in the wedding planning, LauraBeth's father had suggested a totally different use for the TV in this room. "It'll be close to football season," he'd said. We got married on August eighteenth, in the middle of the NFL preseason. "Why not play a video of Eagles highlights during the cocktail hour?" This suggestion, innocuous as it was, depressed me terribly.

Leading up to the wedding, we heard many such suggestions. Well-meaning people had countless ideas for incorporating the Eagles into the wedding. Why didn't you propose at an Eagles game? they asked.* You should hire the Eagles' pep band to play the fight song during the reception, they said.† You should have an

---

* Answer: because it's an unequivocally terrible idea. Even I know that.

† I did look into this, solely out of curiosity, and learned that they charge five hundred dollars for twenty minutes of banjo picking and the barroom-quality singing of one song.

Eagles garter.* Your tables should be labeled with the names of Eagles (i.e., instead of sitting at table 24, you'd be sitting at table Sheldon Brown).

I humored them, but each suggestion made me a little more despondent. There's something deeply sad and unsettling about being so fixated on a football team that you would have to include them in your wedding day. Again, I was forced to face a sad truth: to many people, I was nothing but a one-dimensional fan who allowed a football team to define his being and his self-worth.

If I had desperately wanted to add the Eagles to the event, LauraBeth probably would have gone along with it. Early in the planning, she even suggested a few Eagles-related ideas herself, but I shot them all down. She looked relieved when I told her I wanted our ceremony to have nothing to do with football. Although she would have permitted the Eagles to play a part in the wedding, she also would have been disappointed to think she wasn't enough for me, and she would have always had to fight the lingering doubt that football was more important to me than my own wife. She would always have to wonder whether she was enough to make me happy.

Here's what makes the whole idea seem so upsetting and strange: On my wedding day, why should I want to focus on a group of strangers in tight pants rather than focusing on my wife? Why should I want our guests to be thinking about football during one of the most important moments of my life? If I let football overtake my wedding, does that mean it's all I've got going for me? Doesn't football already infringe on my life enough?

Or maybe I was taking everything too seriously, and I should have just had a good laugh about it. We could have walked down the aisle in jerseys, helmets, and foam fingers while the *Monday Night Football* theme played. We could have written our own vows, invoking great Eagles of the past, declaring, "I love you more than I ever loved Andy Harmon." We could have had beer and popcorn vendors patrolling the room. Maybe it could have been beautiful.

---

* This one was denied on two fronts. No Eagles stuff, and we didn't do the garter thing at all because it's kind of strange and creepy, right?

Leading up to the wedding, I posted a thread on the EMB titled "Eagles-themed weddings: awesome or weird?" Most people agreed that having an overall football-themed wedding is tacky, but also admitted to including Eagles-related elements in their own ceremonies: an ice sculpture of the team logo, an Eagles cake, etc. Essentially, most answers went like this: "It's probably weird, but I think what I did was fine." And what most people did was to let the team sneak into the event somewhere, as we also ultimately did.

In another thread, someone posted an image of their Save the Date invitation, which was designed to look like a ticket to an Eagles game, featuring a photo of the happy couple in their Eagles jerseys, and listing their names as if they were the two teams set to compete: "GROOM vs. BRIDE," it said. This construction seems particularly odd and raises more questions than it answers. Why list the bride on the bottom, as if she were the home team? Does this make her the Eagles, and, if so, who does that make him? Is he a division rival like the Cowboys, the kind of opponent you love to hate? Is he like the Raiders, a renowned cheater whose glory days are behind him? And who is favored to win? Jokes aside, it seems like setting a bad precedent for the marriage when you choose to frame your wedding announcement as an adversarial one*—me versus you, fighting to the finish.

Sometimes people push it further than a simple Save-the-Date, though. In one infamous thread, a poster named dannyb detailed his own wedding ceremony, which featured a tribute to Jerome Brown. During the tribute, he presented an autographed game ball to his wife's parents, like some kind of bizarre dowry. He explained,† "It is best my new wife and her family realize early

---

* Although I suppose that's the same function of slamming a piece of cake into your bride's face, a practice that has always confused me, and seems like a remnant of some era when it was more socially acceptable to publicly degrade and abuse your wife. For the record: LauraBeth made it very clear that no face-smashing would be tolerated, and insisted that it would result in an immediate divorce. I think she was joking.

† All quotes and formatting from EMB posts in this chapter are sic.

in my marriage of the importance Eagles football is in my life."
The first response was supportive: "The Greatest Fans for the
Greatest Football Team!!" Another poster wrote, "Congratula-
tions. A classy move. Even if only the die-hards understand."
Clearly, if you didn't think this move was both classy and admirable, then you weren't a real die-hard fan. If that's the case,
then I must not be a true fan. I've worked hard over the years to
establish my fandom, but I've also learned that there are limits
to my devotion, and I'm okay with that.

Someone finally wrote, "i don't know. it seems kind of weird to
me." Yes, it is kind of weird, isn't it, stopping your wedding mid-
ceremony to present a football to your future in-laws in some
kind of twisted effort to honor the memory of a stranger who
died in a car accident fifteen years ago. It is kind of weird turning
a religious ceremony into the overt worship of false idols. It is
kind of weird to shift the focus of a heterosexual wedding from a
male-female relationship to the worship of the body of an enormous, athletic man.

Dannyb defended himself by saying it's perfectly normal to
memorialize a deceased loved one during the ceremony. And he
was right, to a certain extent: lots of people honor their dead at
weddings. At Kevin's wedding, he and his wife had lit a candle together in memory of Dad, and I'd briefly mentioned him during
my Best Man toast. In our wedding programs, LauraBeth and I
wrote a brief note in tribute to Dad and her mother. In our slide
show, we made sure to include many pictures of both. And in one
corner of the reception hall, we assembled a display with three
framed photos of each: one older photo, one recent photo, and
one from when they last looked healthy. We arranged candles
around the table and left a one-line note in their memories. I liked
this display because it accomplished our main goal—to have both
of our lost parents at the wedding in some way—and I felt it was
respectful without being too weepy or intrusive. No one had to
look at it if they didn't want to, but they could pay their respects
one last time if they felt compelled to do so. Kevin visited Dad
after delivering his Best Man toast. LauraBeth and I made that

table our first stop on the circuit around the room after our dance. We did not talk to the photos, but stood there for a moment to show them we were happy, to let them be a part of the festivities. It was the closest we could come to holding their hands or hugging them.

Mom checked the tribute soon after, and I knew she appreciated it. I've rarely seen her as happy as I did on my wedding day, and this time when she said, "I wish your father were here to see this," I knew it meant something different; before, it meant *I miss your father and can't fully enjoy this moment without him,* but now it meant *This is perfect and I wish your father could have experienced something so beautiful too.* She hugged me, told me and LauraBeth that she loved us for about the fiftieth time that night, and then returned to the dance floor.

Everything had gone as well as we could have hoped—perfect springlike weather in mid-August, the whole ceremony running on time, none of the last-minute emergencies for which we'd been told to prepare—and we took a moment to watch it happening. Our families blending together, everyone legitimately honestly joyous, and the two of us standing beside each other on the precipice of our shared life. Relieved. Content. We had everything we could have wanted, except for one obvious exception. She laughed for no particular reason, couldn't help laughing, and I laughed with her. It felt good to be happy without having to explain yourself, without having to justify it. I had finally reached a point where I didn't feel guilty anymore for being happy, understood that it's part of the process and that you're not dishonoring the dead or being disrespectful by laughing. It's a natural part of living to eventually move on, to stop actively grieving. It doesn't mean you've forgotten your loved ones or stopped caring; it means you're human. Dad, of course, would have understood all of this, probably would have said so if he could have said anything to us.

After visiting with our deceased parents, we returned to the party, which, to LauraBeth's great credit, was a resounding success. I had helped with the planning, finding the seating charts particularly fascinating for reasons I can't really explain, taste-testing all glutenous hors d'oeuvres, and winnowing down the guest list, among other duties. But she's far more meticulous than I am, practical and detail-oriented, which meant all loose ends had been tied up weeks in advance and all we had to do was show up and get dressed. This task wasn't quite as simple as advertised; I showed up about ninety minutes late for our prewedding photos, due to indescribably heavy traffic, but even that didn't cause us much stress. When I called her about the delay, she didn't yell or cry or panic or anything else you might expect if you've watched enough sitcom weddings. She joked about me having cold feet and then told me to be safe on the roads. Don't rush, she said, we'll be here.

After my arrival and the photos, there was the ceremony, which started exactly on time, as LauraBeth had vowed it would. Then the cocktail hour and the consumption of many hors d'oeuvres, the slide show, the speeches and dinner and champagne and dancing and tributes to dead parents and welcoming families and everything all coming together at once in a nearly perfect way that could not have happened without LauraBeth's painstaking efforts. The feeling of being loved, of being accepted, not just by LauraBeth, but by everyone in the room. The sublime notion that, temporarily at least, nothing can go wrong. The clinking of glasses urging us to kiss, the background music of the night.

And we did it all without the Eagles being involved. Almost. Near the end of the reception, everyone was drunk, and I asked the DJ to play the Eagles' fight song. When he played it, we all sang along, spelling out the team name, shouting it through the room. Everyone laughed and smiled and high-fived. I asked him to play it again, and he did. And we all sang along again, pumping our fists on each note, as if we were in front of the stage at a rock concert. I'm not sure why I requested the song. Maybe I felt compelled to prove my die-hardiness, to overcompensate for the lack of Eagles materials elsewhere, or maybe I really did want them to be there. The song capped our reception. Even as the final notes played, even as we spelled out *E-A-G-L-E-S* one last time, workers were clearing out the reception hall. Dad and LauraBeth's mother were wrapped in newspaper and shoved into a box, sealed inside as LauraBeth and I left the room together.

A RECENT thread from the EMB raises an important question:

Subject: Do the Eagles bring you comfort or pain?

Posted by *GreenBleeder:* I take it pretty hard when they lose in the big games and every year ends in disappointment…but I usually feel better after the draft, and there's always next year to look forward to. How do you feel?

Waiting…: both comfort and pain, but isnt that also called love? i think so.

DamnCowboys: alot of comfort, just as much pain.

Sagar110: comfort before the game and pain after games

Fresh Prince: Painpainpainpainpainpainpainpainpainpainpain painpain and nothing but pain. It makes me feel strong, however. I will not feel comfort until our day comes.

Nik3t: The pain usually lasts longer than the comfort. BUT I LOVE IT!

Exit Zero: It's like being married! You just never know whats next!

FlyEagles76: In the end it is ALWAYS pain

I did not respond to this question. Unless, perhaps, this book represents my very long response. And maybe that's the only proper way to answer, because it's much more complicated than it seems. I suppose the truth is that the Eagles bring me a mixture of comfort and pain, but I don't know how balanced it is, and I suspect that the imbalance is not working in my favor. Unlike Nik3t, I do not love the pain at all; it only makes me a worse person. I've always been aware of the pain inherent in sports fandom, but only recently have I realized that I don't have to live with it, that I've got a choice in the matter. This realization is immeasurably liberating. Still, it's hard to walk away from the Eagles, to opt out of the world of sports fandom, not because I'll miss the pain or the heartbreak, but because it would require a total redefinition of myself. Even two years ago, I couldn't have imagined the idea of turning my back on sports, but lately, I've become more aware that this may be my only choice, at least if I want to become a better person than I am now.

The other response to the thread that I found particularly interesting was Exit Zero's comparison to married life. As far as I can tell, marrying LauraBeth—no, to be more accurate, not marrying her, but knowing her, engaging with her, understanding her, finding someone who *wanted* to marry me—has been the complete opposite of everything I know about being a football fan: both commitments make great demands and both make lofty, otherworldly promises, but only one rewards your sacrifices, and only one keeps those promises.

LAURABETH AND I are at a party somewhere in New Jersey. I don't know what the occasion is exactly, but her childhood friend invited us to her apartment, so here we are. It's one of those group-mixing parties, where she's invited friends from home, work, and school, and hoped for quality mingling between strangers. LauraBeth is dressed nicely, kind of a casual elegance, a look she mastered years ago. I'm wearing jeans and my Sheldon Brown jersey.

Despite my objections, people insist on scheduling events for Sunday afternoons in the fall, which leaves me at a lot of these types of things during Eagles games, inappropriately dressed and hunting through strange apartments for a TV. We were the first ones at the party because I wanted a good seat, and I'd been promised that we could watch the Eagles play the Titans. This is a pivotal game we're watching; the Eagles have been floundering

through the season, and it looks like maybe their run of domi-
nance is completely over. We'd rationalized the 2005 season away
as bad luck and bad karma, but a year later they're 6-4, and haven't
looked impressive in any game all season. But, still, if they win this
week, we'll be able to talk ourselves into believing again.

McNabb looks terrible. The whole team looks terrible. The
game is unbelievably boring, and I can tell the non-fans in the
room would rather be watching anything else, or maybe even
nothing at all. People stand in front of the TV to scoop a handful
of chips and methodically dip each one, tapping it on the rim like
a paint brush, and then stopping to consider the taste of each, as
if sampling a fine wine. Etiquette requires that I not yell at them
or shove them out of my way, so I sigh loudly and lean to my right,
wishing I could crane my neck around them like a cartoon character. I've given up on hearing the announcers over the tangential
conversations in the room. To my left, LauraBeth is answering ten
thousand questions about our upcoming wedding, and all the un-
married girls look unnervingly envious, not because of me, by any
means, but because of the *idea* of marriage. They look at Laura-
Beth like she's just scaled Everest or discovered Atlantis, and they
want to know everything. Even things I don't know or care about.
Especially things I don't know or care about.

To my right, people I don't know are having a conversation
about other people I don't know, and as much as I'd like to tune it
out, I can't stop hearing them. And the Eagles are playing like it
doesn't matter whether they win or lose.

A tall, wiry guy breaks free from the kitchen and plops next to
me. "They look like shit," he says. I nod. "Fucking McNabb," he
says, shaking his head.

McNabb does look bad, but I can tell this guy is one of those
Eagles fans who has always hated him, always felt he was a little
too uppity, never thought he was smart enough to handle the
job. He spends the next ten minutes talking in racial code about
McNabb, the way some fans have always talked about black
quarterbacks—*he's a natural athlete, but doesn't have the work ethic;
he doesn't take it serious enough; he just doesn't understand the mental*

part of the game. In another setting, maybe I'd debate him. Maybe I'd say, *Yeah, he looks awful today, but he's one of the best players we've ever had*. But here, he's the only one who will watch the game with me, the only one who will talk to me about football.

Early in the second quarter, McNabb runs out of bounds on a seemingly innocuous play and crumples to the turf. Fighting back tears, he is carted off the field. For the third time in five years, his season is over. The guy next to me—he never tells me his name, but let's call him Sean—pounds his fist on the table. The chip-n-dip bowl rattles and spills. Sean seethes while his girlfriend scoops up the fallen chips. "See," he says. "He doesn't take it serious in the off-season, so now he's too damn fat to play."

The rest of the first half is somehow even more boring. We ride it out and retreat to the kitchen at halftime to fill up on snacks. I don't eat much, because I've been losing weight and I want to make sure I'm in good shape by the time we get married. Halftime is also when I make my rounds with LauraBeth's friends, small-talking and answering questions about the wedding, almost all of which boil down to "Are you excited?" They always seem disappointed when I shrug and say something like "Yeah, I guess so." The truth is, I'm not excited. It's not that I'm worried or afraid; I want to do this. It's just that we're talking about something that's happening nine months from now, and it seems to be a simple formality in which we publicly declare something that we both already know deeply and without reservation. That's not the answer they want,* though, so I give them a schlubby "Sure, yeah, it's cool," and move on, because I know they don't want to ask me any more questions.

Sean has saved my seat for me, and we go over our halftime strategies. We agree that if the Eagles just run the damn ball and force a couple turnovers, they can steal this game. We'll worry

---

* It may not necessarily be the answer LauraBeth wants either, but it's the one she's come to expect. When I assure her that I just don't get overly excited or expressive about anything, she says, "You do about football." And she's right.

about the rest of the season later, as long as they can sneak past this crummy team. I'm feeling more pessimistic than he is, but don't want to argue. I've spent more time talking to him than anyone else at this party, and I don't want to ruin that.

The Titans score a touchdown on a seventy-yard run about three minutes into the half. A torrent of curses streams out of Sean's mouth so rapidly that I wonder if he even knows it's happening; maybe he's just sprung a leak. His girlfriend reaches over to pat him on the back and he shoves her arm away, sliding closer to me. LauraBeth is watching me; I shake my head and say, "Well, there goes the season."

Sean collects himself and insists they still have a chance. I concede that, sure, mathematically, there's a possibility that they could win this game and go on to make the playoffs. But realistically, it's all over. Even they look like they've given up.

Four minutes later, the Titans score a touchdown on a punt return. Sean balls his fists and lunges forward as if to punch the TV. His girlfriend intervenes and tries to drag him away, but he pushes her aside. He storms out of the apartment, leaving his girlfriend behind. She smiles and looks to LauraBeth as if to say, *Men and their football, huh?* LauraBeth does not respond to her, slides closer to me on the couch. I sink deeper into the couch and say, "I wish I could have been born a Patriots fan." My phone buzzes in my pocket, but I don't answer it.

THREE WEEKS before that party, I took LauraBeth to her first Eagles game. We paid double the face value of the tickets to see the Eagles play the Jacksonville Jaguars. In all the times I'd bought Eagles tickets, I had never invited LauraBeth, mainly because I thought it better to keep these two aspects of my life separate (as much as possible), so that I wouldn't embarrass myself in front of her or scare her away. Lately, she'd made it clear how much her exclusion from the games had upset her. She likes football too, watches every game. She's not a fan like I am, but that's probably a good thing. She's one of the few people in my life with whom my bond is not sport-based, a fact of no small comfort to me. Sure, it's nice that she's a fan and we can enjoy football together, but it's nicer to know that if football and the Eagles disappeared forever, I would still have her, and she would still have me.

Big Kev and my brother came with us, and we met LauraBeth's younger brother in the parking lot. We ran a standard tailgate—drinking, grilling, listening to AC/DC—and she saw that it was good. We took a tour of the stadium, and she saw that it was good. We saw the pregame hoopla on the field, and she saw that it was good. We watched the game, and she saw that it was awful.

It was the worst Eagles game I've ever attended. Neither team did anything interesting. It was cold. And the Eagles once again looked like they didn't care who won or lost.

LauraBeth didn't complain, but was obviously bored. I spent the whole day trying to convince her that the games can actually be fun when the Eagles make an effort, and trying to explain that feeling I had when we saw Damon Moore tackle Ron Dixon on the four-yard line to clinch the division in '01. The most interesting thing that happened the entire game was when some guy who was inexplicably dressed like Elvis sat next to us and flirted with her.

As the Eagles strolled complacently off the field at the final whistle, I kicked the seat in front of me repeatedly until the cup holder snapped off and sprayed cracked plastic over the people in front of me. Elvis yelled at me to settle down and I flipped him off. LauraBeth grabbed my hand and pulled me toward the concourse, shaking her head. We filed out of the stadium in silence.

IN 2003, the EMB disappeared. I was nearing a thousand posts, a milestone that I expected to grant me instant credibility. But the site was being redesigned, and they had to shut the place down, start everything from scratch. Everyone's post count was set back to zero, and we all had the opportunity to reinvent ourselves.

Up to this point, most of my posts had been profane or insulting, and I'd spent quite a bit of time agitating people in the political section of the board. Initially, I saw this brief closure as my opportunity to leave the EMB. But when the new board opened, I signed on quickly to see what new features were available. I was, and am, member number 700—a number of great significance to Eagles fans.* I kept my name and began posting immediately. I didn't want to admit it, but I *was* racing to accumulate a high post count. Others, trying to reclaim astronomical counts, desperately responded multiple times in every thread, often with one word, or maybe even a single letter. I didn't do that, because I wanted to impress people with the quality of my posts, but I did respond more often than I used to. Before I knew it, I was one of the post-count leaders; once, I wrote 112 messages in a single day.

If the true measure of an addiction is whether your habit interferes with your daily life, then I am truly addicted to the EMB. Every morning, I wake up around seven A.M. to write, but I do so because I know I'll spend at least an hour scanning the EMB for the latest rumors and arguing with people about whether Sheldon Brown is good enough to cover tall receivers. If I don't wake up early enough, I'll find myself wasting the whole day scanning the EMB, posting comments and checking obsessively to see if anyone responded to them or got the joke I buried deep inside my second paragraph. Some days, I don't even start working until two o'clock. But by then, I'm tired and my eyes hurt, so I decide that I shouldn't type more than a few lines.

This approach has resulted in the production of a handful of complete stories and one dead novel—neglected, malnourished, murdered. Even as I scroll through the repetitive topics—every day, it's *We need a wide receiver, The front office is cheap, I love Dawkins*—I know what I'm doing is wrong. I am very rarely surprised or informed by the posts I read, and I know that my preoccupation with the EMB is crippling me.

A week ago, LauraBeth lounged on the couch with a book while I sat across the room with my back turned to her, scanning the EMB on my laptop. Free agency had just started, and I needed

---

* About a year after the board reopened, I actually received a message offering to buy my member number for fifty dollars. I rejected the offer.

to dig up information on a trade rumor. I found what I was looking for, but during my search I responded to an anti–Sheldon Brown post with a three-paragraph defense of his coverage and leadership skills. While I waited for the response to that one, I checked a few other threads and posted in them. Then it was back to the original thread to see the responses to my response. More responses, more scanning.

An hour later, I turned and saw LauraBeth asleep on the couch, her book still open on her chest, about sixty pages in. If she were awake, I probably would have talked myself into leaving the computer, but since she was asleep, I figured it would be *wrong* for me to wake her now.

Nearly forty-five minutes later, I was still typing. LauraBeth said, "How can you stand being on the computer for so long?"

"I'm looking something up," I said.

"I would feel awful if I wasted that much time on the computer."

"You're the one who fell asleep." I jabbed the keyboard and thumped the space bar.

She sighed and reopened her book. I closed the EMB window and flopped on the couch next to her, staring straight ahead at the TV while she read.

I NOW live in the suburbs of South Jersey, an area I used to call Philly Junior. I have some objections to suburban life, beginning with the fact that every other restaurant is an Applebee's or a Fuddrucker's, but overall it's a nice place to live. I have a deck where I can barbecue or sit with my dogs and read. I have a full-time teaching job at Temple University. We live only a few miles from the Walt Whitman Bridge into Philly. The Linc is ten minutes away. Our families are nearby. And most important, I live with LauraBeth, for whom I would move to any city in the world.

LauraBeth works twelve-hour shifts at the hospital—where she nurses children who are suffering from congenital heart defects—leaving the house at 5:45 and returning at 8:00. On my days off, I feel guilty about our relative workloads, but, hey, it's one of the perks of being a college professor, a job I was lucky to have gotten soon after I moved back from Iowa City. And, unlike my days as a TA at Iowa, I actually do work hard to prepare for my classes, and I do a pretty good job of teaching. I'm much more relaxed in front of the class now, and that confidence is derived mainly from meticulous preparation. Essentially, the main difference between my performance then and now is that I have a plan when I enter the classroom, and I want it to succeed. I don't think I'd be able to look LauraBeth in the eye if I didn't put my best effort into the job, not after she sacrifices so much for her work. Still, I have a lot more free time than she does. After I eat dinner, sometimes I lose track of time and find myself on the EMB until eight o'clock. When I hear her car pull up in the driveway and the dogs begin their barking frenzy, I close the EMB window and scramble across the room to open a book. I pretend to be deep in thought, not even looking up from the book when she walks in the door. I feel like a teenager hiding his porn stash under the mattress.

IN AUGUST '07, a well-known EMB member started a thread about a friend of his who had attempted suicide overnight. He related a long backstory about failed relationships, too many deaths in the family, etc. Standard ingredients for depression/suicide. There was a gathering in the hospital, the emotions of which are difficult to imagine; what an odd mix of joy, fear, and disappointment. The story continued to reveal that the suicidal friend had called the ambulance himself after having consumed countless prescription meds. The poster asked his friend why he would call 911 if he wanted to die, and the friend said:

> Dude I chugged the pills like 5 at a time then cracked a beer, sat down and turned on the Saints/Bills pre-season game... [I] thought man I can't go out like this. I have to see the Eagles win a superbowl. I really think this is the year!

The poster ended by noting that he and his friend had tickets to see the Eagles play the Packers on opening day. As is the standard with any thread like this, the responses were evenly split between self-referential sympathy ("I . . . understand what he was going through. A cousin died a couple of weeks ago, a family friend passed away earlier this week, and my mother got taken to the hospital due to a near heart attack") and self-righteous condemnation ("I have no remorse for someone who tries to take the precious thing called life"). In the end, every person's response is about themselves, and I guess so was mine.

After the season, I dredged up the old thread and asked for an update, but received no answer. The game they had attended was a disaster, one the Eagles lost because of several fumbled punts, and it more or less set the tone for an 8-8 season in which the Eagles' best game was a hard-fought three-point loss to the Patriots. I wondered, did the mediocre season increase or decrease the guy's desire to live? Did the lack of a Super Bowl mean he had to tough it out a little longer, play through the pain for another couple seasons just in case they win one? Or did it confirm his belief that the world is hideously bleak and hopeless, driving him toward more pills or maybe even a more effective means of suicide? Maybe the lure of the Super Bowl was enough of a lifeline to compel him back to land, and, once there, he found something else to sustain him. If so, what did he find that helped him forget about the Eagles?

One of the odd things about being a fan is the constant, nagging fear that tells you you're going to die before this team ever wins a championship. While your ashes sit in some nondescript box in someone's attic, you're going to miss something amazing.* Your life will end unfulfilled. The only choice is to stubbornly hang on and hope for the glorious payoff that you're promised

---

* In 2005, Eagles fan Christopher Noteboom tried to address this problem when he charged onto the field during a game and dumped his mother's ashes on the fifty yard line before genuflecting. He was arrested, but later said it was worth it, because "I know that the last handful of ashes I had are laying on the field, and will never be taken away. She'll always be part of Lincoln Financial Field and of the Eagles."

when you first become a fan. It's one of the most common refrains among Eagles fans—"I just want to see them win a Super Bowl before I die." And if they don't, you can bury me in my jersey so I can root for them from beyond the grave, so I can still be invited to the party when they finally do win. Whenever the Eagles win a Super Bowl—*if* they win a Super Bowl—thousands of sick and elderly Philadelphians will submit and die simultaneously. Nursing homes throughout the city will be abandoned. The city will be beset by a grief equal to the ecstasy of victory. We'll go to the championship parade dressed in black.

WHEN I'M in my office at school, I sometimes close the door and open the EMB to see what's going on. There's no rule against my looking at the EMB, but I would rather not have the department chair see me arguing the relative merits of the 3-4 defense with a guy named PuffPuffPass. I do this with a stack of student essays to my left, but I never grade anything in the office. If someone knocks on the door, I minimize the window and shuffle the papers to make it look like I'm working. When they leave, I close the door and continue posting. I feel like a drunk sneaking swigs from the flask between classes.

LAST CHRISTMAS, LauraBeth's father bought me an autographed photo of Sheldon Brown's unforgettable hit on Saints halfback Reggie Bush. The hit, a YouTube favorite also deemed by *Sports Illustrated* to be one of the biggest hits of 2007, occurred in a playoff game. The ball, jarred loose on impact, floats in the top of the frame while Bush's body is being driven downward so forcefully that it looks like Sheldon may push him through the bottom of the frame onto my floor. When Bush tried to jump back to his feet, he fell immediately to his knees and crawled toward the sideline. It was the perfect hit: violent, impeccably timed, awe-inspiring. And the picture is snapped at the perfect time too. The photo hangs in my office next to the autographed Bednarik jersey, across from two Eagles rally towels, and beneath a panoramic shot of Veterans Stadium's interior. My Sheldon Brown picture measures twenty by twenty-four, larger than my wedding photo.

THE OBVIOUS unspoken epilogue to any memoir is "And then I wrote this book and sold it to a publisher. The End." I hadn't written anything substantial for about eight months when I saw Tra Thomas buying oranges at Whole Foods. So I wrote an essay about it, thinking it would be a short funny piece, and it turned out to be about how much I missed my Dad. Lee read it, told me I had to make it longer, and suddenly I was writing more than I ever had. Every morning at seven o'clock, I go upstairs to my office and work for at least three hours, the routine Frank Conroy prescribed to all of his students at Iowa. And sixteen months after I saw Tra and his oranges, I've sold a memoir to a major publisher and I'm officially a writer, just as Dad had always expected. I think he would probably like this book; although he was generally more of a sci-fi kind of guy, I'm sure he would have made an exception for me. Even now, I imagine him asleep in his recliner, wearing his Eagles T-shirt, smiling faintly as he snores, my book splayed open atop his chest. Everything back to normal.

JANUARY 2008—LauraBeth and I are at another party. This time, it's a neighborhood Christmas/Hanukkah/Holiday gathering, and we're mingling awkwardly with the neighbors. We've lived here for about a year and a half, but we rarely interact with them in meaningful or even meaningless ways because our schedules are such that our comings and goings don't often intersect with theirs. They're nice enough people, and it's good of them to invite us over, even though we're clearly the youngest couple on the block and our dogs bark pretty much all day every day.

Luckily, I'm feeling pretty good today, so I'm able to handle all the conversation with strangers, and I may even be borderline charismatic. I've got a beer in hand, but am drinking it mainly out of politeness and social obligation. I may have one more if it's offered, but after that, I'll switch to water, not because LauraBeth will make me stop, but because I've been learning how to have a couple drinks without having a dozen.

We're chatting with somebody about our jobs in that passive-aggressive competitive way people do when they want to make sure everyone in the room knows their job is challenging and tiring. During the conversation, one of the other neighbors reveals that he is also originally from Philly, so we're naming random people and places to see if the other person knows them too. As with any discussion of the city, the conversation turns to crime, the escalating murder rate. He says it used to be a good place to live, but "now you got all the wrong kinds of people there." I say something bland like "Yeah, it's rough." He goes on to explain that just the other day, a colored family* tried to move into his old neighborhood, and the neighbors trashed the house, spray-painted racial slurs on the walls, the whole skinhead treatment. LauraBeth gasps and says something about what a terrible story that is.[†] My buddy from Philly nods and says, "Yeah, it's all over the news now. If you wanna do it right, you gotta be more subtle about it. Put glue in the locks, that kind of thing." LauraBeth and I begin actively seeking another conversation.

Behind us, someone mentions Donovan McNabb, and I drift toward the voice, just like I followed James Thrash's name at the barbecue in Iowa City. A group of four guys is talking football, so I figure this is my chance to really endear myself to the neighbors. I've spent my whole life preparing for exactly these kinds of conversations, and I have hundreds of opinions on how the Eagles can improve next season. One stubby guy with swollen hands

---

* His actual words.

† She is legitimately shocked. She spent her whole life in the suburbs, where things like that don't happen. But it still happens now and then in Philly. When I worked at the steak shop, one of the waitresses asked me to sign a petition to keep a black family off her street. I did not sign it. Not that it mattered; a week later they staged a rally to drive the family off, and, of course, the family moved away.

dominates the conversation. He's talking about how McNabb sucks, he's too much of a whiner, you can't win with him, all the standard criticisms. He complains about how McNabb's parents are too involved in his life; they disrupt his focus on football.

This is a common complaint about McNabb, who is very close to both of his parents. They're at every game and often in the background at his public appearances. Some see this as meddling, but I have a tendency to view it as being kind of nice. He's a successful grown man in a stable, loving family; this, it seems, would be the kind of positive example we're always demanding from our athletes. But when the team's not winning, everything becomes fair game. And it seems perfectly reasonable to WIP callers and EMB posters to insult McNabb's parents and insist that he give them up, at least until he gets us a championship. It's a sacrifice none of us would make—losing your parents for the sake of your company's success. But it's a sacrifice fans feel entitled to demand from their star players. What matters, in the end, is how fast he can run, how high he can jump, and how far he can throw the ball. Everything else has to be abandoned, at least until we're satisfied.

I have this whole rant prepared—*have* had it prepared for years—but spare everyone at the party. I let the stubby, swollen guy go on his own rant against McNabb. When he's done with that, I interject and say I think it's important to upgrade the tight end position this off-season, an observation designed both to change the subject and to impress them because it's different from what the mainstream media is saying. The ringleader shakes his head and insists that we need a new coach more than anything. He mocks Andy Reid for not even having control of his own home, since his two adult sons have been involved in a very public drug trial over the past six months. Most of the criticisms of Reid's parenting strike me as gross oversimplifications of the issues of parenting, discipline, and addiction.* I've heard all of

---

* Unsurprisingly, my favorite public take on the incident was articulated by Sheldon Brown: "[Reid] has done everything he could. He went out, worked his butt off to make sure he made a good life for his family," he said.

these arguments before, railed against them before. LauraBeth
squeezes my hand and leans into me. I take a deep breath, swallow
my anger.

The guy's comments are so familiar that I'm sure he's an EMB
regular. The others might be too. Sometimes this happens—we're
out in public and we run into people who are almost definitely
EMB posters. My first impulse is to identify myself as swamistubbs, ask them their identity. Then, quickly, my next impulse is
to pretend I never heard of the EMB in my life. How do you follow that introduction? And how do you deal with the disparity between reality and one's online persona? Worse, what if this is one
of the guys who hates me, or what if he's one of the guys I can't
stand, the posters who send me flying into a rage every time they
say something ignorant or inflammatory? What if we've held long
debates over the Internet, and now find out that we've been doing
so from across the street, and this guy's nothing like I pictured
that poster anyway, and do we now have to greet each other by our
real names or our screen names? The more I think about it, the
more exhausted I am.

I'm looking for a good excuse to exit gracefully. The stubby guy
says, "You know, the problem with the team is they don't appreciate the fans," echoing a popular sentiment in Philly. The idea is
that we're the greatest fans in the league, and, sure, we get out of
control sometimes, but you can't deny the passion. Passion, it
seems, is our blanket defense for ignorance and incivility, and we
expect to be praised for cheering for the team, as if there should
be some kind of reciprocal reverence between fans and athletes.
When that doesn't happen, we say the team and the players "just
don't get it." But, pretty obviously, we're the ones who don't get it.
We always brag about our devoted fandom, how we always sell the
stadium out even when the team is terrible, and sometimes I don't

---

"Through that he showed his kids . . . It is up to the kids to learn from it."
Then he added, in phrasing so reminiscent of Dad that it's a little bit creepy,
"At the end of the day, each individual makes his own decision and has to be
held accountable for his own actions."

understand how this makes any sense. Our greatness as fans is measured, apparently, by how much suffering we're willing to endure, and how much sacrifice we're willing to demand. In the end, it's hard to see how anyone wins with that deal.

All that said, I'm still a fan. I'm probably more devoted to the team than I've ever been. I can't rationally justify this dichotomy, and maybe that's enough to explain it; once you become a fan, a true fan, rationality goes out the window and you give yourself up to the mob. So, as much as I try to look down on other fans, I know I'm just like them, if not worse.

LauraBeth shakes her hand free of mine. I didn't realize how hard I'd been squeezing it. She looks at me, then toward the door. I remember how Dad hated these gatherings, the small talk and the wasted time. We used to joke that he was unpopular, didn't have a lot of friends, but now I understand why he felt the way he did: he had Mom, and that was enough, more than he ever wanted. Sometime before I was born, before Kevin was born, he'd experienced a similarly epiphanous moment with Mom—a kiss maybe, or a quiet night watching TV while she ran a hand through his hair, or a fleeting smile in response to a bad joke—when he decided that it was time to grow up, to move on from all the petty, inconsequential distractions and to overhaul his priorities. I lock on to LauraBeth's eyes, a lifetime of stories written into one glance, and I know exactly how Dad felt. I nod to her, and we break away from the group, no longer concerned about graceful exits. We tell the hosts we've got other plans tonight, and then we're gone. I could have stayed and argued about the Eagles, but I'm going home with my wife instead. As we cross the street, she looks beautiful bathed in the suburban starlight. I stop to kiss her. We lied when we left; we have no other plans, and that's okay, because there's no place I would rather be.

CHAPTER
TWELVE

THIS FUCKING GAME IS OVER

LISTEN, THIS is important: this is not a story about the redemptive power of sport, or the transcendence of connecting with my heroes. It is not a story about how football saved my life. It is not about how football helped me overcome my grief, nor how football *caused* my grief. Sports had nothing to do with saving me, but it's taken me a long time to figure this out. This is about isolation and the things we do to overcome our loneliness. This is about emptiness, and not knowing how to fill it.

It's still February 6, 2005, and we're still in Swanson's basement, still watching the Super Bowl, still reeling from Tedy Bruschi's interception. I want to break something. I want to put my foot through the TV screen. The interception was bad enough, but for it to go to Bruschi was too much.

I've never particularly cared for Bruschi—always considered him smug, thought he looked like the kind of All-American boy who is the president of the fraternity, pulls good grades, captains the debate team, stars on the field, and then, one day, it turns out to everyone's shock and dismay that he's a date rapist. The Patriots have a lot of guys I would describe that way—date rapist smug—but he's the worst of the bunch. Which made it even more unbearable when, during the endless pregame hype, the broadcast team devoted several minutes of fawning coverage to Bruschi's parenting skills. They had a shot of him sitting on the field, at least five hours before the game, playing with his children in the most conspicuous manner possible. About thirty seconds of banal footage showed him sitting on the ground while his children ran toward him. These thirty seconds led to obscene amounts of praise for being a wonderful father and role model for other fathers out there. What a great man, playing with his children. What a wonderful father he was, they told us, because, *even on a day when he has to work,* he played with his damn kids for a minute in full view of twenty cameras. Am I too cynical? Maybe. But fuck him, and fuck their insane, deifying coverage. Playing with your kids before work? That's not some wildly virtuous and unselfish act. It's something you're supposed to do. It's what my Dad did, and he didn't need an audience or masturbatory football analysts to keep him going, not when he worked sixteen-hour shifts every day, nor when the cancer was killing him and it made him nauseous just to walk from one room to the next. Tedy Bruschi did something all good fathers do—except he did it in front of a thousand cameras—and they force-fed us this sickeningly overplayed story. While they were putting him on a pedestal for taking a minute to play with his kids, we all cursed at the screen, and I called Kevin, who was at my aunt's house, a block away, watching with Mom, among many others. I needed to vent about how stupid the whole Bruschi thing was. He said it reminded him of the Brett Favre thing, how they deified him for doing what any normal person would after their father died. It infuriated both of us, just as the Favre story had—both men were normal people being treated like superheroes just because they were on camera—and while neither of us said it, I know we were both thinking about Dad the whole time.

The game should be over at this point—the Eagles are down ten with about six minutes left, and Bruschi's interception has given the Patriots the ball. But we're still holding out hope, because it's all we've got. The defense forces a punt and the Eagles have the ball back on their own twenty-one-yard line. They move the ball easily, but they also move slowly. We're all screaming at the TV, begging them to go into a hurry-up offense, to run to the line and forget about the long huddles.

They score a touchdown, but it takes them almost four minutes when they could afford to use only about two. The two-minute warning has passed, and the Patriots have the ball. It's still possible that the Eagles will win, but not very likely, and we're all silently resigning ourselves to the loss. For two weeks, I looked forward to that moment when we would run out of Swanson's basement and celebrate in the streets, pouring beer on one another like we were in the locker room ourselves. I had spent two weeks envisioning that stream of green, everyone running downhill and pooling at the bottom of the road in delirious glory. But now there will only be a trickling of desultory fans, wandering aimlessly down the street carrying unopened bottles of champagne.

All of us are visibly deflated, the weight of the disappointment enough to crumple us forward. Everyone, even Big Kev, looks small. I'm leaning on my hands, wishing I hadn't flown home to watch a stupid football game on TV.

I think about what I'm supposed to do next. When I fly back to Iowa City, will anyone be waiting for me? Will they commiserate with me, or will they dance around the topic like you do when someone is diagnosed with cancer? What will I look forward to now? Everything is a question. We were supposed to have left this game with answers.

The Eagles get the ball back, but they're in an impossible situation. On their own four-yard line with only forty-six seconds left, their only hope is for all of the Patriots defenders to suffer heart attacks simultaneously. The Polish had a better chance against the invading Germans than the Eagles do now. The game ends on an interception and the Patriots all prance on the field, mimicking Terrell Owens' wing-flapping celebration. It's officially over now, and so is the party. We clean up our messes silently. I look no one in the eye. I don't want them to see how much this hurts me, although I'm sure it's obvious in my posture. The Eagles turn me inside out; I can't hide anything. I say my good-byes, tell everyone I'm not sure when I'll be back in town again, and head toward the door.

Instead of celebrating, we will spend eternity wondering why they took so long to score that final touchdown, why they couldn't move with any urgency. Why didn't they care as much as we did? It's a question that will ultimately unravel the entire franchise, and a city with it. The Patriots have won their third Super Bowl. They celebrate in Boston, and we do not. I leave my Molson behind because now it tastes bitter and I can feel it choking me when I gulp from the bottle. The only sounds are distant sirens and the crash of the storm door closing behind us as we leave. Everyone shuffles home, heads hanging.

I stop in the middle of the road while bitter winds whip tears from my eyes. I see my reflection in a car mirror—I'm wearing my stupid sweater, my ragged jersey, my tired old sweatshirt, every other green thing I own, and I look ridiculous. Childish. The person in the reflection looks tired. Confused. Frightened. Angry. He's still young, but too old to be playing the fool anymore. He doesn't look at all like his father, and he won't, no matter how hard he stares into his own eyes and wills it. He looks lost.

I take off my hat and think about where I'm supposed to go next. I don't want to stay here, but I don't want to go back to Iowa City either. All I really want is to go away, but I know I can't keep running. I'm miserable and broken, but I don't yet understand what I've lost, or how to replace it. I was hoping for the game to heal all my old wounds, but it's only opened up new ones. If the game and the day offer any hope, it's that maybe I'm finally beginning to realize I've been looking in the wrong place for answers all this time. Rather than handling my problems myself, I've been looking for the Eagles to solve them, to help me cope. My football obsession may have brought me closer to Dad, but now it is driving me further from the man he wanted me to be. I've used football as an excuse for immaturity, used it as a mask when I was afraid, hid myself from the real world. Still eyeing my reflection, I call LauraBeth to tell her I love her, and I wish I'd watched the game with her. She tells me she loves me too, and, unhappy as I am, I feel a little better.

ACKNOWLEDGMENTS

Eternal gratitude to Mom and Dad, to whom I owe everything. This book wouldn't have stood a chance without you. Nor could I have done it without my wife, LauraBeth, whose patience and support know no bounds. Thanks also to Lee Klein, who knew three years before I did that I had to write this book; to my agent, Katherine Boyle; and to my editor, Ryan Doherty.

Countless others have conspired to help me complete this book, through some combination of friendship, manuscript reading, inspiration, and instruction. Sincerest thanks to all of them, including: Kevin Brockmeier, Frank Conroy, Justin Cronin, Jim Hynes, Mike Ingram, Vince Kling, Nam Le, Kevin McAllister, Chris Offutt, and Matthew Vollmer.

ABOUT THE AUTHOR

TOM MCALLISTER is a graduate of the Iowa Writers' Workshop, and La Salle University in Philadelphia. His work has appeared in numerous publications, including *Barrelhouse, Black Warrior Review,* and *Storyglossia.* A lecturer in the English department at Temple University, he lives with his wife and two dogs in New Jersey, a ten-minute drive from Lincoln Financial Field, where the Eagles play their home games.